A TOUCH OF THE MEMOIRS

A TOUCH OF THE MEMOIRS

DONALD SINDEN

HODDER AND STOUGHTON
LONDON SYDNEY AUCKLAND TORONTO

Πολύ φοβᾶμαι, ἀγαπητέ ἀναγνῶστα, πῶς κάποιος περιμένει
ἀπό σένα νά μεταφράσῃς στά ἀγγλικά αὐτό τό σημείωμα
᾽ελπίζοντας πῶς τοῦτο περιλαμβάνει διανοητικό περιεχόμενο
ποῦ σχετίζεται μέ τό κείμενο τοῦ βιβλίου.
    Μετέφρασα τίς παραπάνω γραμμές ἀπό τό ἀγγλικό κείμενο
παρακλήσει τοῦ συγγραφέως.

Th. Aghnides

(Sometime Greek ambassador to the Court of St James)

British Library Cataloguing in Publication Data
Sinden, Donald
  A touch of the memoirs.
  1. Sinden, Donald 2. Actors – Great
  Britain – Biography
  I. Title
  792'.028'0924   PN2598.s/
  ISBN 0 340 26235 4

For Diana

CONTENTS

ILLUSTRATIONS

With Akim Tamiroff (*You Know What Sailors Are*)[6]
How to carry a live alligator (*An Alligator Named Daisy*)[6]
Four depressed medical students (*Doctor In The House*)[6]
Rankery contract artists[6]
Above Us The Waves[6]
At the Venice Film Festival[6]
A Royal Command film performance
Jeremy, Diana and Marc[7]

Acknowledgments
1 Ed Dann
2 Rockefeller Center, NY
3 Ron Loadsman
4 By courtesy of EMI Films
5 By courtesy of Metro–Goldwyn–Mayer Pictures Ltd
6 By courtesy of The Rank Organisation Ltd
7 Times and Post Newspapers

FOREWORD

Over the years many friends have suggested that I should commit my memories to print but I always hesitated, mainly because I feared they would not fill a small exercise book, until Ion Trewin twisted my arm. So here they are.

Dining one evening with Sir Sidney Nolan, he asked me what I had been doing that day.

'Writing' I moaned.

'Writing what?'

'Oh – a touch of the memoirs.'

'What a good title,' suggested Sidney.

I am most grateful to:

my daughter-in-law Joanne for transforming my longhand scribble into a typewritten text,

Ion Trewin for his invaluable help: he has expertly sharpened my punctuation, relaxed my tenses, joined my infinitives, assessed my syntax and graciously accepted my insistence on the use of Capitals

my sister Joy for similar diligence in checking the proofs.

Lastly but not leastly thanks to my wife Diana for her forbearance during the seemingly endless hours it has taken to complete my unaccustomed task.

PROLOGUE

Near the Palace Pier in Brighton stands a row of motor-coaches; beside the steps of several are placards advertising MYSTERY TOURS. Will you join me on one? Mine will be a real mystery tour because as yet I don't know how it ends.

Off we go, passing old Sir Harry Preston's Albion Hotel, leaving the sea behind us to proceed north up the Steine. Look over to your left and at the top of North Street you can see the Clock Tower in the centre of the road: in the gentleman's lavatory beneath it, my Grandfather Sinden died of a heart attack in 1930. My sons believed that the tower was put there as a memorial to him, but actually it commemorates Queen Victoria's Golden Jubilee. Over to the right is the fine parish church dedicated to St Peter, designed by the young Charles Barry in Gothic Revival style (he was later to design the Houses of Parliament). In there that same grandfather married Caroline Cadby in 1894. (Her uncle was a piano-maker at Cadby Hall, Kensington, later the headquarters of J. Lyons.) How my grandparents would have loved today's outing! Behind the church we soon find Ditchling Road. The road is very steep and immediately we begin to climb past endless terraces of houses built at the turn of the century. Up and up we go – what a hill! – we have to keep in low gear. At last we are free of the town, at least we were when I was a boy, but what were once green fields are now covered with the creeping eczema of brick and concrete created by Brighton's bulging limits. Still we climb until the ground levels out. Grass as far as we can see. Over there on the right those trees, skirted by a low flint wall, hide a great mansion called Stanmer Park House in whose grounds the University of Sussex has been built. The wind blows the curiously springy turf in waves. Do up your coat if you feel chilly. We are now on the top of the Sussex Downs. We always expect hills or mountains to be topped by a peak, but here we are on a plateau. Away to the right these massive chalk hills will fall majestically into the sea at Beachy Head. Our road, which is now very narrow, was originally built by the Romans and only at given spots can two cars pass each other. In the 1920s it was rarely used; only very few people would risk the journey. Yes, it is strange to see a pond on *top* of a hill – it is a dew-pond, dug by man possibly a thousand years ago and lined with clay; no spring feeds it, only the condensed morning dew and it never dries up however much the fat Southdown sheep drink.

Don't be alarmed – the road ahead has disappeared – just prepare yourself for something that will take your breath away. I want you to leave the road for a moment and climb on foot a little higher to our left . . . We are now on the highest part of the South Downs, Ditchling Beacon – so called because in olden days here, and at other vantage points all over the country, fires were lit at times of national celebration or apprehension. Now, look to the north – don't talk – just look . . . The whole range of the Downs slopes sharply away into the vast Weald of Sussex. The great valley is some thirty miles across to the North Downs – not as impressive as 'our' Downs – which stride away to the east where they will fall into the sea at Dover. The silence is eerie, broken only by a slight rustle of the wind in the grass and the bark of a dog from a house possibly a mile away. You would hardly know it, but scores of villages are tucked away in the wooded landscape – if you look carefully you can pick out the stubby church spires pinpointing their parishes; those immediately below us are Westmeston, Ditchling, Keymer and Clayton and a little further to the left is the railway line linking Brighton to London. It was easier to see in the days of steam; a racing plume of smoke cut straight through the irregular countryside: it was then called the Southern Railway, but even in the late Twenties much of the rolling stock still bore the magical initials LB & SCR – the London Brighton and South Coast Railway. However you can just see an electric train drawing into the local station, Hassocks. It was there in 1924 that my father Alfred Sinden decided to open a chemist's shop. He had already served his apprenticeship in Hove when in 1916, at the age of twenty-one, he volunteered for the Royal Navy and served for the rest of the war in a destroyer, HMS *Defender*, in the Mediterranean.

He later told us many stories of his time at sea. I still have a vivid picture in my mind of the time when his ship went to the aid of a blazing oil tanker. It was impossible to quench the fire so they began picking up the survivors, but the cries could be heard of a poor man who tried to get out through a small porthole and became jammed; no matter how much he wriggled he could neither get out nor back in. *Defender* came alongside and a ladder was straightaway placed against the side of the burning ship so that a doctor could climb up and administer morphia to the man who was slowly roasting.

On his infrequent returns to England my father's ship docked at Devonport, and, my mother, whom he married in 1916, went to live in St. Budeaux, a suburb of Plymouth, so that precious hours should not be wasted when he was on leave. The war over, the young couple decided to stay on in Devon and there, infuriatingly, my sister, Joy, and I were born. Infuriatingly, because on all sides of our family we come from Sussex – we are Suxonians to the core – but on our passports it says 'Place of Birth – Plymouth'.

We moved into a small house, Fernlea Villa, just east of Hassocks station, but Pop speculated – wrongly as it turned out – that the future development of Hassocks for the growing population of commuters would be west of the main line, so there, with the financial assistance of his father-in-law, premises were fitted out with a splendid fascia board which read *A. E. SINDEN LTD*. Why did I never ask what *LTD* meant? For years I speculated on the difference between those shops that proudly sported *LTD* and those – obviously inferior – with no such appendage. To get to the shop from the house meant crossing the railway line – ideally through the station, down the steps and up the other side – but the station staff resented us using this short cut, so mostly we used the longer route along the road, under the bridge and up a flight of wooden steps.

In 1927, as my mother was pregnant with my brother, Leon, Fernlea was too small and we moved to The Limes in Ditchling, a village one and a half miles east of Hassocks.

So the moment has come to visit Ditchling. Ditchling as I knew it in my boyhood.

Sussex was the territory of the South Saxons and one of their Kings, Dicul, owned land hereabouts known as Dicul's Ing which over the years was corrupted to Ditchling. (Dicul is buried along the coast at Bosham.) We must now make the treacherous descent from the Beacon into the Weald, using the narrow road which winds down in a series of hairpin bends. Even today I cannot use this road without horror, remembering that as a boy we were not considered eligible for the 'gang' unless we had been initiated by coming down this terrifying route on a bicycle from which the brakes had been removed. It was necessary to walk the course like a jockey preparing for the Grand National: you had to know exactly where to leave the road and bounce up the bank in order to slow yourself. On the outer side of the road the ground just falls away, but here and there a grass verge could be used to throw you back on course. Do boys still do it? I hope not – there is now too much traffic.

Down, down we go – keep in bottom gear! Down, down and at last the final bend, now we cross another narrow Roman road, which follows the foot of the hills, and there, ahead of us, is Ditchling. In that house on the left lived Nancy Simmonds: like a puppy I trailed round after her, but she never noticed and went off and married Marcus Smythe. Opposite lived Mrs Mairet, who almost alone revived the art of hand-loom weaving. Now on our left is the main road to Brighton which will cross the Downs in a cleft at Clayton (I brought you on the scenic route) beside the two windmills, Jack and Jill, where the golfer Henry Longhurst lived.

The large house and garden we see next on the left is called The Jointure, once the home of Ditchling's most famous resident (Sir) Frank Brangwyn. He was a prolific painter of vast murals, who at various times used almost every inhabitant of the village as a model. His technique was to pose his models, who were then photographed, developed and printed by Pop. Brangwyn painted from the photographs; and we still have copies of most of the prints.

The Sinden family feature quite regularly, especially in the murals at the Rockefeller Centre in New York. I was posed once as the Boy Carpenter for a series on The Life of Christ. I have the photograph, but I wish I knew the whereabouts of the finished painting. Only a few years ago I was shown a delightful oil painting of his, depicting a Venetian scene with the Bridge of Sighs in the background and in the foreground a laughing group of Venetians – every one of them recognisably a Ditchling villager.

Brangwyn was the first person I heard use 'bloody' as a colloquial swear word. His conversation was laced with it. 'Yes, that's a Rubens,' he would say. 'Bloody marvellous painter.' When I met him he was no longer young; a wisp of straight grey hair attached to his chin, he sat behind an oak refectory table and busied himself with an elaborate procedure: having lit a match he twirled the cork tip of a cigarette in the flame until it was quite black. Only then would he place it in his mouth.

Today I find Brangwyn's etchings much more satisfying than his

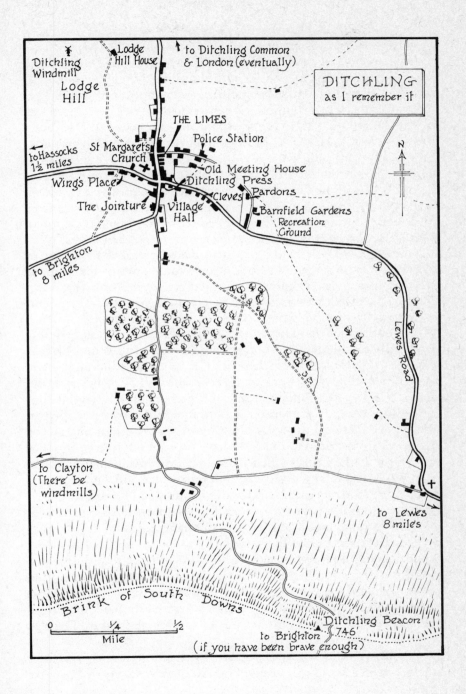

Ditchling Windmill

Lodge Hill

Lodge Hill House

to Ditchling Common & London (eventually)

DITCHLING
as I remember it

THE LIMES

Police Station

to Hassocks 1½ miles

St Margaret's Church

Wing's Place

Old Meeting House
Ditchling Press
Cleves   Pardons

The Jointure   Village Hall

Barnfield Gardens
Recreation Ground

N

to Brighton 8 miles

Lewes Road

to Clayton
(There be windmills)

to Lewes 8 miles

Brink of South Downs

0   ¼   ½
Mile

Ditchling Beacon
746'
to Brighton
(if you have been brave enough)

other work. There is a monumentality about them; a quality of Piranesi which is awesome.

A steam-powered lorry once got out of control on the steep High Street and ploughed into the beautiful timbered house at the corner of the crossroads – which is why the ground floor is now rebuilt in brick. On the opposite corner are the comparatively new premises of the Ditchling Press, founded (under the name St Dominic's Press) by Eric Gill and H. D. C. Pepler. In my time Pepler was in sole charge, but Gill, who was primarily a sculptor, continued to design and cut woodblocks for illustrations, fleurons and capitals. The products of the early days of the press now command vast sums at auction. Pepler's son Mark was a fine cricketer and became an early hero of mine, and I worshipped from afar Pepler's daughter Margaret who became a ballet dancer. Oh, those early loves!

Turning to the left, we pass the baker's shop backed by its bakehouse from which old Mr Cutress would emerge like a portly white ghost, with rivulets of sweat cutting through his flour-covered face to greet his customers. His sons John and Tony were members of our local 'gang'.

We soon notice that Ditchling is built on a series of bumps – you can hardly call them hills – and here the road rises to Wings Place at the top. It is also known as Anne of Cleves' House, because it and the surrounding land were given to Henry VIII's Queen on her divorce. When the Sindens came to Ditchling this splendid timbered house was divided into four cottages, but just before the war all four were bought by an antique dealer from London for £1,500 and lovingly restored to their original splendour as one house. The large field at the back, which had been used as allotments by the previous occupants, was slowly built into a beautiful Tudor garden with York stone paving, balustrades, statues and fountains. Years later the house was again put up for sale and the property was advertised as having 'a genuine Elizabethan garden'. But I know. I helped to carry much of the Tudoralia.

Opposite, on its own special hill, stands the largely thirteenth-century parish church of St Margaret. If you require a short rest, in the churchyard is a seat with a delightful view of the Downs. It was placed there in memory of my mother whose ashes are interred in the corner of the graveyard beside her mother and father, Hannah and Albert Fuller.

Past the war memorial designed by Eric Gill and round the village pond, a lane leads up to Lodge Hill and it is well worth the extra climb. I think I knew every tree and ant-hill in the surrounding fields. The steep western side of the hill was thick with head-high bracken in which one could be quite seriously lost – only a glimpse of the white windmill at the top could give us our bearings. Near the windmill lived Mr Kenning, his head like a ball perched on a tweed jacket. Quite bald except for two tufts of ginger hair just above his ears, his head and face were covered with freckles. He was, in fact, one large freckle. Mr Kenning had built his house on this prominence because from an upper room he could just see, with the aid of a telescope, trains on the London–Brighton and the London–Eastbourne lines. In the middle of a conversation he would rush away, and on his return comment that 'the four fifteen is two minutes late', before carrying on the conversation as if nothing had happened. All around the upper floor ran a small train set powered by real steam; under beds and wardrobes and through 'tunnels' cut in the walls. Unfortunately children were never allowed to touch it.

One evening Mumps – as I called my mother – and I had walked up to his house, probably to deliver something. After our conversation had been interrupted as usual, he said, 'I'll run you back to the village', in a tone of voice that expected no dissension. He had a lovely old Riley sports car, yellow, with a brass bull-nose radiator and large brass headlamps and wire wheels. He threw out a hen coop and vigorously turned the starting handle. It failed to start. He tried again and failed again. With not another word he took from the wall a notice and hung it over the bonnet. It read, 'OUT OF ORDER'. 'Goodnight,' he said, as if the subject of driving us home had never arisen. Perfectly in character, he died of a heart attack while climbing to a bird's nest. His body became wedged in a cleft and had to be extricated by the fire brigade.

A short walk takes us to the very top of Lodge Hill. Here is the best view of the village, cuddled protectively under the arms of St Margaret's with the majestic heights of the Downs as a green green background. Immediately below us is a natural amphitheatre in which a colourful pageant is performed by the villagers every ten years. I could quite happily sit up here all day but there is so much more to show you; we must retrace our steps to the crossroads. (Oh – there is Mrs Morley, an old family friend, whose sons Jack and Dick were also members of the 'gang'.) We pass Hoadleys, the Grocers and Hardware shop, managed by the Cottingham family (Dick, Jim and David, more stalwarts of the 'gang'). I want to save the High Street till last, so let us cross straight over.

This road leads to Lewes and around there were living many members of the Bloomsbury group, Clive and Vanessa Bell, Duncan Grant, Maynard and Lydia Keynes, Leonard and Virginia Woolf – I was walking in Lewes the day they found her body floating in the River Ouse. Just on our right is the Village Hall – the hub of all village activities, dances, whist drives, exhibitions, jumble sales; the Ditchling Players perform on the stage, the library was underneath and here the Women's Institute meets – my mother was a keen member and one-time President. It was here that we were given our gas masks in 1938. It seemed so large to us then, but what was once the whole hall is now merely the stage of the rebuilt hall.

A hundred yards along lived a man I wish you could have met. Ditchling was – and in a way still is – an artists' colony ('Artists, cranks or sods,' as someone once described the inhabitants) and most of the inhabitants who were not artists were eccentrics – or sometimes they were both, as in the case of Edward Johnston. A gaunt man with a great domed forehead, a walrus moustache and hollow eyes, he lived with his wife and their three daughters in a 'secret' house called Cleves behind high hedges on the Lewes road. You don't know of Edward Johnston? You should! He was a calligrapher typographer and illuminator. He it was who designed the lettering for London Transport. Every London bus and underground station displays his work. (I must admit that it took me years to realise that every letter one sees – even the print you are now reading – had to be designed by someone in the first place. This is called Bembo and was designed by Stanley Morison.)

It was Edward Johnston who first interested Eric Gill in typography from which resulted many aesthetic delights we now take for granted, such as the lettering over every W. H. Smith bookstall (Alas! They are now being replaced with a new design by Guyatt-Jenkins. However good it is, the loss of the Gill is tragic), and the Latin inscription in the main hall of the BBC's Broadcasting House in London.

When the Duke of Windsor as the Prince of Wales was made a Freeman of the City of London he was presented with a silver casket containing an illuminated address. Johnston was commissioned to execute the document. But time meant nothing to him and he did not finish the address until late the night before the Prince was due to receive it at a banquet in the Guildhall. Now there are many ways in which Johnston might have effected the delivery of his precious workmanship, but he was nothing if not eccentric. He sat on a stool at Ditchling crossroads, stopped each car travelling north – and, remember, it was not a main road – and asked if the driver was going 'near the City'. At last he found a taker and incredibly enough the manuscript was delivered. What faith!

There must have been something peculiar in the Johnston genes. His brother Dr Johnston, who lived further along the road, had severe curvature of the spine so as he walked his face was parallel to the road. To counterbalance this he held his arms like two sickles stuck out behind him. When he died Grahame Martin Turner moved into his house. A director of De La Rue, the printers, he and his wife Pat had two small girls and a Great Dane which would allow the baby to pull at its slobbering lips when it put its great head into the pram. Grahame Martin Turner was also the captain of the Ditchling cricket team.

In my teens there were many groups in the district one could join and it was not an easy choice: they all had attractive uniforms: the Scouts, the Communists, the Boys' Brigade, the Fascists and the Church Lads' Brigade. I rather fancied the last but they were all Church of England and my family were Congregationalists. I had been a Cub and didn't like it so avoided the senior branch, the Scouts. A great sneak at school had joined the Communists so they were out, as were the Fascists because the school bully had just joined them. This left the Boys' Brigade, with which the Sindens had long been associated. They took me in. Once a year we raised funds by making a house-to-house collection. We carried a card which had to be signed by the donor with the amount given. I always started with Mr Martin Turner who I could be sure would give five shillings. This set a precedent for another six selected houses before the amount dropped to two shillings and sixpence and so on down to sixpence. I have remained grateful to Grahame Martin Turner.

Further along still we meet the end of East End Lane: in that house on the corner lived George Milsted, a publisher. I was delighted to read Anthony Powell's description of him in his autobiography, *Messengers of Day*:

. . . small, thickset, white moustached, his turnout was always intensely sporting. Together with a brown bowler, he wore, all the year round, tweeds of the loudest check, most uncompromisingly horsey cut; in winter, as for hacking, a fawn covert coat

21

. . . the ensemble suggesting a prosperous bookie on the way to Newmarket.

He would frequently stop me in the street and give me reams of 'good advice' which bored me considerably.

That narrow turning on the right leads to Barnfield Gardens. Here lived Mrs Hilton Philipson who, as Mabel Russell, had enchanted audiences in the great days of George Edwardes' Gaiety Theatre. She had two sons and a daughter, Anne. I fell in love with Anne's photograph which stood on a piano when I first visited the house with my mother. She was away in Switzerland. Would I ever meet her? At last I did . . . she never knew how much I loved her. Why did she have to marry that other chap?

Behind the Philipson's house is the Recreation Ground: pitches for cricket and stool–ball, and an arena for athletics by day and a snogging ground for young couples by night. We are frequently required to state our Place of Birth; how much more entertaining if we were asked for our Place of Conception. Just imagine – 'Behind the pavilion at Ditchling recreation ground.'

I suppose here I must admit the awful fact . . . A couple whom I will call Mr and Mrs Heath lived in the village. They had a dog which I frequently took for walks. Mr Heath was often absent on business and one day when I called I heard the voice of Mrs H. saying, 'I'm in the bedroom, come up.' She stood there . . . Oh! . . . her body was beautiful . . . She moved towards me . . .

She was thirty-two and I fifteen. Life took on a new meaning. This blissful existence lasted for two years until, sadly, the Heaths moved from the village.

East End Lane is quite the prettiest part of Ditchling, winding its way along, past Pardons, one of the few houses singled out for mention in Pevsner's *Buildings of England*. Here on the left is The Twitten, an enchanting name, found only in Sussex, for a small passageway. Let us turn up it for twenty yards to the Old Meeting House, built in 1740. In 1933 my father happened to be passing when a wedding was taking place quietly; luckily he had his camera with him and after enquiring the names of the bride and groom he took a photograph of the couple as they left the chapel and sent it to a county newspaper. Pop had a scoop. The bridegroom was Dr Adrian Boult and playing the harmonium had been Sir Walford Davies. For the next thirty years my father covered all the local events for a variety of newspapers at a penny a line. He worked long into the night typing separate versions of the same story for different papers. But it was the war that inspired his masterpiece.

A major event in Ditchling was the annual Gooseberry Show, accompanied by all the fun of the fair – roundabouts and swings, the vegetable and flower show – but the Gooseberry Show was the centre of attraction. And what gooseberries they were. Many different varieties were entered, with and without hairs, of different colours and all enormous. Pop could easily write half a page on the event, but during the war the show was not held and to him this would mean quite a financial loss. But Pop had flair; each year he still wrote an article beginning, 'In Ditchling, but for the war[!] today would have been the two hundredth and thirty-sixth Gooseberry Show . . .' and then would follow column after column of descriptions of past glories.

During the last war Pop also became a War Reserve policeman and put in eight hours a day at the police station just across the road from the Old Meeting House.

Past the post office, East End Lane now joins the High Street and the house on the corner is . . . No. Wait till we turn the corner into the High Street. There, now you can see it properly. The house is called The Limes, because three pollarded lime trees once stood at the edge of the pavement.

It is a perfect Queen Anne house; every child's idea of what a house should look like – a door in the middle with a window on each side and three windows above. Unseen from the High Street are two long rooms built into the roof and here my brother Leon (who was born soon after we moved in) and I originally slept and had our playrooms. From one of these rooms was the only view of the Downs. If the day was to be fine, they would appear miles away, but if rain was expected they seemed close enough to be about to fall on us. From this window it was only a two-foot drop on to the roof of the house next door. It was then possible to climb around a chimney stack and up a valley of our roof, over the ridge and down into a secret valley on the other side. This was the place for special conferences over a tin of Nestle's milk. It was to her eternal credit that Mumps did not collapse in a heap on the day she saw us from the street below, astride the ridge of the main roof – three storeys up.

One of the rooms facing on to the street was converted into a shop by removing the existing window – my parents had the good sense not to interfere with the brickwork – and appliquéing a large frame of plate glass over the front. This also bore the legend A. E. SINDEN LTD. The entrance was via the front door of the house. We now had two shops.

My mother looked after the Ditchling shop, fed us and got us off to school. Doctors' prescriptions handed to her in Ditchling had to be telephoned to Pop in Hassocks on the private extension. I sometimes thought my parents only conversed in pharmaceutical Latin. The price of everything in the shops was marked in a 'secret' Sinden code. Pop discovered that the longest word in which no two letters were duplicated was ANTIMSULPH, and by adding YZ he brought the number of letters up to twelve – necessary for the number of pence in a shilling. I still associate those letters with their equivalent numbers: M/Y is 5/11.

Every morning Pop left Ditchling in time to open the Hassocks shop at nine. I loved watching him there dispensing prescriptions. Today most medicines are a proprietary brand, but then each had to be made up individually: Dec Aloes, Zingib Rad, Inf Buchu, Pot Cit, Quassia Wood, Pulv Cinchon, Oxym Scillae, Pulv Jalapae, etc., a little of this, a gramme of that and the mixture poured into a bottle, thousands of which were stored in racks, all different sizes, 6 oz., 8 oz., 10 oz., and so on. (The task of washing these bottles was frequently allotted to we young ones.) A cork was rammed in and then, as the bottle was held with the cork against the edge of the counter and the other end against Pop's stomach, it was tied over the top and around the neck with pink string, the ends of the thread carefully trimmed with scissors. A label was stuck exactly – and it had to be exact – on the front, headed A. E. SINDEN LTD., and the dosage written out in a legible hand. A little pleated paper cup was added over the top of the cork and this too was tied. Finally the bottle was wrapped beautifully in white paper and the fold at top and bottom sealed with wax, softened by a gas burner which flickered continually, and the name of the recipient written lengthwise on the paper.

It was quite often our job as children to deliver these and other goods, and as the houses had names instead of numbers, the name of the occupant became linguistically attached to the house. I can still hear RawlinsTheMount; WoodCheals; EllisNorthEnd; Hobbs-WhiteGates; PhillipsRuxley; BuzzardTheLag; and NewmanRollscroft.

Life must have been very difficult for my parents. Money was always short and my father tried to supplement his chemist's income with various sidelines. Radio sets were then powered by accumulators. So at Hassocks Pop installed 'The Power Unit', a great machine which hummed and to which dozens of accumulators could be attached by wires and charged overnight – this was one of the many 'Services to his Customers' which he devised. He also started a developing and printing service for films in a dark-room built at the back of the Hassocks shop. But closing time was always late, as he had to wait until the last of the doctor's patients brought in their prescriptions, before starting work by the light of a small red bulb, first putting the films in a tank, then hanging them up to dry and finally printing them on a machine that could do dozens at a time. Anyone could be sure that a film dropped in by nine in the evening would be ready for collection by nine the next morning. Somehow he managed to keep all these extra jobs going at the same time. But when did he sleep?

If only we had time I would take you two miles north on to Ditchling Common. We would go past the place where a giant crucifix, carved by Eric Gill, marked the wooden hutted community of Roman Catholic handcraftsmen founded by Gill after he left his house in the High Street two doors down from The Limes, and on to a spot where a gallows once stood on which a murderer called Jacob Harris was hanged. Here I would ask you to turn round with your eyes closed. When you open them you will see a sight at which my heart sings every time I see it as I drive to Ditchling from London. I have seen the Himalayas, the Alps, the Andes, the mountains of Scotland and Wales, but nothing matches the smooth green undulating line of the South Downs as they rise steeply from the flat Weald.

Ditchling, its inhabitants and its environs have coloured my whole life.

I

BARGE-'ILL AND HARDS-HEE

At the age of two and a half I contracted chicken pox after which I developed asthma. It quite blighted my early life. I grew into the classic 'seven stone weakling'. Modern remedies such as Ventolin and Medihaler were unknown then, the only relief being an injection of Ephedrine. My attacks mostly occurred at night. I would awake fighting for breath and the miserable sound of my wheezing would awake my parents. My room was totally dark until the door opened; framed against the light from the corridor I could see the figure of Pop holding a charged hypodermic syringe. Although this brought instant relief it has left me with a fearsome dread of injections. I get in a complete state of panic when I need to be inoculated. My dentist is now accustomed to filling my teeth without any form of anaesthetic: I prefer the pain of the drill to the horror of the needle.

I was sent to a series of private schools, but recurring attacks of asthma kept me away quite regularly and I always fell behind my classmates. I just could not keep up scholastically and I had to be excused from all games. I was a weak, asthmatic loner.

At the age of nine I was sent to join my five-year-old brother Leon at Hassocks Primary School. I had a bicycle with fourteen-inch wheels and he had a tricycle with which to do the mile and a half journey. I was furious because by myself I could get up a good speed, but I was subjected to 'looking after' him: in practical terms this meant pushing him along with one hand. I also had to 'look after' him at lunch and playtime to the derision of my contemporaries. Leon was an encumbrance. As I was bullied, so I bullied Leon. Mumps had been a committed suffragette and a pacifist. We were brought up to believe that all fighting was wrong – and this extended to school, where I was always being hit by other boys and denied the satisfaction of hitting back (not that I would have been very effective). Therefore I hit Leon. The four-year gap in our ages was unbridgeable. We were made to play together, but naturally wanted to play different games. Joy was older and anyway she was a girl who was placed in the invidious position of having to 'look after' us in the absence of Mumps. We thought her bossy. She and Leon were clever, which was not conducive to good relations with someone who wasn't. Only when we became adults did we recognise each other's good qualities.

Mumps hero-worshipped her father, Albert Fuller, who was Assistant Borough Surveyor at the Hove Town Hall. His hobby was to sketch buildings – especially churches – and details such as fonts, doors, windows and mouldings. Each holiday he and his family would set off by train to some centre from which, on bicycle, they would search out anything of architectural interest and return home with filled sketch books. I imagined that his whole family shared his obsession, but many years later my aunt explained that only Mumps enjoyed these excursions; the others were bored out of their minds. I hardly remember him, but his presence permeated my childhood. I was six when he died and his effects were divided between his three daughters with The Limes becoming a veritable Fuller museum. The best of his drawings were framed and hung on every wall. He had also collected old scientific instruments and these were displayed in a Boule cabinet. He had, I am ashamed to say, gutted a William IV spinet, which had come from the Royal Pavilion in Brighton, to house his surveyor's plans: this now stood in our drawing room. His ornaments, bronzes and ceramics were displayed on our shelves. From him came my own obsession for ecclesiology, so let me digress for a moment.

Almost every English village revolves around its church and the traveller need have no fears of getting lost, the rolling landscape is interrupted by beautiful spires and towers to signpost his way, although I must admit that sometimes he can be misled. My collateral ancestor 'Mad Jack' Fuller once wagered that he could see thirteen church spires from his house in Brightling and then found that he could see only twelve so he built a fake steeple on the horizon and won the bet.

Architectural details and the building materials that are used vary geographically. To the practised eye it is possible to place a particular county by the design of the church. Then we start to look at the details which can be read like a book. The rise and fall in the prosperity of the parish can be deduced by the size of the building, the quality of the workmanship and the periods in which it was done. Most dramatic is to see how all work suddenly ceased at the time of the Black Death (1348), which carried off so many stone-masons. When resumed, the work was much plainer and produced the Perpendicular style, unique to England.

From my grandfather came the splendid advice that one should always look upwards as one walked along. What a lasting effect that has had on me. The top of a tree fretted against the sky is so much more beautiful than the pavement at one's feet. Above many a cut-price supermarket in any town can be seen the windows and roofs of Georgian houses sadly bemoaning the fact that their ground floors have been gutted. Actually my wife would have me believe that by looking up I may tread on something nasty on the pavement: I must admit that I have done just that on three occa-sions – a small price to pay for the pleasures I have had from 'looking up'.

All this was transmitted to me by Mumps: a walk down the High Street was packed with adventure and discovery. What would we discover today? A gas bracket, a barge board, some pargetting, or knapped flintwork?

She brought us up to believe that we were scions of an honour-able family temporarily embarrassed financially: envy was un-known – we were a family who 'fortunes, buffets and rewards have taken with equal thanks'. Family problems were private. She was known and loved by all the villagers, by whom she was known simply as Mrs Sinden – I doubt if anyone knew her christian name. She was disabled for five years before she died in 1959, during which time I behaved in a rather cowardly fashion – I could not bear to think that this was the woman I had loved and admired and who was once so vitally active.

Pop we hardly knew until his later years – he was always work-ing. He had an extensive collection of platitudes: 'If a job's worth doing it's worth doing well'; 'Today is the tomorrow you thought about yesterday'; 'If you want a job well done, do it yourself'; 'Try to leave the world a better place than you found it'.

Naturally I failed the Eleven Plus examination, so I was des-patched to the nearest Senior school at Burgess Hill, two train stops north of Hassocks. This station boasted a porter with the loudest voice on the south coast. During wartime blackouts and when station name plates were removed, commuters returning from London could sleep happily knowing that they would be awakened by a stentorian voice bellowing 'BARGE-'ILL'. One night he was sent as a last-minute relief to the next stop up the line, Haywards Heath. As the last train drew in it disgorged many Burgess Hillians, who had leaped out on hearing his voice, discovering too late that he had shouted 'HARDS-HEE'.

Mr Woolcock was my new headmaster – his name, inevitably, gave rise to many ribald jokes among the boys – who believed in a liberal use of the cane. I cannot think why so much fuss is made today about corporal punishment. We all knew what the penalty would be if we infringed certain rules, but we took that calculated risk. The choice was our own. We never grumbled. If we were caught, we stoically took six of the best and proudly showed our weals while secretly wondering if what we had done had made it worth being caught. The school was coeducational, but at that age girls were 'silly' (except, I often thought, for Valerie . . . Oh, Valerie . . . ! But Mrs Heath was still to come).

I was extremely fortunate in my teachers. Mr Pretty succeeded in kindling a flame of interest in mathematics. 'Budge' Farley developed in me a love of wood and woodwork and, most important, I came under the influence of Jack Freestone. He should have been a professional singer. He still sang the leading tenor role in the annual production of a Gilbert and Sullivan opera (at his old school, the Brighton and Hove Grammar, where my cousin Frank was then a pupil and also took part). I saw many of these performances.

At Burgess Hill he taught English and Music, and I hung on his every word. He must have detected in me some seam that he thought worth mining. To him I owe my life-long interest in Renaissance art and in music – English as a subject bored me. He took me to my first opera, *The Barber of Seville* at Sadler's Wells. Was I bored? I think not, because I now spend all the spare time I can at the opera. One day he asked if I would join him at a recital to be given in a village hall at Haywards Heath, where a young singer he knew of was to sing some songs composed especially for him by another young man who would be accompanying him at the piano. The singer was Peter Pears, the composer was Benjamin Britten and I understand that this was the first public performance of *The Seven Sonnets of Michelangelo*. I was competely captured by Britten's music and Pears' voice and bought the 78 rpm records immediately they were released – I still have them now, worn nearly smooth. Years later I thrilled to hear some of Britten's many operas and his magnificent *War Requiem* with Pears singing the English soldier,

Dietrich Fischer-Dieskau, the German, and Galina Vishnevskaya as the soprano soloist. Later, in 1970, I had the pleasure of meeting Britten and before his untimely death he wrote me many splendid letters. I owe so much to Jack Freestone.

I spent several holidays with my mother's sister Florence who was one of the original policewomen, then stationed at Croydon. Each morning I would set off by myself on a tram to Westminster to discover London on foot – the only way. So started another of my obsessions, a love of the Metropolis which I now list as one of my principal hobbies. Keeping to Grandpa's dictum of always looking up, I roamed the streets of Westminster, the City, St James's, Mayfair – all magical names to a country boy. Looking one day at the enormous nude statue of Achilles at Hyde Park Corner I heard a Londoner saying to a visitor, 'No, no, dear – Big Ben is a clock.' I spent hours in the British Museum, the Victoria and Albert and the Maritime Museum, Westminster Abbey, St Paul's and the many City churches. Pop had introduced me to the Sir John Soane Museum, which has remained my favourite refuge. He also took us all to see the rehearsal of George VI's coronation, and I have never regretted not seeing the real thing. The bands and marching feet of the Guards were thrilling and during a temporary halt we were able to study, and even touch, Kent's magnificent fairy-tale golden state coach with its decoration by Cipriani.

One other characteristic that I inherited from my grandfather is colour blindness. I am not totally colour blind, but I find it almost impossible to differentiate between certain browns, greens and reds and there comes a time when 'egg-shell' blue is identical to 'egg-shell' green. My wife will try to draw my attention to a 'green' sea or a 'russet' tree in a wood. I fail miserably to appreciate the hue. Traffic lights do not present the expected problem: I see two reds and a blue, so quite safely stop on either red or go on the blue.

As a result of this deficiency I find myself more attracted to sculpture than to painting – my sense of line and form is considerably heightened and for this same reason, of the painting schools, I am more attracted to the Florentine – which explains, I imagine, why I began to be interested in the statues of London and to take a pride in knowing their whereabouts ('Name the statues in Trafalgar Square in a clock-wise direction').

To a Ditchling boy, Brighton, only eight miles away, represented the bright lights. I became an enthusiastic supporter of the Brighton Tigers Ice Hockey Team and used to go skating myself every Thursday night. After which I would catch the last train to Hassocks and walk the mile and a half home.

I regret to say that due mainly to my asthma I still remained scholastically backward. There was no point in staying on at school, but what job could I do?

To the delight of my mother, I had shown some ability at geometry and actually enjoyed drawing geometric projections. Perhaps I could be a draughtsman? Mumps applied to some of my grandfather's old colleagues at Hove Town Hall, but, alas, I needed to have passed my School Certificate examination. Someone suggested that we should try T. B. Colman and Son, a large firm of shopfitters, who employed draughtsmen – perhaps there was a vacancy? Off we traipsed to be interviewed by Arthur Colman. No, he did not have any vacancies, but he would like to help Albert Fuller's grandson. If I would like to be apprenticed in joinery I could then attend evening classes in draughtsmanship and he would allow me the run of his drawing office and if and when a vacancy occurred . . .

All was agreed, and my indenture was drawn up which

witnesseth that in consideration of the covenants and agreements hereinafter entered into by the Guardian and Apprentice the Employers hereby covenant with the Guardian and Apprentice in the manner following that is to say that the Employers will take and receive the Apprentice as their Apprentice for the term of Five Years from the Sixth day of March, One Thousand Nine Hundred and Thirty Nine also will during the said term to the best of their knowledge and power and ability teach and instruct or cause to be taught and instructed the Apprentice in the trade or business of Joinery and in all things incident or relating thereto and the Employers will pay to the Apprentice Wages at the rate and in the manner following that is to say for a term of Five Years during the first year Six Shillings per week during the second year Ten Shillings per week during the third year Fifteen Shillings per week during the fourth year Twenty Shillings per week during the fifth year Twenty Five Shillings per week . . .

I was required to provide my own tools, so – at the age of fifteen – and with the initial minimum requirement of a hand saw, a smoother plane, a one-inch chisel, a hammer, pincers and screwdriver, I reported for work on the Sixth day of March One Thousand Nine Hundred and Thirty Nine.

2

SKIRTING STEPS AND CORNICE KNEEPADS

I had to catch a seven twelve a.m. train from Hassocks to reach the factory in time for an eight a.m. start. The large building was on three floors. On the lowest – the Mill – was all the machinery: circular saws, band saws, planers, spindles and the like. The top floor housed the metal workshop, the veneering department and the french polishing shop, while the middle, in which I worked, was one enormous room with large windows and about twenty work benches down each side of a centre gangway. At one end of the room the foreman had his office. A fine demarcation line was drawn between those employees who had known him before he became foreman and who called him Bill, and those more recent arrivals who called him Mister Bellingham. A window in his office allowed him to oversee the whole floor.

Three of the joiners were entrusted with the tutelage of apprentices: my 'master' was Frank Verral. A kind man of medium height and enormous strength, he had a decided paunch which he always claimed was 'not a paunch but a hollow back'. A bachelor, he had lodged in the house of his own master joiner for twenty years. They both spent every spare minute on their adjoining allotments, where they cultivated chrysanthemums which always won prizes.

At this time Colmans were mainly concerned with the making of revolving doors. A Mr Van Kannel had invented a safety device whereby a set of revolving doors could be snapped open to allow free movement through the exit (prior to that, these doors constituted a hazard should the building catch fire). Colman had acquired the patent and cornered the market: each of their products bore a push-plate engraved COLMAN – VAN KANNEL.

My job was to assist Frank, and another apprentice named Ted Cushnie, in the making of soffits, the large circular ceiling of the revolving doors, between seven and eight feet in diameter and twelve inches deep (to house the bearings and trolley). A circle of one-inch-thick blockboard was cut and to this was glued and screwed nine by two inch joists – my first job was to bore the holes and make a channel to allow the screw to be turned. Two feet long segments of two by two inch deal had been roughly cut on a band saw and the ends mitred, these were then glued and nailed to the edge of the blockboard to form a perfect circle and gradually the rim was built up. The 'drum' was then passed over to the veneerer who covered the flat surface with oak, mahogany, walnut or teak veneer. It then came back to us to fix, with great accuracy, bands and mouldings of similar wood to the circumference. Then began the laborious task of removing all imperfections, first with a plane, then a scraper, followed by coarse glasspaper. The surface was then damped to raise the grain and then gone over again with fine glasspaper. My first disaster occurred when I became too enthusiastic and scraped right through the veneer. It took the french polisher hours to match the bald spot with the oak.

All the veneering was done by one man, Jack, brilliant at his job but cantankerous and belligerent, and therefore often lonely. On one occasion, by muttering antagonistic remarks he picked on one of the joiners who could stand it no longer and, taking Jack by the throat, forced him backwards over a bench. I saw his hand grope out and pick up his razor-sharp veneering knife. Someone shouted and the joiner leapt back; knife in hand Jack advanced and the joiner picked up a chisel. They circled one another and, suddenly, like two cats, they leaped at each other in a flurry of arms and legs. All work stopped and the other men stood around helplessly until Frank forced his way between the fighting figures and, taking each by the hair, held them apart long enough for them to be disarmed. He then cracked their heads together and by the time the foreman had made his way to our end of the workshop everyone was hard at work and pretended they knew nothing of any incident.

One of my jobs was to prepare the glue – 'Glue cold won't hold. Glue thick won't stick'. Another job was to make the tea, which was criticised until one of the older men told me how they liked it: 'Fill the kettle with cold water, add six teaspoonsful of tea, twelve of sugar, quarter of a pint of milk and put it on the gas till it boils, you idiot.' This was intended to be taken seriously, but at other times gullible apprentices were teased unmercifully: they would be sent to borrow 'the skirting steps' or 'the cornice kneepads'.

We apprentices were also general dogsbodies – when a lorryload of timber arrived we had to unload and restack it; our hands became tough and impregnable to the rough-sawn planks. Again, every week we had to take a bicycle load of brass hinges and push-bars to an electro-plating workshop where they were 'bronzed' or 'chromiumed'.

To be sent down to the mill on the ground floor was particularly exciting. In the dust-laden atmosphere it was quite impossible to see from one end to the other. Try to imagine yourself standing in the works of a vacuum cleaner with the blades and wheels, magnified fifty times, whirring around two feet above your head. The noise was incessant and the clattering wheels and shafts were driven by two giant, juddering electric motors. From the spinning wheels belts led down to drive screaming machines which chewed and gnashed long lengths of timber and spewed out the remainder in the form of chippings and dust. Eerie figures in caps moved around, feeding wood into these insatiably devouring monsters. Because of the dust we learned to identify the three mill-hands by their shapes. Alf, a large bull of a man but kindness itself, operated the spindle. From the drawing office came the outline of a proposed moulding; Alf would then grind a cutter to match it, fit it into his spindle, throw the lever which engaged the canvas belt to the spinning wheels and feed in a length of square section timber and from the other side would emerge a beautiful cyma-recta or cyma-reversa or a simple ovolo; only the strength and steadiness of his hands preventing any ridges – this was difficult enough on a straight length of wood, but it was sheer artistry to watch the swoop of his arms as he worked on a curved piece. Alf had an eagle eye for a 'shake' in timber – cracks which appear during the seasoning process – as such timber could only produce very second-rate mouldings. But more vital was to spot a 'cup shake', which occurs in a growth ring: if hit by the cutter it could send a long, spear-shaped piece of wood flying down the length of the mill. A workmate of Alf had been killed by one – 'It went right through 'im'.

Then there was the thin angular outline of Maurie who worked the circular saws. He and the saws were equally dangerous – Maurie had two fingers missing on his left hand. He would manoeuvre great baulks of timber, twenty or more feet long, on to the bench and edge them into the saw, which screeched as it ripped through. It was often our dubious task to receive the two pieces that emerged from the other side. Several times I saw Maurie perform a terrible trick on a new apprentice: as the saw bit through the last inch he flicked his end on to the spinning blade, which wrenched the wood out of the apprentice's hands and sent it somersaulting over his head. From Maurie I originally heard every four-letter word. Everything to him was down to basics.

'How long you been married, Tom?' he asked the lorry-driver.

'Three years.'

'Just started farting in front of yer missus then.'

The medium-sized outline was Ernie, who operated the planer, which grumbled and chattered as it reduced a piece of 'nine b' two sawn' to 'eight 'n' threequarter by one 'n' threequarters finished', and the band saw which dealt with everything but a straight line. He was the shop steward for the Amalgamated Society of Wood-workers which we were encouraged to join – but there was no closed shop. Ernie lovingly showed me around the hardwood store and explained the properties and usages of the various woods. Budge Farley at school had first encouraged me to appreciate the tactile values of timber and now Ernie took it a step further. He showed me the differences between the grain of English oak and the 'flower' of Japanese; the varieties of mahogany, from Spanish and Honduras to the inferior sapele, luan and utille; the weight of lignum vitae; the qualities of beech, sycamore, maple and the uses of rosewood, burr-walnut, yew and zebra-wood; the sand in teak which would blunt my plane. He showed me how to look down the length of a piece of wood to detect any 'winding' (twisting). I still get a positive thrill from the feel of good timber.

'All right,' said Frank, 'so you think you know all about timber. Each plank you work on has a "way of the grain". In its natural state does the grain run up or down a tree? – You don't know? The grain runs both ways, but a tree tapers to the top and the "way of the grain" is produced when it is sawn into parallel planks.'

I cut my fingers with the chisel, bruised my thumb with the hammer, made my arms ache with the screwdriver (have you ever tried screwing for four hours at a stretch?), and got enormous blisters in my hands, as I helped to fashion the beautiful timber.

I was happy, but on the international horizon, war was imminent. The declaration came on 3rd September, 1939. Six weeks later I celebrated my sixteenth birthday. For the first few months of the war Colmans carried on much as before. Customers continued to order revolving doors, which on several occasions I was sent with Frank to fit at London hotels, the Cumberland for instance, and stores such as Bentalls in Kingston. But it was a sign of my lowly rank that I had to travel in the back of a lorry with the dismembered doors, whereas Frank sat with the driver. The windows of our factory had to be fitted with blackout frames which was a job that could be given to the apprentices, and we all had to take our turn at firewatching duty. This was enormous fun as I had never before stayed up all night. Tin hats and coffee were provided, but we brought our own food. Meanwhile the factory was slowly being turned over to the war effort, with Colmans making endless ammunition boxes and instrument containers.

One day in 1940 I received a telephone call that was to change my life. My cousin Frank had, from his school days, been a keen amateur actor and joined the Brighton Little Theatre Company. In the middle of rehearsals for a new play he received his call-up papers for the RAF and he was now asking me if I would take over his part.

'Don't be damned silly,' I said. (Both my sister and brother were devotees of The Drama, but I was a philistine.)

'It's dead easy,' Frank pleaded, 'all you have to do is learn some lines and go on.'

I could not think of a good enough excuse (Frank knew I couldn't) so I agreed.

The play was called *A Modern Aspasia* and had been written especially for the company by a local resident, Hamilton Fyfe. Frank introduced me to the enthusiastic company. The theatre held some seventy people and the company specialised in plays written mainly by foreigners, with names that meant nothing to me, Chekhov, Ibsen, Strindberg and Shaw. I learned my lines and went on. It was not as frightening as I had expected. I encountered the camaraderie always to be found among actors: Evelyn Bannister, Cicely Atkinson, Geoffrey Spence, Tom Gowling, Doris Sabine and Una Todd all guided my inexpert steps. I had fallen among friends. I was asked to do another play; and another; and another. Each took a month. One Sunday evening a young professional actor came to talk to us; he had recently been called up in the Navy and was training at HMS *King Alfred* in Hove, where I had previously fitted all the panelling in the ballroom. This was my first meeting with Alec Guinness.

One of my performances was seen by Charles F. Smith, who wrote to me on writing paper headed Mobile Entertainments Southern Area (MESA, as it was known) to ask if I would come and see him at his office at the Theatre Royal, Brighton.

The son of a Leeds mill owner, Charles Smith hated the idea of following his father into business and had devoted most of his time to fostering theatre in Yorkshire. He founded civic playhouses in Leeds and Bradford, as well as the Leeds Arts Theatre. He engaged the services of Edith Craig to produce a spectacular *Everyman* on the steps of Leeds Town Hall, discovered and employed Eric Portman and persuaded Nugent Monck (of whom more anon) to come from Norwich to produce several plays. Smith had retired to Brighton and after the outbreak of war was horrified by the A, B, C, and D system of allocating entertainment adopted by the newly-formed ENSA (as the Entertainments National Service Association was known). 'A' shows were virtually complete London productions which could only play in garrison towns with already well equipped theatres, whereas the 'D' shows comprised merely an accordionist and singer or conjuror who were sent to isolated ack-ack sites. Charles Smith thought that all service personnel were making equal contributions to the war effort and therefore all should receive the same quality of entertainment. To this end, he started and financed MESA and for four years sent out two plays, two concert parties and a film show nearly every night, using as a base Brighton's Theatre Royal, of which he was a director.

Charles rose from his desk as I was ushered in by his attractive secretary Patricia Brent. (I later discovered she was also an actress in his company. She is now a BBC producer.) He looked surprisingly like an older Noël Coward with twinkling eyes, a slightly protruding lower lip and no upper lip. As he walked with short steps, he leaned forward, giving the impression that he was about to topple, with only the quickness of his steps preserving his equilibrium.

The formalities over, Charles went straight to the point, and, to my astonishment, asked me to join his company (not, I was to discover later, because he thought I was brilliant, but because he could not get anyone else). I tried to explain that this was quite impossible. I had just received my call-up papers, and at my medical examination I had been pronounced unfit because of asthma, but I was still required to do war work of a lower grade and had been offered the choice of ambulance attendant or answering a telephone in a Report Centre. 'In that case there is no problem,' said Charles. 'My company qualifies as the same grade. I will get in touch with the authorities.'

My parents, to my surprise, raised no objections, probably because I had no intention of leaving Colmans and during the day would still be working off the remaining three and a half years of my apprenticeship, to leave me qualified for something at least. On my Colmans' wages I had to be subsidised. As Mumps had a theory that she could feed a family for one pound a week per head, each of us paid her half of our wages until that sum equalled one pound. In my first year at Colmans I had been giving her three shillings a week, but as she paid for my lunches, which cost one shilling and sixpence a day from a shop opposite the factory, and also my train fares, I was not exactly pulling my weight as far as the family exchequer was concerned. I was sixteen and my three shillings a week pocket money hardly allowed for much high living. Charles Smith was prepared to pay me seven shillings and sixpence a performance, for a maximum of five performances a week. This could add one pound seventeen shillings and sixpence to my second-year wage which had now risen to eight shillings – I could give Mumps her one pound and still be left with one pound five shillings and sixpence. I would be rich.

For the next three and a half years I held down two jobs: from eight a.m. to five p.m. I was a joiner, and from five-thirty to midnight I was an actor. It being now quite impossible for me to travel to and from Ditchling to sleep at home, I stayed for most nights of the week in my grandmother's house in Hove. But I never divulged to my friends at Colmans that I had another job. I led a totally schizophrenic existence and used two accents, as my MESA voice would have met with derision at Colmans.

My first part for MESA was Dudley in Gerald Savory's *George and Margaret*, which was directed by Winifred Shelley, who also played my mother. Winifred, who hated the abbreviation Winnie, but was known to all as Winif, was the wife of H. Jack Keates, the manager of the Theatre Royal. A friendship was born which lasted until their recent deaths. They became surrogate parents to me and I loved them both. Years later when my second son Marc was born they became his godparents. They were a devoted couple and their flat at 18, Montpelier Place, Hove, became a second home to selected MESA young ones. They vetted our girl friends and any of whom they disapproved were icily cold-shouldered, but those who passed were absorbed into the fold with incredible warmth. One's first impression of Winifred was of reserve, there was no hint of her bubbling warm sense of humour. She gave the semblance of being top heavy, her round face topping a bosom which tapered suddenly to finely shaped but thin legs.

Jack could be seen every evening welcoming his patrons in the foyer of the theatre. Short in stature, his bloodshot eyes, with dark rings beneath them, protruded slightly. These eyes lit up and sparkled at the sight of his 'popsies', but he adored Winif. Those of us who were privileged to be of their circle could always obtain complimentary tickets or be squeezed into the management box if the house was full – but not if we turned up with someone of whom they disapproved. Back stage there was a small bar known as The Single Gulp and to this we would be invited at the end of the performance to join the cast of the current play.

Rehearsals for *George and Margaret* took place in the Keates's sitting room. Winif told me years later that she despaired of my performance which did not come alive until the first night – a characteristic of many amateurs. We opened on 26th January, 1941 to an audience of soldiers.

We would set out for a performance in a Southdown bus from which half the seats had been removed to allow room for our scenery and furniture. On arrival the men erected the scenery and the girls made themselves responsible for the props and furnishings, because we carried no stage managers. Sound effects were produced by whoever happened to be in the wings at the time.

Our theatres and stages varied enormously in size: one night we might play in a building seating 2,000; the next in a Nissen hut capable of seating seventy with a stage ten feet square. Mostly our venues were village halls. I think I have played in more of these in Kent, Sussex, Hampshire and Surrey than any other actor. More often than not we all had to share a dressing room and I would find attractive girls on all sides removing their clothes – or most of them. At the end of the performance we had to pack everything back into the bus and return to Brighton.

After Dunkirk the whole of the South Coast was barricaded and only residents were allowed within fifteen miles of the coast. Gun emplacements had been dotted along the shore. We heard at first-hand the story of General Montgomery coming down to inspect the defences and asking a young subaltern if there were any problems: 'Yes, sir,' he said pointing to his map. 'There are Howitzers here and here with a range of X yards, twenty-five-pounders here and here with a range of Y yards and anti-tank guns here and here with a range of Z yards – this leaves a stretch of coast twenty yards long quite undefended. Suppose the Germans were to land there! – what should we do?'

'Count them as they come ashore, ring me up, tell me how many and I'll tell you what to do,' replied Monty.

We took our plays to these gun emplacements and to ack-ack sites on the Sussex Downs. Never since have I known such enthusiastic reception or such audience participation. We were at one with them: from the hilarious moment in *Private Lives* when, shortly after Elyot has uttered the delightful Coward line 'Don't quibble, Sybil', he handed her a cocktail and as she raised it to her lips a voice from the audience shouted, 'Don't dribble, Sybil', to the uncanny experience we had when playing Terence Rattigan's *French Without Tears* to an RAF audience.

The performance was going splendidly and the audience were on their toes, responding to every nuance when suddenly halfway through the second act the laughter ceased. Silence . . . What had happened? We cast questioning looks at each other. We continued the dialogue haltingly . . . and then . . . stopped. We became aware of a concerted murmur . . . Wrrr . . . Trrr . . . Thrrr . . . Frrr.

Unbeknown to us a squadron had set out from that RAF station during the afternoon. Now they were returning and the entire audience was counting them in as their ears picked up the drone of the engines . . . Five . . . Six . . . Seven . . . Thank God – on that occasion – they all returned. As the last was heard a cheer went up. We had all been facing each other for – what? – thirty minutes? The audience had never ceased looking in our direction, but were oblivious of our presence. Now we could breathe again and we continued with the scene to much laughter – laughter tinged with a certain hysteria – laughter of a quality I will probably never hear again.

This was the time of the Home Guard. A friend of mine in the regular Army had to deliver a highly important message to headquarters in the middle of the night. Sitting in the back of a staff car, he was being driven at top speed through the Sussex lanes when a waving red light from a Home Guard post could be seen ahead. The driver started to slow down, but was ordered to drive straight through. Muffled figures leaped out of the way. Fifty yards further on a bullet shattered the rear window. Seconds later a second shot missed my friend by inches and buried itself in the backside of the driver. The car swerved to a standstill. Up came an elderly and panting Home Guard waving a smoking Lee-Enfield rifle and shouting, 'It's a good job you did stop – I wouldn't have fired the third shot in the air!'

George and Margaret remained a permanent standby, but many other plays were included in our repertoire: *Fresh Fields, Private Lives, Good Morning Bill, French Without Tears, The Man in Possession* – for this play MESA was joined by Winifred Shotter and Laurence O'Madden, who were both to appear with us off and on for the rest of the war. Laurence was one of the finest comedy actors I have ever seen. What a technician! One day at rehearsal I was seated next to him in the green room as he was working on his script. He was reading through a long speech and after some thought he pencilled four crosses at various points in the text. I was intrigued, and, being young and eager to learn, I could not resist asking him what the crosses were for.

'Mmm? Oh! That's where I am going to get the laughs.'

I tried a fairly knowing 'Ah', but I was bemused.

Up to that moment I thought that an author wrote funny lines and if spoken clearly enough by the actor the audience would laugh. I bided my time. The play opened and sure enough where he had placed the crosses came four laughs. A couple of nights later I plucked up courage and asked, 'How did you *know* that at those points the audience would laugh?'

'It was my decision,' he replied, and turned to the page in his script. 'For instance I could have got laughs there, there, there and there, but I think the others are better.'

'Oh, come off it,' I said.

'All right. I'll show you what I mean,' he countered. 'Tomorrow night I'll give you the alternatives.'

Sure enough at the next performance he cut the four laughs he had been getting and got four new ones. I was watching goggle-eyed and as he came off stage he said, 'You see what I mean – the others are better.'

He became my hero. He never proffered advice unless asked and I never stopped asking. Every night we had a post-mortem on the performance. 'Don't drop your voice at the end of a sentence – hit it for six', 'Kill that laugh – it's not worth it,' etc. I experimented and when I succeeded I received a wink from his upstage eye. He would metaphorically hold my arm as he willed me to 'wait for it – wait for it' during a laugh and then, a flash of his eyes: 'NOW!'

During one of our periodic returns to *George and Margaret* we took the production to the docks at Newhaven. The Navy had erected a corridor of lavatories in the customs hall for the benefit of their personnel, made of matchboarding fixed to alternate sides of timber framing, open to the roof. On my way to one of the cubicles I heard a plaintive cry of 'Help! Help!' Winif, I discovered, had locked herself in and was now unable to undo the latch. I had always fancied myself as a knight errant and shouted to her, 'Don't panic – I'll get you out.' I went into the next compartment and managed to climb up the framing and then dropped down to her side. I tried the latch, but – disaster – it would not shift, but, worse still, her cubicle had matchboarding on both sides. There was no way out. Presently two plaintive voices could be heard calling, 'Help! Help!' We had a lot of explaining to do.

We also played in Dover during the time the Germans were shelling the town from Calais. For years I kept some pieces of shrapnel that came through the roof during a performance. On another occasion we arrived in Pevensey and were told that the play could not start for two hours. Being on the coast I thought this would be a delightful moment for a walk on the sands. I had ventured some way down towards the sea when suddenly a stentorian voice roared, 'STAND STILL!' I turned, to be met by 'DON'T MOVE!' An officer was standing there, back on the road. 'You're in the middle of a minefield; stay right there till I get back,' and he disappeared into a building.

He came back with a detailed plan. Consulting it, he said quietly but ominously, 'Take two steps to your left . . . stop . . . come towards me . . . turn to your right . . . a little more . . . stop . . . towards me to the right a little . . . good . . . as you are.' As I put my foot on the road the voice cracked and I was treated to a torrent of invective.

As D-Day approached vast numbers of troops began to be assembled in South-East England and a veil of secrecy masked all movements. We would set out as usual from the Theatre Royal, but we were not allowed to know our destination. At an established rendezvous we were taken over by two soldiers – one to drive and the other to see that we did not peep when all the blinds were pulled down. I became the one member of the company who could tell the others where we were; I had spent so many years bicycling round the lanes that I only had to feel the sway of the bus to know each corner: Ah yes, left at the crossroads: towards Uckfield; right at

Uckfield; left at Cross-in-Hand; no left turn so it must be Mayfield.

If the Germans had really wanted to know where our troops were massing they should have asked me.

All this time Charles Smith, like a Chinese Mandarin, hovered around and guided my steps, professionally and socially. He became my mentor. Earlier I may have given a wrong impression to the reader: my initial arrangement with MESA was for a 'maximum of five performances a week'. Sometimes there were only two. As D-Day approached sometimes six. Sometimes, because of troop movements, performances were cancelled. On my evenings off Charles arranged for me to have voice production lessons from a Brighton teacher, Leslie Charteris Coffin. Although I could be heard, my voice was then what can only be described as mouse-coloured. Leslie gave it timbre and forced it down in register. I became a bass.

Charles also guided my theatregoing and insisted that I studied certain actors. He once arranged for me to go to every performance during a week at the Theatre Royal. 'I want you to watch this actor, watch his movement, watch what he does with his hands, listen to the way he uses his voice. And never, never do it!' Alfred Lunt was the one actor who could do no wrong and was given top priority as a model to be emulated.

Charles had seen and known every actor of note in the twentieth century – he had begun his own theatregoing at the Lyceum and Henry Irving remained for him 'the master' – and when they visited the Theatre Royal, he arranged for me to meet them, usually at his flat on Marine Parade. Charles had done several world tours and his rooms bore a decided eastern influence: Chinese tables and chests, Japanese scrolls, carvings from Bali, Eastern rugs littered the floor, and paintings by Jacob Kramer, whose talent Charles had fostered by commissioning portraits of his own family and friends. There, among actors, I met a cross-section of the professions, many drawn from Charles's younger days in Leeds: Norman Newman, who has now been my doctor for thirty-five years and understands my metabolism better than anyone else: when I am feeling at my worst and near death's door he merely says, 'Come and see me' (why doesn't he come to see *me*?) and then says there is 'nothing wrong with you – get back to work'; and Mick Baker, who we knew as a doctor, but not for years did we discover that his specialisation was VD. 'Never acknowledge me in public,' he was to remark, 'people will automatically assume we know each other professionally.' I once asked him how business was: 'Oh it comes along in dribs and drabs.'

On Sunday nights there were parties given specifically so that we should play The Game which was quite new then, but is better known through television as *Give us a Clue*. We young actors were expected to show our paces, but Charles, who was our host and would sulk if he were not given two turns, was quite abysmal: he would face us and after an interminable pause would flutter one hand in the air. When asked how many words there were in the sentence he was trying to enact, he would pause and then flutter his hand in the air again. At long last a member of his own side would whisper the answer to us, which would be something totally unexpected, such as 'The Birth of a Nation'.

Alcohol was available, but rarely consumed – endless cups of coffee were necessary to keep us on our toes – but here, at the age of twenty, I had my first alcoholic drink, a half pint of beer. And hated it. Both my parents, and their parents before them, were confirmed teetotallers and 'drink' was never allowed in the house. To this day I do not really enjoy it. The prime effect of alcohol seems to be to produce a sense of euphoria: an other-than-now-ness. This must necessarily presume that one is unhappy with one's normal state. I always feel worse, not better, after imbibing. I'm sorry if that sounds pi. I really have tried to like it.

Marine Parade was not my only source of social contact. Colmans expected me to attend evening classes once a week at the Brighton Technical College. One evening I passed a beautiful girl in the main hall; she had jet black hair and was wearing a pillar-box coloured suit. I arranged to meet her the next Sunday. Her name was Joanne Coates and she was studying Fine Art – I dropped a few names, like Giotto and Massaccio, which I had learned from Jack Freestone and I was in. I had hitherto avoided the ballet, thinking it rather wet, but she was a devotee and together we saw everything the Theatre Royal had to offer. (She passed the Keates test.)

During the war in Brighton one could die of a surfeit of *les pliès*. We had the Sadler's Wells ballet with Fonteyn and Helpmann; the Ballet Rambert with Sally Gilmour and Walter Gore; the Ballet Jooss; the Lydia Kyasht; the Anglo-Polish with Halama and Konarski; the International with Mona Inglesby and the Wonderland Company (in which I first met Wendy Toye, Tommy Linden, Beryl Kaye, Daphne Anderson, and fell head over heels in love with Barbara Jdanova).

Some years before my parents had tried to foster in me a friendship with a boy from Hassocks, largely because he too was a
weakling and had been excused games. He wrote poetry (I didn't
realise that people actually did it: I thought it just a boring subject
for schoolboys) and took me to a meeting in Hove of the Sussex
Poetry Society, whose secretary told me the history of the society
and mentioned the poets who lived locally. The only name I reacted
to was 'Lord Alfred Douglas'.

Someone at the Little Theatre had loaned me a biography of
Oscar Wilde (with malice aforethought, I now think) and, in it, of
course, Alfred Douglas featured prominently. Through Charles I
had discovered that 'famous' people were still alive; previously I
imagined that all 'famous' people were dead. Now here was a
'famous' person, living in Hove. I would make it my business to
meet him. Some days later I surreptitiously discovered his address
and set off. It was, to my surprise, only a few hundred yards behind
Colmans' factory, a street of very small houses built shortly after
the First World War – two rooms and a kitchen on the ground
floor, with two rooms and a bathroom upstairs. The front door led
straight into a passageway with the stairs running up ahead. Beside
the door a small bow window supported the bow of the room
above. (*The* Lord Alfred Douglas living *here*?) With some trepidation, but tingling with excitement I rang the bell. A long pause. The
door was wrenched open and there stood a vast gorgon of a woman
wearing carpet slippers and rumpled woollen stockings. She had
wide hips and pendulous breasts at her waistline, sloping shoulders
and a large head with a fringe of mangy black hair, but nearly bald
on top. Her lower jaw jutted, disclosing no teeth on her upper jaw
and four fangs on her lower, which must have completely bypassed
her upper dentures when they were there. This was Eileen. 'Yes?'

'I – I – I – would it be possible to speak to Lord Alfred Douglas?'

'Who are you?'

My name seemed of so little importance, but I stammered it out.

'Can I help? Good morning,' came a frail voice from the darkness
of the passage.

Reluctantly the gorgon gave way and retreated to the kitchen.
Her place was taken by a little stooping man, not more than five
feet, four inches tall, with grey hair, bleary eyes and pouches under
them and a bulbous nose. 'Please come in,' said Lord Alfred.

I was taken in to the back room which overlooked the small

garden. The furniture was Edwardian; a mahogany glass-fronted bookcase, a sideboard with mirror over it and a dining table, with four chairs. I was invited to sit.

By sheer luck I opened by talking about his poetry, having done my homework and borrowed and read his sonnets. (I was to learn later that he would shut up like a clam if a newcomer embarked on the subject of Oscar Wilde.) He must have known I had no knowledge of what I was talking about, but I think he was flattered that a young 'actor' had been brave enough to call on him and he responded charmingly. I was invited to tea the following week and so began a series of visits during which he would talk of his childhood, his time in Oxford, the actors he had known – not many – his court cases, books and writers, and gradually the subject of Oscar Wilde, whom he always recalled with great affection. Tears sometimes welled in his eyes.

One day in a Brighton second-hand bookshop I saw a book entitled *Oscar Wilde and Myself* by Alfred Douglas. He had never mentioned this book so I bought and read it. I was shocked. It was full of vitriol and he abused Wilde on every page. I could not understand. On my next visit I took it with me. 'I've just been reading this,' I said, and produced it from my bag . . .

Bosie leaped to his feet, his whole body twitching, his face became deathly white and his eyes glared, he spluttered and mucus ran from his nose and mouth. He seemed to be choking and his eyes grew larger and sightless. The

> walls suddenly seemed to reel,
> and the sky above my head became
> like a casque of scorching steel

At last he managed an intake of breath and screamed, 'WHERE DID YOU GET IT? WHERE DID YOU GET IT?'

I was deeply shocked but tried to explain. He snatched the book with jumping hands – for a moment I thought he was going to throw what had cost me two shillings and sixpence on the fire. I was seeing the Douglas I later read about.

He embarked on the explanation that after Wilde's death Arthur Ransome had written *Oscar Wilde, A Critical Study*, and quoted passages from *De Profundis*, the letter (then in the possession of Wilde's literary executor, Robert Ross) in which he posthumously accused Douglas of being the sole cause of his downfall. Douglas sued Ransome. Ransome pleaded justification and produced the manuscript. Douglas lost the case and with the assistance of T. W. H. Crosland rushed into print with his own version of the story, *Oscar Wilde and Myself*.

With the mellowness of age he saw things in a different perspective. The book had been out of print for thirty years and had been wiped from his memory until I thoughtlessly brought it back into his life. He threw the book on the table, grabbed a pen, wrote a repudiation of it down the flyleaf and thrust it back into my hands.

I feel rather disloyal recounting this story, because on every other occasion he behaved impeccably. In my reduced circumstances I found it difficult to repay his hospitality. On two occasions I scraped enough money together to take him to lunch at the Pavilion Hotel (the haven of MESA) praying that he would not stray from the three shillings and sixpence table d'hôte. Once a child was bawling at another table: 'Portrait of a bloody child,' he grumbled. I proffered a drink. 'No, thank you. The wages of gin is breath, as Oscar would have said.'

I was probably not alone in finding it quite extraordinary that Douglas should have been so ridiculously careless as to have left the famous 'love' letter from Wilde in a suit which he gave away (another version of the incident is that the letter was stolen). The letter –

. . . it is a marvel that those red rose-leaf lips of yours should have been made no less for music of song than for madness of kisses. Your slim gilt soul walks between passion and poetry. I know Hyacinthus, whom Apollo loved so madly, was you in Greek days . . . Always with undying love, Yours Oscar.

– later became a central piece of evidence in Wilde's trial. I questioned Bosie about his apparent stupidity, but he said, 'My dear Donald, you must realise that this letter was by comparison with others insignificant – I had received scores of letters from Oscar far more beautiful, far more personal than that one. I kept them locked away – but I burned them after the Ransome case.'

Bosie later moved to the farm of Edward Colman (no relation to the shopfitter) at Lancing; I had left Sussex, but we corresponded. I only saw him once more, when he was confined to his bed. I sat beside him for some time, but he was very weak and conversation was difficult. He signed a photograph for me – the last thing he

1

This book (nearly all of which was written by T. D. H. Crosland) has long since been repudiated by me. It does not represent my real views about Wilde as I have explained in numerous places. I much regret that it was ever published. Alfred Douglas

Sep. 1944.

Lord Alfred Douglas's dedication on my copy of *Oscar Wilde and Myself*.

ever wrote. A few days later, on 20th March, 1945, I received a telegram, 'LORD ALFRED DOUGLAS DIED EARLY THIS MORNING. COLMAN.' Not more than ten of us gathered at his graveside in Crawley as we buried Oscar's 'Rose-lipped youth'.

To me, a very kind old man.

I have moved ahead of myself. Let us go back twelve months to spring 1944. Things international and personal were reaching a climax. Preparations were advancing apace for the invasion of Normandy and many more performances a week were required of us, but of relatively greater importance to me was my personal D-Day – on 5th March I would complete my apprenticeship at Colmans. I could then leave. But should I devote myself to the theatre or remain a joiner?

I could not understand what Charles meant when he asked me, 'What have you got to offer the theatre?' – I was still taking too much out of it. I now know what he meant and always ask the same of aspiring actors.

One persistent visitor to Charles's flat was the celebrated drama critic of *The Sunday Times*, James Agate. A homosexual, who had the appearance of a prize-fight promoter, he was a short, bulky man with a large bony head, whose protruding upper teeth made his 'S's difficult to pronounce – they sounded more like 'TH's. I met him many times at Marine Parade. He too had begun his theatregoing by watching Irving.

'Did you ever *speak* to Irving?' I once asked.

'Certainly not,' glowered J.A. '*Greatness* is not to be spoken to – I don't know how you can sit there speaking to *me* like that.'

He was fond of giving advice on acting to the young, and would begin by asking a question. If we knew the answer he would override us. *He* wanted to tell *us*. 'Now if I asked you for a match for my cigar what would you do? The aristocracy would throw me a box; the middle class would pass me a box; the lower class would take out a match and light it for me.' He once asked if I had noticed that the higher the social scale the straighter the fingers and the nearer one gets to the artisan the more curled they become. I knew exactly what he meant: my own fingers were always clenched around an imaginary hammer.

He was a wonderful raconteur. He told me the story behind C. E. Montague's oft-quoted review of Frank Benson's *Richard II* in the *Manchester Guardian*. Montague wrote that Benson's Richard was more obsessed with the *idea* than the *deed*, following this through to his final lines,

> Mount, mount, my soul, thy seat is up on high;
> Whilst my gross flesh sinks downward, here to die.

at the end of which Benson, who was lying down, faltered, then raised himself, and repeated the words 'to die'. The *idea* of dying.

Agate questioned Benson about this and asked why in his present performance he was no longer repeating the words. Benson then told him that he had often wondered about the nonsense that Montague had written. A busy man, running his own company and with many other things on his mind, at that particular performance in Manchester he got to the end of the play, but could not recall saying his last words so roused himself and said them again.

Of such are legends made.

Another favourite Agate story concerned the time when he was in a chauffeur-driven car going north up the old A1. He had started late for an appointment in the Midlands. Ahead lay a sleepy village astride a crossroad, with a thirty m.p.h. sign and the derestriction sign hardly a hundred yards apart. The driver started to brake, but Agate insisted that he kept moving. Sure enough, hiding around the corner was a police motorcyclist who gave chase and flagged down the car. The policeman slowly got off his machine, removed his gauntlets which he placed on the saddle, came over to the car and bent down at the open window. On seeing the driver his demeanour suddenly changed: 'Hello!' he said and, putting his head in the car, gave the driver a smacking kiss right on the lips and added, 'Get going and don't get caught again.'

The car started off.

'Do you know him?' asked the astonished Agate.

'I can't remember his name sir,' replied the chauffeur, 'but we were in the Guards together.'

Surprisingly one of J. A.'s main interests was keeping a string of trotting ponies, which cost him a large amount of money. He rather dressed the part with a brown bowler hat and a covert overcoat. One day he invited the President of the All England Trotting Ponies Association, an archetypal Brigadier, to lunch at his flat in Grape Street. It so happened that at that time almost every resident in the block was homosexual, including the staff.

After lunch, which had been served by J. A's 'man servant', they decided to go for a walk. Arriving in the lift at the ground floor J. A. realised he had left his walking stick behind, and, in a tone of masculine thunder, he asked the hall porter, 'Get through to my man and tell him to bring my stick.'

The porter picked up the house phone and, overheard by the Brigadier, President of the All England Trotting Ponies Association, said: 'Is that you, Emma? – She's forgotten her wand again.'

Charles had faith in my ability as an actor, but not feeling qualified to advise me that I should make a career in such a precarious profession, he asked J.A., who had previously seen several MESA performances, to come down to Brighton specifically to give his opinion. He stayed at the Pavilion Hotel and Charles and I met him at the Stage Door Club on Saturday evening. It was arranged that we should foregather at Charles's flat after lunch the next day for a serious session.

After some coffee J.A. thrust a copy of Shakespeare into my hands open at Wolsey's farewell speech from *Henry VIII*. I had neither seen nor read the play before, but I dived in . . . There was a long silence and then he growled, 'Yes . . . it's an interpretation – it's the *wrong* one – but it's an interpretation.' He then asked me to read Buckingham's farewell, in which I did not fare nearly so well. Then, to my consternation, he asked me to 'do something modern'. I had nothing up my sleeve but a scene from Frederick Lonsdale's *On Approval*, which I had mugged up some time before as an audition piece. I did it nervously and badly. He ruminated for a few minutes and then said, 'Yes, Charles, let him do it, but,' and turning to me, 'you must get into Shakespeare – it's the *only* way to learn your job. Good luck.'

Agate's own version of the interview appeared in his autobiography *Ego 7*, for Sunday, 20th February, 1944:

Excellent lunch, after which I am persuaded to interview a boy of twenty, Don Sinden, who has been playing in Charles's repertory company. He is the son of a chemist, and according to Charles has some notion of acting. Will I say whether, in my opinion, he should go on the stage or stick to cabinet-making, to which he had already served his apprenticeship? Murmuring 'Stick to your fretwork, young man!' I prepare to go to sleep. But Charles won't have it, and presently I find myself taking stock of the boy. Enough height, an attractive head, something of the look of young Ainley, a good resonant voice, vowels not common, manner modest yet firm. Straightway and without fuss he gives me a taste of his quality – Wolsey's Farewell – and after a bit I am playing Cromwell! We then go through Buckingham's last scene, and I find myself suggesting that even the 'mirror of all courtesy' can't be supposed to enjoy going to the block, that the whole of the 'All good people' speech should be spoken in the light of this, and that 'Lead on, o' God's name!' is not a pious command but shows Buckingham at the end of his tether. Afterwards the young man does a scene from *On Approval* quite badly, and I tell him to stick to Shakespeare, beginning at the bottom of the ladder. Which advice may ruin his career; the giving of it certainly wrecks my afternoon.

On the fifth of March I bade farewell to my colleagues at Colmans and on the sixth of March 1944 I took the plunge – I became an actor.

3
TUM LAKHRI LAKHRI TUM

'I will not allow you to climb into the West End on the backs of actors who through no fault of their own are in the services,' said Charles. 'You will stay in MESA until the war is over.' He knew that I had had one or two offers from London managers I had met at the Theatre Royal. I now had three and a half years of experience, but if I was going to do Shakespeare I was deficient in certain areas. My voice was powerful – I used to go on the Downs with a friend, pace out a quarter of a mile and then make sure he/she could understand what I was saying from the other end – but it lacked variety. My movement was not exactly fluid. I could not fence. I could not dance. (I still can't.) It was arranged, therefore, that I should go to the Webber-Douglas School of Dramatic Art which had been evacuated to Hampshire. At that time male students were in short supply and as I had no money and I could not fall back on parents, a scholarship was arranged: board and tuition for a nominal fee of nine pounds for a term of twelve weeks. Charles gave me three pounds a week pocket money, which I insisted should be treated as a loan. He laughingly agreed: 'Pay it back, if and when you can' (when I did so in the Fifties, Charles told me that I was the first actor to repay him a loan).

I buckled down to learn all I could in as short a time as possible, but life was hardly easy with thirty-one beautiful girls and only six men – three of them not in the running (and they would have us believe that the permissive society began in the Sixties). I shared a room with Bill Pyman and one embarrassing morning he was there when the matron brought some shirts back from the laundry. While putting them in a drawer she exposed a packet of contraceptives. 'What are these?' she demanded of Bill. Resourcefully he replied, 'They're something Donald uses for his asthma.' A widow of many years, she accepted the explanation apparently without a qualm.

'Lights out' was officially at ten thirty p.m. and at ten thirty-five p.m. half the students changed rooms . . .

The Principal of the school was W. Johnstone-Douglas to whom I was devoted: he taught voice-production superbly. Within weeks he had increased the range of my voice by at least an octave.

An elderly retired actress, Ellen O'Malley, who had appeared in the original productions of some of Bernard Shaw's plays (she was the first Ellie Dunn in *Heartbreak House*), taught us in 'period' plays by continually illustrating how it should be done. 'No, *NO* – like THIS,' and she would leap on to the stage; her knees sagged, her arms sawed the air and her voice thundered. We could never do it like that, nor did we want to, but our attempts, though half the size, were then an improvement on our previous efforts. One day we crossed in a corridor: she suddenly called me back and peered into my face. 'Yes, YES! I see it! You have a face exactly like Beerbohm Tree's (I swelled with pride) – without make-up it is *nothing*, but you can do anything with make-up.'

My favourite on the staff was Renée de Vaux, who was blind in one eye. She had, I understand, been a very good actress, but marriage, children, and then a sick husband had forced her to give up professional work. She was the first person to make me worry about the psychological side of a character. What was he doing this morning? Where has he come from? Where is he going? She laughed at Stanislavsky, but at heart she approved of his methods. She quickly sorted out the wheat from the chaff: at an early rehearsal she would close her eyes and appear to be asleep. Those who continued intelligently with the rehearsal would afterwards receive her closest attention; those who played about she never bothered with again.

I had an alarming experience during *Romeo and Juliet*. One of the male students was mentally sub-normal – like me he was unfit for military service and had been sent by his parents to the school in an attempt to occupy him. He was Tybalt, I was Romeo and we had to fence before I killed him. He was quite hopeless and was unable to learn the fight. For rehearsals we used walking sticks but he could do no more than Cross – Cross – Cross – Under the armpit – Dead (very boring – I was hoping to show my prowess), but for the performance we had real swords . . . A maniacal gleam came into his eye, he came at me slashing to the right and left. I managed to parry his every move, but when I thrust under his armpit he flatly refused to 'die'. Back he came striking at my head, body and legs. The audience thought it was splendid. At the first opportunity to get at close quarters I dropped my own sword and succeeded in wrenching his from his hand. I then wrestled him to the ground, knelt on his chest and impressed upon him that he should 'die, you twerp!'

On another occasion he failed to enter on his cue. Ten of us waited. The line was repeated and still he did not appear. I went to the door and found him just outside. 'It's your cue,' I hissed. 'No, it isn't,' he countered and shut the door in my face.

At the end of term I rejoined MESA for the holidays. On 6th June the Allies had landed in Normandy – D-Day. Laurence O'Madden had discovered a play called *French Leave* written by Reginald Berkeley during the First World War. Now he quickly got to work and brought it up to date (where the General called for his horse in the original, the Brigadier now called for his jeep) and, with scant acknowledgment to Reginald Berkeley, he renamed it *The Normandy Story*. Again we had Winifred Shotter in the feminine lead, and with Laurence as the Brigadier and me as the juvenile – I was working with my hero again – we raced into rehearsal and opened in a week. Place names were changed nightly to keep abreast of the Allied advance. It was a 'scoop'.

After a month I returned to the Webber-Douglas for another term, at the end of which *The Normandy Story* was resurrected. Meanwhile ENSA headquarters in London had heard about it and the entire production was requisitioned to go under their official banner to France. Within days I was fitted with a uniform – all ENSA personnel were given the honorary rank of Second Lieutenant and wore the equivalent uniform with a flash, ENSA, on the shoulder – then on to a boat and over to France, where we followed the Allied advance at a discreet, though sometimes unnerving, distance.

I had never been abroad before. We moved across Europe playing in huts and tents and were in Schleswig-Holstein when peace was declared. We continued playing, but now in larger centres. I 'discovered' Paris and was there to watch de Gaulle and Eisenhower in the victory parade. I realised that I had an insatiable interest in towns. Indeed I still spend my holidays in towns, going over them inch by inch. I have returned many times to Paris, but I have discovered very little more than on my first visit.

It soon dawned on ENSA that a war was still going on in the East. Hence we were all bundled into a Sunderland flying-boat at Poole harbour to arrive, by stages, three days later in Karachi. One more day in a Dakota and we were in Calcutta. This was my first

THEATRE ROYAL

Tel. BRIGHTON **4118**

Week commencing MONDAY, 14th AUG.

NIGHTLY at 6.30

MATINEES: THURSDAY and SATURDAY at 2.30

Box Office open 10 a.m. to 8 p.m.

M.E.S.A.

(Mobile Entertainments for the Southern Area)

presents

FRENCH LEAVE

By Captain REGINALD BERKELEY

WINIFRED	LAWRENCE
SHOTTER	**O'MADDEN**
David Ashe	**Douglas Quayle**
John Blaine	**Don Sinden**
Peter Tennant	**Ann Trevlar**

WHICH HAS BEEN PLAYED TO OUR BOYS
IN H.M. FORCES UNDER THE TITLE OF

A Normandy Story

A Topical Comedy of the Beach-heads

S.P.Co.—D4830

encounter with extreme heat and extreme humidity – if one squeezed on shaking hands the dripping sweat made a pool on the floor.

We played in exotic places such as Dacca, Jessore, Barrackpore and Comilla. We had absolutely no opportunity to do any sight-seeing or to meet any Indians (or Pakistanis as they now are). We were on the go the whole time.

A strange custom existed in the RAF who were operating from makeshift runways cut in the jungle. When they were required to pack up and move forward there seemed little point in taking the contents of the bar – far better to drink it now. The morning after such a night we were taken to the airstrip in a jeep. None of us had been to bed and everyone was far the worse for wear – the Flight Lieutenant driving the jeep especially. He was driving at breakneck speed and sometimes found himself leaving the track altogether, then driving through the trees in circles trying to find it again.

He looked very ill as we drew up beside the plane.

'Poor fellow,' I said. 'Is he coming with us?'

'He has to,' came the reply. 'He's the pilot.'

Our take-off and landing, I might say, were perfect.

During another flight, which took us across the top of the Bay of Bengal to Chittagong, I was invited up to the flight deck. The pilot was explaining how 'George', the automatic pilot, worked. I asked if it was possible manually to countermand the instructions given to 'George'. 'Oh yes – look, if I do this,' and he thrust the joystick forward and we hurtled down towards the coastline . . . He pulled out just in time and then took us hedge-hopping. Phew! and Ugh!

'Go on and tell your colleagues that you have been steering.'

I returned elated to the cabin, threw back the curtain and announced, 'I did that.' Such a sight met my eyes! People had been sick. Girls had screamed. Men had prayed and now they all believed that I had been responsible. I was never allowed on the flight deck again. Most unfair.

While we were in Rangoon the atom bomb on Hiroshima finished the war in the East and emaciated prisoners of war were released from the Japanese camps. Our entertainment was now required by a new, pathetic, yet wonderful audience. After each performance we joined the spectators, all of whom were eager for news of home, and talked way into the night. One evening we attended a concert given in a football stadium in the centre of which a platform had been erected. Gracie Fields was the star attraction and etched in my mind's eye is the sight of thousands of ragged ex-prisoners with tears streaming down their cheeks trying with croaking voices to join in as she sang 'Sally'.

Our job with the South-East Asia Command completed, we were to be returned to England. But the waiting list for places on the ships was long, and naturally actors were at the back of the queue. Some of our waiting time was spent in Calcutta. We were invited to the Tollygunge Club, where we joined a group of sahibs and memsahibs who were sitting on a large verandah in cane chairs sipping their chota pegs. A young subaltern languidly rose to his feet and proceeded to recount some jokes which were so old that when I had told them my father had told me he had heard them from his father. These were received with gales of laughter, led by an Indian Army Colonel seated on my right. He coughed and spluttered and beat his knee: 'He tells a damned good story,' he wheezed in my ear. 'Mark you – his father told 'em better.'

The order eventually came that we were to catch a nine twenty a.m. train to Bombay where we were to embark. Our baggage was collected the night before, but the next morning I overslept (I have always had difficulty in waking up) and arrived at the station at nine twenty-five a.m. to be greeted by an irate officer who informed me that the next train didn't leave until nine twenty the following morning. I caught it, but nobody had told me that the journey took three days and nights. I did not have even a toothbrush – everything had gone on ahead. The train carried only troops and we talked and sang the whole journey. They had learned a kind of pigeon-Urdu – as, for instance, the Urdu for WOOD is LAKHRI and YOU is TUM so 'Tum lakhri lakhri tum?' means 'You would, would you?'

Seventy-two hours later, with dust caked on my sweat, I arrived in Bombay to find that the rest of my company had been put straight on a ship the day before and were already on the high seas bound for England!

I registered at Greens Hotel, the ENSA hostel, where I found my baggage, and waited for the next ship. Three days later a company arrived from England headed by John Gielgud, who was to play Hamlet. But they were without a 'ghost'. John suggested that I could do it, but the wheels of bureaucracy were in motion – I had been allocated my place on the next ship. I was, however, allowed to attend all the rehearsals and each performance during the following weeks.

I have abject admiration for John Gielgud: he is everything I could not be. If Olivier is a physical actor, Gielgud is cerebral. I had seen him in *Hamlet* in London and in *Macbeth*, in *The Importance of Being Earnest*, *Love for Love*, *A Midsummer Night's Dream* and *The Duchess of Malfi*. John speaks Shakespeare's lines as if he had written them himself; we understand them because he understands them; if we do not it is our fault, not his.

The untold depths of misery he could dredge up in any of Hamlet's lines: the gravity he gave to 'A little more than kin, and less than kind'. After Hamlet had seen and talked with his father's ghost he says to himself:

> The time is out of joint: O cursed spite,
> That ever I was born to set it right!

then he turns to Horatio and Marcellus and says, 'Nay, come, let's go together'. I wish I could describe how many facets Gielgud gave to that simple line. ('Please go with me.' 'I don't want to let you out of my sight.' 'It would look better if we arrived together.' 'Let us leave this awesome place.' 'Don't leave me.') I learned from that one line what infinite possibilities are open to an actor.

John and I were walking along the coast and with all the innocence of youth I asked him what he considered the most important elements of acting. He thought for a second and replied, 'I should say *feeling* and *timing*,' and then he flashed me a look out of the corner of his eyes and gurgled, 'I understand it's the same in many walks of life.'

Many, many years later the magazine *Tit-bits* discovered an Indian palmist who was supposedly so brilliant that they arranged to test his claims and publish the results. I was asked to participate. To ensure utter secrecy I was to meet the editor at the Savoy Hotel and then be hustled across the road to an office where the editor's secretary was to telephone another secretary who was sitting with the assistant editor and the palmist in some other part of London. My hand prints were taken and sent by messenger to the palmist. So far he had no means of even knowing my sex. Everything he then said to the assistant editor was relayed to the secretary, to the other secretary, to the editor, to me and replies went back the same way. He opened by stating my sex and the exact month in which I was born! He told me about my asthma, when I left school and the type of work I had done ('working wood with your hands'). He knew when I started in MESA and then said, 'I see you in the East.' I thought that was a bit too spacial so queried, 'Where in the East?'

'Not the *Far* East – more like India,' he replied via the chain. There seemed nothing he did not know about me. Sometimes I got confused because he always prefixed his remarks by saying, 'When you are X years old . . .', while I remember everything by the year in which it happened.

Twice I thought I had caught him out: he said, quite dogmatically, that a 'close relative is very ill' (yes, but the year was wrong) and that at another time I was 'involved in litigation – over buying a property' (again the year was wrong). But later, my wife corrected me: my mother had contracted diabetes in that year and we took a lease on the house four years before we bought it!

After the session was over we all met for lunch. He asked where I had been in India. 'Mostly around Calcutta,' I replied, 'although I spent four weeks in Bombay.'

'I thought so,' he beamed. 'Did you meet any Indians in Bombay?'

'Many,' I said.

'Anyone in particular?'

'Yes. A gentleman by the name of Bukari who was the head of the radio.'

'Did you go to any of his parties?'

'Yes.'

'Did you once take home the daughter of the Maharajah of —?'

(I did – and what an escapade that was! But neither of us had breathed a word to a soul – should I now admit it?)

'Er – yes,' I replied most innocently.

'Well, I escorted her to that party.'

After four weeks of idyllic idleness in Bombay I eventually embarked for England – my first and only 'cruise'. We stopped at Cairo, where I had the opportunity to see the Pyramids, the Sphinx and the treasures from the Tomb of Tutankhamun which were being brought out from dusty wartime vaults, and at Malta and Gibraltar.

The ship was officially 'dry' – no liquor was to be sold on board, but each evening a call would come over the tannoy: 'Will Captain X, Lieutenant Y, Corporal Z report to the first officer's cabin *immediately*.' He was a short round man with a 'baby's bottom' face, known as 'Pinkie', and in the absence of any branded alcohol, he mixed a cocktail called Pinkie's Revenge. You must believe me when I tell you the ingredients: a base of brandy made in Cairo, rather more than a few drops of 'bitters', a splash of Eau de Cologne and, to provide a cloudiness like an egg nog, a dollop of Brylcreem. It was lethal! It tasted innocuous enough, but I was warned that the effect would strike me about three hours later, so to be safe I retired to my cabin. I sat on my bunk happily reading when something seemed to hit me on the back of the head. I came to seventeen hours later in the heat of the Red Sea. I have never been so ill.

Charles had not been idle in my absence. He had written – and persuaded Agate to write as well – to an old friend of his, Sir Barry Jackson, the founder of the celebrated Birmingham Repertory Theatre, who, it had just been announced, was to become the Director of the Memorial Theatre at Stratford-upon-Avon in 1946. Would he give me a job? With such guns brought to bear, poor Sir Barry could hardly say no.

There was one slight problem: rehearsals were not due to start for another six months, but again I was in luck. J. Baxter Somerville, the lessee of the Theatre Royal, Brighton, also ran theatres in Hammersmith, Leicester, Margate and Llandrindod Wells, and he kept a flat at each place. He was always 'somewhere else' if you wanted to pin him down.

I asked if he could fit me in. Yes, he had a vacancy in Leicester, but how much would I expect to be paid? Having known him as a friend for four years, I told him, quite straightforwardly, that ENSA had paid me ten pounds a week and, feeling that I was worth it, I would ask him the same.

J.B. wore heavy horn-rimmed spectacles which kept slipping down his nose and which, just as regularly, he pushed back with the middle finger of his chubby hand. He now smiled at me, his eyes twinkled and down came the glasses. He chortled, and as his finger pushed them back he said, 'Six' as if to say 'Done'. I thought he had misheard me so I repeated, 'Ten'. He chortled once more and again the glasses slipped and again he pushed them back as he said, 'Six'. Surely J.B. wouldn't do this to me, so I explained. '*Ten*, J.B.'. The glasses; the chortle; the finger, preceded '*Six*, Donald'. So off I went to Leicester for six. As a parting present Charles gave me the hat that Sir John Martin-Harvey had worn as the Dickens character, Sydney Carton, in *The Only Way*. This was to start me on my craze for collecting theatricalia.

On my way through London I stopped at the Haymarket Theatre to see *Lady Windermere's Fan*. While talking to my old friend Michael Shepley at the stage door the great Lilian Braithwaite sailed in.

To follow this story it is necessary to know that in her youth Dame Lilian had had a long-standing affair with Sir George Alexander. Lady Alexander (who was famous for wearing large hats) knew of the liaison, but in the tradition of the time accepted the situation, although from that moment on she refused to meet Lilian Braithwaite.

She now bore down on us. 'Michael; I'm *terribly* worried about Lady Alexander. I've just been down to Brighton for the weekend, staying at the Royal Crescent Hotel. On Sunday morning I decided to have a little walk along the front and on my way out, as I passed the lounge, I saw, sitting under a hat, Lady Alexander. I went over to her, extended my hand and said, "It's Lilian Braithwaite . . ." She shot up and roared, "WHERE?!" '

At Leicester a different play was presented every week. As a routine we read through the play and set Act I on Tuesdays; rehearsed Act I (having learnt it overnight) and set Act II on Wednesdays; rehearsed Act II (having learned . . .) and set Act III on Thursdays; rehearsed Act III (having . . .) and ran through the play on Fridays; ran the play on Saturdays; polished our lines on Sunday; and opened the play, after a dress rehearsal, on Mondays.

And we had afternoons off, except for matinees!

Saturdays were the worst because, after rehearsal, we had to give three performances at two thirty p.m., five p.m., and seven thirty p.m. This meant that each play could only run for two hours if we were to get one audience out and the next in. On Friday evening a list of 'cuts' was placed on the notice board, but with no time to rehearse them, the next day's two thirty p.m. show was sheer panic. A glazed look would come over the actor's face as his colleague intimated with his eyes that 'that' was all he was going to say. It always amazed us that we got to the end and it was with some relief that we started on the five p.m. show. Knowing looks of confirmation were then passed around. But the seven thirty show was chaotic: we all had the feeling that we had 'just said that line' – we had; twice in the last five hours! Hysteria set in, but, thank goodness, people came regularly to that performance knowing that it would be something like *Hellzapoppin'* – and it was! The audience expected lunacy and got it.

I shared a dressing room with another young actor who joined the company as leading man on the same day as I did – I was the juvenile. It transpired that it was his first job – and it showed. Within four weeks I was the leading man and he the juvenile. Some weeks later as we sat removing our make-up he said, 'This is bloody hard work for fifteen pounds a week, isn't it?'

'How much?!' I enquired, incredulously, 'Do you know how much they are paying me? Six pounds a week!'

Neither of us would believe the other, so the following Friday we exchanged pay packets. It was true. I thought it most unfair. I complained about my salary to J.B., but the outcome was not what either of us had expected: mine was increased to eight pounds, but my colleague's was reduced to eight pounds. J.B. had saved five pounds a week.

I must not be too hard on J.B. Although notoriously tight on money he always looked after his old friends and he would always find them a job somewhere. Henry Irving had been the same: one day an elderly actress came to him for a job. He had no vacancy, but sent for his manager, Bram Stoker, and told him that she was to be put on the payroll for looking after the theatre cat. 'But we already have an actress looking after the cat,' argued B.S. 'Then,' insisted Irving, 'let this lady look after the lady who is looking after the cat.'

My colleague made a memorable gaffe in Emlyn Williams' play *The Druid's Rest*. In one scene, for reasons best known to the plot, most of the cast are asleep on the stage while he and a young boy are talking. 'Thank you,' he had to say, 'that's very kind of you. It's a nice feeling to be wanted.' On this occasion he failed to say the last seven words. The boy had not been given his cue and would not continue until he had. After a very long silence one of the 'sleeping' figures whispered, 'It's a nice feeling to be wanted.' My colleague turned towards the voice and said, 'Yes, it is, isn't it.'

I think it was at this time that a new ASM arrived. One of her jobs was to sit with the script and prompt us when necessary. On her first day the manager was in his office during the performance when she suddenly raced in with the script and, pointing to a page, bleated: 'They've *stopped* – there!'

You may have noticed that I have not mentioned my health for some pages. I had outgrown my asthma, which had been diagnosed as being of the allergic variety. I now knew what caused it (Dust. Feather Beds. Musty clothes and, oddly enough, the fumes of sealing wax.) As long as I avoided these things I was fine. In its place, however, I now contracted cystitis which, I understand, is not usually a man's complaint. An inflammation of the bladder causes one to spend a penny with terrible frequency and great pain. More often than not the desire to go is greater than the necessity. While playing leading parts and unable to leave the stage I would hop from one foot to the other and then dash for a bucket kept in the wings – and then – nothing.

Let me digress here for a moment. A young actor in weekly rep hated his leading man. He kept a diary and in it he daily confided all the details of his obsession. 'Tonight HE killed my exit round.' 'Tonight HE ruined my finest scene.' 'Tonight HE coughed on my best laugh line.'

Then came: 'Monday. 6.15 p.m. Dear Diary. Tonight I think I am going to get the better of HIM. We open a new play and I have a speech fifteen minutes long. Downstage. In the light. Facing the audience – and HE is upstage, seated at a desk, with his *back* to the audience, writing a letter. I think I must win . . .'

A slightly drunken hand added, '11.45 p.m. *HE* DRANK THE INK.'

Our Sundays in Leicester were free and every week we would go to a concert at the De Montfort Hall, which reminded me of the first time I had seen a symphony concert advertised in Brighton. I asked my mother what it was. Knowing her son, she said, 'A symphony concert? Oh, you wouldn't like that.' Perversely, the next Saturday I went to The Dome. I was bored silly, but dared not admit it. So I went again. And again. It was the recitals that really converted me, especially those given, quite regularly, by Richard Tauber, and I began to collect his records.

One end of the De Montfort Hall was stepped like an Italian vineyard and when not required for choirs or to raise the tympani and brass players above the strings, seats were placed there and sold to the public for one shilling. This was where we always sat enthralled as we listened to Solomon, Moiseiwitsch, Menuhin, Ida Haendel, Leon Goossens, Mark Hamburg, who I remember announcing in his gruff, wheezing voice, 'I will now play Beethoven's Country Dance – he called it "Contra" dance, but it's a country dance all the same' and 'Chopin wrote the Minute Waltz to be played in one minute. I will attempt to play it in half that time.' And to John Barbirolli, George Weldon, Herbert Menges and so many others.

We learned a splendid technique: not to waste our energy applauding when the soloist was on the platform, but to wait until he reached the wings; then to lead the rest of the audience in a storm of applause to bring him back for an encore, after which we would redouble our efforts and get him back again. We got many looks of 'you bastards' from the performers, but we got our shilling's worth.

One aspect of the theatre of which many people are unaware is the fact that, until recently, for all 'modern' plays, actors had to provide their own costumes. In weekly rep an actress could be called on to provide fifty-two outfits in a year, so much borrowing went on. It was easier for a man; by now I had two suits, a dinner jacket, several pairs of trousers, two sports jackets and several cardigans, all of which I had paid for out of my own money. As these were the tools of my trade they were looked after with loving care. But we had a rather scruffy actor in the company and one week the director asked if I would lend him one of my suits as he was expected to look 'well dressed'. Reluctantly I agreed and, to my horror, each night he just dropped it on the floor in the dressing room. I found myself following him around picking up the pieces, dusting them off and hanging them up carefully. He never noticed.

My six months at Leicester were almost up. On my last night I had to make a speech from the stage and presents were handed over the footlights by the regular playgoers, to whom we were all part of a family. Having been a big fish in a small pond at Leicester, I felt more than a little apprehensive at my next engagement: the Shakespeare Memorial Theatre at Stratford-upon-Avon.

Sadly there are now practically no weekly reps, which is an irreplaceable loss in the training of young actors. They taught one to see and aim at the essentials of a character – the equivalent of graffiti in a fresco. Of course if one stayed too long one picked up bad habits, but we also learnt how to cope with any emergency, as when our leading 'character' actress Edith Devonshire entered on a first night wearing one of those long period dresses which were form-fitting down to the knee and then flared into a fish tail. But a pouffe had been placed directly in her line between a settee and an armchair and, only seeing it at the last moment, and forgetting her dress, she tried stepping over it . . . it became jammed up her fish tail. She had to fall sideways on to the settee and after several attempts succeeded in shaking it out.

4

IF THAT FAILS
YOU CAN ALWAYS TRY ACTING

Before the war a strong demarcation line existed in the theatre: (indeed in a way it still does): an actor was deemed to be either classical or modern. The classical actor would spend his whole life in the comparatively small classical repertoire and he was expected to know most of the parts within his range – in much the same position as an opera singer is today. If, shall we say, a Mercutio fell ill, at least twenty actors could be called upon at a moment's notice to replace him.

Until only a few years before, even classical actors had to provide their own costumes and as they became too old for a range of characters these costumes had to be adapted or passed on to younger actors. When Sir Henry Irving died in 1905, his company's entire wardrobe was taken over by his son H. B. Irving, and when he died, his widow Dorothea Baird sold them at auction. Actors thronged the room at viewing day – many of them could remember 'The Guv'nor' wearing certain items. Russell Thorndike, who was present, discovered a costume that was far too small to have been worn by Irving, but the sight of it stirred something in his memory. He went home, consulted his reference books and the following day bought it for ten pounds. It was the original costume worn by Edmund Kean as Richard III which must have been handed down from actor to actor. (It is now in the Guildhall Museum.) But Russell's researches were not yet over. Shortly before his death he told me that he was now convinced that this same costume had been worn previously by David Garrick as King Lear (it was not until the 1840s that any attempt was made at historical accuracy in theatre design).

In London Sir Henry Irving dominated the British theatre, to be followed by Johnston Forbes-Robertson and Beerbohm Tree. In

the provinces Frank Benson toured for the best part of forty years
with his own company. Benson was also a splendid athlete. He
believed that an actor should be as alert physically as mentally and
within his company he organised a cricket and hockey team. It is
said that he once advertised, 'Wanted: a good fast bowler able to
play Laertes.' He also suffered wonderful lapses of memory. As
Caliban one of his effects was to swing by his ankles on suspended
ropes as he beat his chest, Tarzan fashion. Madge Compton as
Miranda was waiting to make her entrance when she noticed
Benson's dresser trying to attract his attention as he looped across
the stage. 'Psst. Psst. – Sir – Psst.' When Benson looked towards
the wings Madge could see that apart from his whole body covered
in his half-fish, half-animal make-up, he still had his pince-nez
perched on his nose! Benson carried a minimal amount of scenery
on his tours and several elements did service in many plays. In
Henry V for instance there was a section of wall six feet high, over
which Benson would pole vault and immediately launch into 'Once
more unto the breach dear friends'. This same section of wall was
used in the Rialto scene of *The Merchant of Venice*. One night
Benson, as Shylock with his staff, came sailing over the wall and
after landing with great agility, realised his mistake and embarked,
'Ah! "Three thousand ducats – Well." '

Of the many members of his company I was privileged to meet
over the years my favourite was Baliol Holloway, who became a
great friend. His small London flat on an upper floor in Thayer
Street, Marylebone, was reached by a narrow staircase lined with
framed theatre playbills of Charles Kean and Macready. For me the
inside of the flat was an Aladdin's Cave. The walls were lined with
books on the theatre, prints and photographs of actors of the past,
and theatrical 'props' – such as his *Henry V* shield, crowns, swords
and daggers – hung from hooks. On the floor was an old, hand-
wound gramophone and piles of records of Gilbert and Sullivan –
he knew the complete lyrics of all the operas. One was greeted at the
door by his too-indulged dog Joey and then . . . there was Ba. (Oh,
the honour of being allowed to call him Ba – which was pronounced 'Bay'.) Very tall, he had a wonderful leonine head, large
and bony, with a splendid nose (so many of the old actors had
splendid noses. Did they become actors because of their noses? Or
was there a long-lost secret for enlarging the proboscis?). Behind
that nose must have been a cavity the size of the Albert Hall which
produced the most astonishingly resonant voice. In his time he was

the finest Othello, the finest Richard III and the finest Falstaff, but always on tour or at Stratford or at the Old Vic – to his detriment, only his Richard was seen in the West End.

While his wife Emil produced tea and biscuits, he stretched out his gaunt frame in a gaunt chair while I sat and listened to his anecdotes of a theatre tradition that had passed: the following story in particular.

Soon after the turn of the century Ba read in a theatrical newspaper that a leading man was required for a stock company in Northampton. In answer to his letter an appointment was made for the following Saturday. Ba put on his best suit, caught the train to Northampton, asked his way to the theatre and presented himself outside the manager's office. 'Come in,' a voice bellowed. Standing behind a desk was a portly man with his jacket off, braces supporting his trousers and a bowler hat on his head.

'My name is Holloway sir – Baliol Holloway.'

'Yes, well I'm glad you've come, 'olloway – I want you to start Monday.' He then opened a drawer, took out six scripts and threw them one by one on the desk: 'There you are; Monday night. Tuesday night. Wednesday matinee same as Monday. Wednesday night. Thursday night. Friday night. Saturday matinee same as Thursday. Saturday night. Six wonderful parts 'olloway. Monday night's the best one – forty-two rounds [rounds of applause] in it. And you've got the best line in the play: I'll give it to you. "I may be only a trooper, Kendrick, but I would rather be a trooper – ten times rather – than an ensign with an 'eart as black as Villiers." Brings the house down, 'olloway. Good luck.'

Considerably shaken, Ba found himself some digs and started to swot up his six leading parts over the weekend. On Monday night he opened and at the end of the performance the manager appeared in his dressing room. 'Not bad 'olloway, not bad. Thirty-six out of the forty-two. But 'olloway, " 'eart as black as Villiers" – what 'appened to it?'

'I don't know, sir,' said Ba. 'I shouted it as loudly as I could.'

'SHOUTED IT!? It's yer right arm. YOU DROPPED IT! . . . Look, I'll give it to you again: "I may be only a trooper, Kendrick, but I would rather be a trooper – *ten times rather* – [the manager here raised his arm ominously and pointed] than an ensign with an 'eart as black as Villiers." Hold it; keep yer arm up there till they do applaud.'

On each of my visits Ba would produce some fascinating relic of the past to show me, such as an envelope containing scraps of wallpaper from Irving's dressing room. From his wonderful library Ba would press me to borrow a book. He then entered the details and the date in an exercise book. If the book was not returned within one calendar month from that date I would receive a reminder. Two weeks later would follow a snorter, threatening dire proceedings.

And then there was Robert Atkins. What actor has not tried to imitate his voice – the essence is there but never that idiosyncratic timbre wherein all his bass vowel sounds came through a cavern and down his nose. He it was, at the Open Air Theatre at Regent's Park where the stage is of grass surrounded by real trees and bushes, who stopped a rehearsal and, advancing on an inept young actor, delivered himself of a resounding Johnsonian phrase: 'Scenery by God. The words by the greatest poet the world has ever known. A director – not bad, and then . . . *YOU* come on.'

I would love to have been present when he and the actor Ralph Truman were walking beside the docks in Bristol as they espied a four-masted schooner. 'Look at her,' mused Atkins. 'That beautiful barque has sailed the seven seas bringing us tea from Ceylon, jewels from India, silks from China, spices from Samarkand and there she lies about to depart at our behest.' He called to a deck-hand: 'Sailor! Whither sailest thou?' Hardly bothering to turn, the deck-hand replied, 'F – off.'

He was incredibly perceptive over theatrical matters. He could immediately put his finger on a fault. He attended the first night of Peter O'Toole's *Hamlet*. The settings by Sean Kenny, directed by Sir Laurence Olivier at the Old Vic Theatre, the first home of England's National Theatre Company. Expectation was in the air. The house lights lowered. In the stygian gloom of the battlements Francisco and Bernardo began the play . . .

'Have *you* had quiet guard?'
                    'Not a mouse stirring.'

Atkins turned to his companion and in his hollow boom, ventured, 'That's a *very interesting* intonation – I don't think I'm going to like this.' Theatrically he was right. You cannot be so particular in the first ten or fifteen lines of a play.

Again when John Neville was playing Hamlet at the Old Vic

during the Fifties, Atkins was asked later what he thought of him. 'Well, with a little more sex and a little less sanctity he'd make a very passable Laertes.'

At Stratford-upon-Avon it was always the custom for the leading actor to read the lesson in Holy Trinity Church on the Sunday nearest Shakespeare's birthday. In 1945 Atkins was not asked. Extremely annoyed, he cornered Canon Prentice in the High Street. 'Can you adduce any cogent reason why *I* should not read the f – ing lesson?' The Canon humbly tried to explain that some- one else had been booked earlier, etc. 'Well,' grumbled Atkins. 'You can stuff yer church and you can stuff yer steeple! – except of course the bells which I understand are the most melodious in Warwickshire.'

The Memorial Theatre at Stratford-upon-Avon was built in 1879 and in its very first season, which lasted ten days, the actor Barry Sullivan presented four plays. From 1886, when Frank Benson began bringing his own company to the theatre for the annual Festival, to the end of his reign thirty years later, the Festival was still of only two weeks' duration.

But by the time the next Director, Bridges-Adams, left in 1935 he had lengthened the season to six months during which the company presented eight plays, each of which could be seen during any week (six evening performances and two matinees).

B. Iden Payne and Robert Atkins continued this policy until the end of 1945. Using actors who knew their classical repertoire, they were able to rehearse the eight plays in eight weeks and open them all within a fortnight.

In 1946 when I joined the company Sir Barry Jackson had just been appointed Director. The nearest the British have come to producing a Diaghilev, he was blessed with a private income, derived, I believe, from Maypole Dairies. At the age of twenty-seven he started the Pilgrim Players. At thirty-three he founded the Birmingham Repertory Company, only a few years after Miss Horniman had started the repertory movement at the Gaiety Theatre, Manchester. There he fostered a formidable array of talent. Plays by Yeats, St John Hankin, Drinkwater, Shaw, Ibsen, Besier, Eden Phillpotts, among many others, and performed by the then unknown Cedric Hardwicke, Edith Evans, Ralph Richardson, Felix Aylmer; the list of people who subsequently became world famous and who owed much to Sir Barry is legion. Still continuing at Birmingham he became, in 1929, the Director of the Malvern

Festival where he supervised the birth of many of Shaw's later plays.

Although he adapted some plays for the stage, Sir Barry was not really a practitioner, but in all aspects of the drama he recognised quality. Only the best was acceptable. If the National Theatre had become a reality when it was first mooted, Sir Barry would have been an ideal Director. He who was the mildest of men, swept through the Memorial Theatre like a tornado. All the heads of departments, who thought they were in safe jobs, were axed and for his company of actors he refused to employ anyone who had acted in Stratford before. It was a clean sweep for the new broom.

Every play was to have four weeks' rehearsal and each a different director. The season was to open in April with three productions and the other five plays would follow at monthly intervals, the last three becoming the first three of the following year. Seats would cost eight shillings and sixpence (42½p) for the stalls, one shilling and sixpence (7½p) for the gallery.

Our leading lady, Valerie Taylor, had never before appeared in Shakespeare, unlike our leading man, Robert Harris, who had spent many years in the classics. His load was back-breaking. He was to appear as the Chorus (in *Henry V*), Macbeth, Angelo (in *Measure for Measure*), Prospero and Dr Faustus. Halfway through the season he had cause to return to London. One of his calls was on his bank manager who greeted him with, 'Ah, Mr Harris . . . now let me see . . . you're up in the Midlands somewhere, aren't you?' Meanwhile Sir Barry's white hope from his Birmingham company, Paul Scofield, was to be given his chance of promotion as Henry V. Paul was another product of Sussex and, although we had never met, our parents knew each other. Also from Birmingham came twenty-one-year-old Peter Brook to direct *Love's Labour's Lost*.

We were all young and we were all eager, Sir Barry was our father figure and we felt privileged to be working in the idyllic surroundings of the Warwickshire countryside, where we could walk in the fields, punt on the river and – for me the newest joy – speak Shakespeare's magical lines. Had I really been taught this at school?

Endless pedants have tried to prove that the plays were written not by Shakespeare, but by various other contenders. I attended a lecture once where the speaker set out to prove irrefutably that they were written by the then Earl of Oxford, his main evidence being found in *Romeo and Juliet*. Throughout the play the lovers are referred to as Romeo and Juliet until the last line.

For never was a story of more woe
Than this of Juliet and her Romeo.

So the play ends with the letters EO = Earl of Oxford!

You only have to spend a season playing Shakespeare in Stratford-upon-Avon, in the heart of Warwickshire, to know incon-
trovertibly that those plays were written by a man who had actually
lived in Stratford and who had walked the Warwickshire lanes.
Also there is much internal evidence in the plays. For instance
Shakespeare must have walked many times over the bridge, then
only recently built by Sir Hugh Clopton, who was criticised
publicly for his ostentation in building a structure with eighteen
arches to span what was then a narrow stream. In *Much Ado About
Nothing*, Don Pedro says, 'What needs the bridge much broader
than the flood?'

A member of our company was one day watching some farm
workers 'layering' a hedge. This is done by cutting the side-shoots
off a sapling, slicing halfway through its base, bending it sideways
and staking it down, so that next year's growth will then grow
vertically through it. Impressed by their expertise, the actor asked
one of the men if they always worked as a team and received as
answer, 'Ay. I shapes their ends – he rough-hews 'em.

And if you don't know your *Hamlet*, see page 247.

The old theatre of 1879 was burned out in 1926 and the present
theatre, designed by Elisabeth Scott, opened its doors in 1932.
Originally disliked by almost everybody, it has acquired a certain
patina and historical architectural interest over the years – it looks
rather like the old Cunarder, *Queen Mary*, built in brick. We called it
the Ham Factory.

Miss Scott's intentions for the stage area, where she had installed
sophisticated mechanical equipment, were ambitious: behind the
proscenium arch the stage was to be three times the width of the
part visible to the audience with a platform on wheels on which two
complete sets could be built (one in view, the other hidden). At the
press of a button this platform could slide across, bringing the
second set into view. The first could then be dismantled and a new
set erected ready for the return journey. Alternatively the two
halves of the platform could be divided to enable another complete
scene to arise from below stage level. More scenery could be
dropped in from an enormous fly tower above the stage.

Unfortunately, when digging the foundations the contractors

encountered problems with flooding and were restricted in the depth of usable basement area, with the result that the lift from below the stage was four feet too short for the scenery. (Many years before, when W. S. Gilbert was building the Garrick Theatre in London, an underground spring was disclosed and Gilbert is reputed to have said that he 'couldn't make up his mind whether to continue building or sell the fishing rights'.)

Money, unfortunately, ran short and Miss Scott was forced to reduce the overall width of the stage with the result that the sliding platform had to be hinged and six feet on either side ran – at great expense – on rails up the walls. Yet nobody seems to have realised the impossibility of putting scenery on a section of stage which would become vertical. It was another minor defect that the gallery queue assembled immediately outside the windows of the principal dressing room, so that eminent actors could plainly hear caustic comments on their personas and performances.

This then was the theatre in which Sir Barry launched his first season with his highly publicised troup of young hopefuls. And the first night was a disaster.

The curtain rose – Stratford had a curtain then – on the first scene of *The Tempest*, to show a ship, complete with masts and sails, which rocked as it appeared to sink, accompanied by superb sound and lighting effects. At the end of this five-minute-long scene the curtain fell. With so elaborate a set it was essential that everything went right – on this occasion everything went wrong. To change the scenery ready for Scene II took twenty-five minutes. The audience grew restive and it was impossible for anyone, even Robert Harris as a superb Prospero, to recapture their attention. By the final scene he had nearly succeeded when the unexpected happened again.

The part of Ariel was being played by a brilliant boy actor, David O'Brien, and when Prospero says farewell, 'Then to the elements be free' he was to walk a few paces, turn back to Prospero, tears in both their eyes, turn away again then actually *fly* up into the air. (Anyone who has seen *Peter Pan* will know that this effect is created by Kirby's Flying Ballet, attaching a practically invisible wire to a harness worn by the actor who is then pulled into the air.) But something went wrong. Instead of disappearing silently he crashed into the scenery and came swinging back to Prospero, before being yanked off his feet again to take some of the scenery with him as he was propelled into the wings.

Cymbeline was to open on Shakespeare's birthday (23rd April) and to direct it Nugent Monck had been invited from his own Maddermarket Theatre in Norwich which he had built as a small replica of Shakespeare's Globe Theatre and in which he had presented every one of his plays. He was a small man with a bald head and what hair he had was cut very short. Rather hunched shoulders gave him the appearance of having no neck – he looked indeed a little like Picasso. He spoke in a carefully articulated but high voice which would pipe up from the back of the stalls. At this stage of my life I was always the scapegoat of a company – the whipping boy – for several reasons: I appeared to have a skin as thick as a rhinoceros (I hadn't really but I didn't want anyone to know). I had a sense of humour and could always see the funny side; and, lastly, I deserved it – what I was expected to do came too easily to me. If I was reprimanded I was inwardly mortified but my reaction was to laugh, which infuriated those in authority. Now I became Nugent Monck's scapegoat.

I was playing Arviragus, with another young actor from Sir Barry's Birmingham Company, John Harrison, as Guiderius, and in the last scene we had very little to do. During a rehearsal John whispered something which caused me to smile. Immediately from the stalls came, 'Is the second brother going to giggle *all through* this scene?' (I think John and I were smiling about Valerie Taylor as Imogen, who earlier in that rehearsal, instead of reading aloud from a letter, 'Thy mistress, Pisanio, hath play'd the strumpet in my bed', actually said, 'Thy mistress, Pisanio, hath play'd the *trumpet* in my bed'.)

At another rehearsal his voice came from the back of the empty theatre 'Donald – you have a *beau*tiful voice – ' he gave me only just enough time to register the compliment before he continued – 'but it's like having a Bechstein if you're only going to vamp on it.'

Nugent kept the action of the play moving at a cracking pace: each full stage scene was followed by one on the forestage and he insisted that we were to enter as the curtains were being drawn and to overlap the previous scene. 'Do it!' cried Nugent, 'the audience may be bewildered but they won't be bored!'

Tea was an important social part of one's life and the company haunted the Cobweb and Hathaway tearooms. One day at the Hathaway a group of us, including Nugent, were recounting theatrical anecdotes concerning the skills required of actors, when I said, 'An old friend of mine, Charles Smith, said that to be a good juvenile you must make half the audience want to mother you and the other half go to bed with you.' Nugent cut in, 'Of course if that fails, Donald, you can always try acting!'

Vernon Fortescue, who played Belarius, the father of Arviragus and Guiderius, was an actor of the old school who shared our dressing room. We young ones got to the theatre an hour before curtain-up to put on our elaborate make-up, but Vernon, who had a face like a mountain crag, introduced us to the Soft Brick. I never knew it existed before but since that time I have checked the facts. On the outside of any old theatre, somewhere near the stage door can be found a brick which, due to its original manufacture, is softer than its neighbours. Old actors would hold an envelope against the wall and by rubbing a finger over the brick could dislodge the coloured dust into the envelope. Vernon had found the Soft Brick at Stratford. This dust he used as rouge for his cheeks. He then ran a finger along the top of the door and applied the dirt to his eyebrows. The only greasepaint he possessed was a stick of dark blue which he smudged on his eyelids. His make-up had cost virtually nothing and he was ready in two minutes.

It was in *Cymbeline* that I received my first mention in a review in a national newspaper. John Harrison and I had to speak the wonderfully moving dirge, 'Fear no more the heat of the sun', over the body of the (supposedly) dead Fidele, and the critic J. C. Trewin picked us out. Oh the excitement! Copies of the paper were sent to every uncle and aunt. Charles wrote to congratulate me and said that Agate had seen it. John and I walked around ten feet tall.

The Tempest had been a disaster, *Cymbeline* rather pedestrian, but Sir Barry's policy and reputation were completely vindicated by Peter Brook's production of *Love's Labour's Lost* which, given a setting based on the paintings of Watteau, was intensely beautiful. Paul Scofield's astonishing performance as Don Armado gave haunting melancholy to lines such as 'Rust rapier, be still drum, for your manager is in love, yea he loveth'. During rehearsals it was anarchically funny to watch Peter Brook, only twenty-one and his whole body stiff with nerves, trying to show David O'Brien (who was playing Moth), no more than fifteen years old, yet a 'natural' actor, how he wanted the part played. Every sinew of Peter's body tightened to such an extent that one could almost hear them creaking as he tried to move his arms and legs. Young David, who understood nothing of Peter's self-consciousness, studiously copied Peter's spastic-like mannerisms. 'No, no,' cried Peter. 'Not like that – like this!' until both of them were jerking around the stage like puppets.

I cannot think why David King-Wood gave up being an actor. In this production he gave a splendidly romantic performance as Berowne. I understudied him as well as playing my own part of Dumaine.

My contract with Stratford had stated that I was 'to play as cast' but with the understanding (unwritten) that I should play the Dauphin in *Henry V*. The evening before the first rehearsal for *Henry*, several of us had been to a little party after the performance. The next morning the alarm went off and I gave myself 'a few more minutes'. I was due at the theatre at ten thirty a.m. I looked at the clock: good God! I shot out of bed and ran . . . I got there unshaven but on time – in fact at ten twenty-five a.m. We all congregated in the rehearsal room to meet the new director, Dorothy Green, an old Bensonian and the finest Cleopatra of her generation. As we shook hands she said, 'I don't think you've shaved this morning.' I tried to explain but she continued, 'We can't have that. I'm afraid I cannot allow you to play the Dauphin.' And I didn't. Cleanshaven John Harrison got the part and I must confess to a wicked delight when one night during the performance, in which he wore magnificent gold armour, he was unaware that his foot had caught in a loop of rope; he took up the slack as he marched on, but when he got to the centre of the stage he was brought down with a crash.

I have never since turned up unshaven to a rehearsal.

Under Sir Barry, personal discipline and respect for others were very important. The company were given instructions that they were 'not to hold hands or link arms outside the theatre'! As Sir John Gielgud has recalled, 'When I was young we wore our best suits to rehearsal and called the leading man "sir" – now they wear jeans and call me John.'

Instead of the Dauphin I was given three small parts and understudied Henry. I rather fancied myself as Henry and it is the one part I should like to have played – I'm now too old, sadly – but since that time I have always avoided the question, 'What would you like to play?'

I was grateful to Dorothy Green for pulling me up while I was young and she and her husband Alfred Harris, another old Bensonian, became my good friends. One day he asked me what plays were being done the following year. I mentioned *Romeo and Juliet* among others, 'R. and J.? – it's a good play. I could never make up my mind whether to play Mercutio and get home early, or Friar Lawrence and keep my trousers on.'

For me *As You Like It* was memorable, because I was given two small but stunning parts, Le Beau and William (Alec Guinness had played the same double in 1937). For the former I forced my voice up an octave and made him a very 'affected' character. On the first night I got a 'frog' in my throat and my last line

> Hereafter, in a better world than this,
> I shall desire more love and knowledge of you

came out in my normal register. One or two critics remarked on the sincerity thus shown by the character in the otherwise false surroundings of the court!

Faber and Gwyer, the publishers, had issued some of Shakespeare's plays individually printed in a facsimile of the First Folio. I bought these one by one and for the first time I discovered some advantages in working from this early text. In the part of William his words 'Aye Sir' are twice spelled 'I Sir'. I was able to use this to good advantage, making them a question instead of a statement.

Let me digress again for a moment to mention something that I found of enormous interest. There was no complete edition of Shakespeare's plays during his lifetime, but many of them were privately printed from a pirated text. There are two main theories as to how these were obtained by the printers: either an employee sat in the theatre and took down the dialogue in a form of unreliable shorthand, or one of the actors was bribed to divulge what he knew of the text. (Until quite recently actors were only given their own lines plus two or three words that preceded them as a cue – not the complete text.) One of the best examples of the latter is the pirated *Merry Wives of Windsor*, in which the only reliable words that equate to later authorised texts are spoken by the Host: next best are those spoken by Falstaff. The supposition is that the 'informer' was the actor who played the Host and understudied Falstaff, but had a faulty memory as to what the other actors said.

Not until seven years after Shakespeare's death did his fellow actors John Heminge and Henry Condell bring together all his plays (bar one) into a splendid folio edition and it is presumed that this was printed from Shakespeare's original manuscripts. Here it must be remembered that a hand press was used. Two blocks of movable type were set up side by side, one for Page 1, the other for Page 12, and were impressed upon a single large sheet of paper. 1,500 or so copies of these were printed. Then the type for pages 2 & 11 were impressed on the reverse (and so on, 3 & 10 on the back of 4 & 9, and 5 & 8 on the back of 6 & 7). These were then folded and when placed together gave continuous numbering, 1–12. This process was repeated again and again until page 400 was reached.

Let us imagine the original printers, Jaggard and Blount, working as fast as they can – they will not be paid until these books are sold. The first two pages have been set up and Blount is pulling at the heavy lever of the hand press: he hands the first pull to Jaggard who starts to check it against the manuscript while the next is being printed. 'Just a minute!' says Jaggard. 'You are printing "if" and it should be "of".' Blount removes the offending 'i' from the fount and replaces it with an 'o'. But three of those sheets have now been printed with an 'i' – not worth throwing them away. The press starts working again. Ten sheets later Jaggard notices that a full stop should have been a comma. Again a change is made. Twenty sheets later he spots another mistake . . . it is some time before he is perfectly satisfied.

These sheets have been placed in a pile – the *first at the bottom*. Now they begin on the reverse to print pages 2 & 11, taking the paper from the *top of the pile*. Again Blount hands the first proof to Jaggard who, six sheets later, notices that 'there' should have been 'their' and so it goes on. Thus the best imprints of 1 & 12 become the worst of 2 & 11.

This strange but elementary fact was first noticed by scholars at the Folger Library in Washington D.C., which houses more copies of the First Folio than anywhere else in the world. The best available pages were brought together and published as the Norton Facsimile in 1968, but even in this we can see an example of where Jaggard slipped up – Page 399 is printed as 993.

Now isn't all that fascinating? No? All right then, let me tell you about our next play, *Macbeth*. This is supposed to be a notoriously unlucky play, but it was not always so. Before the days of repertory companies most towns had a stock company – a group of actors whose job it was to support visiting stars who toured around the country. The visitor occupied the centre of the stage and everyone else had to keep a respectful distance – Edmund Kean used to say 'Keep out of my circle'. William Charles Macready was furious when, after condescending to appear as Macbeth, the resident actress who played Lady Macbeth, 'Thanked me for my *support!*'

If any of these companies was doing badly they would put on *Macbeth*, which was a sure-fire box-office winner, to recoup their losses. As the theatrical newspapers carried details of the plays to be performed, the entire profession would know which companies were failing. Macbeth, therefore, became synonymous with ill fortune. But once give a dog . . . Actors now look for trouble.

I must admit that our production started badly. The designer had set the play in the Jacobean period and had provided two vast staircases like the arms of a horseshoe, which swept round on to the forestage in an effort to cross the line of the proscenium arch which some believe divides the audience from the actors. Only when they were erected was it discovered that they obliterated the view from sixty seats on either side of the auditorium: these could never be sold.

I was once again playing three small parts, one of them Young Seward who, after a brief verbal exchange with Macbeth (Robert Harris), is killed in a duel. I was young and athletic so I volunteered to enter at the top of the staircase and, on seeing Macbeth and hearing his name, to leap eight feet down on to the stage, to fight with sabres and, after being disarmed, to have my throat 'cut' and my 'lifeless' body kicked to the edge of the battlements, then roll off to crash the imagined hundreds of feet to the raging seas at the bottom of the orchestra pit. (In fact it was another eight-foot drop and a mattress was placed there on which to land.)

One night I was waiting in the wings for my entrance when a commotion broke out, people started to run around and I heard the stage manager order someone to 'get the First Aid! – Robert Harris's eye is cut'. I looked on to the stage and there was Macbeth with blood pouring down his face. Some idiot did a quick calculation and announced that it was the thirteenth performance! Oh God. I still had my scene to play. Of course . . . I will break my leg as I jump! I made my entrance. I said my line. I jumped . . . No, my legs were still in one piece. So watch out in the fight. The sabres clashed, I was disarmed, Macbeth put his left arm round my neck and placed his sword across my throat. This is it, I thought. He drew the sword across . . . No that was not it. He kicked my 'lifeless' body and as I rolled it dawned on me: tonight they have forgotten to put the mattress at the bottom of the orchestra pit . . . As I got to the edge I funked it and vaulted off. I bounced quite happily on the mattress. When I returned to the wings the idiot had done a recount – this was the *fourteenth* performance and Robert Harris had actually only grazed his eyebrow.

It is not just *Macbeth*: the theatre is inundated with superstitions and all of them are founded on good common sense. For instance at least until 1900, during a performance, instructions were always given to the stage staff by short peeps on a whistle. One peep: fly the scenery out. Two peeps: fly the scenery in. A different peep would open the trap door, and so on. A superstition grew that it was unlucky for actors to whistle backstage. Indeed it was worse than unlucky – you might be killed if your whistle opened the stage at your feet or brought scenery down on your head. I thought the practice had died out until my son Marc told me that in the theatre at Salisbury the scenery was still being changed by whistle in 1980.

That it is considered unlucky to have real flowers on a stage has a practical explanation. For centuries the stage area was covered with green-coloured canvas, which did service as a green carpet for indoor scenes or as green grass for outdoor scenes. (Thus, among actors the stage is still referred to colloquially as 'The Green' and the waiting room beside the stage as the Green Room.) Under the heat generated by the lights – worse when they were gas – real flowers wilted and their petals fell to the canvas-covered ground, so an actor, who practically never looks down when he is walking during a performance, could easily slip and break a leg. (As a director, the late Jack Minster once said, 'It's no good looking at the floor – there's nothing there except the play!')

Personally I never bother about any superstitions, because I always carry a rabbit's foot.

Shakespeare's plays are full of stumbling blocks for the unwary actor; *Macbeth* has several, two of them occurring within four lines. The king has been murdered and members of the household are told the terrible news as they arrive. His two sons Malcolm and Donalbain appear and Donalbain asks 'What is amiss?' to be told, 'You are and do not know't'. (Hitherto his sex had never been in doubt.) Macduff then tells them 'Your noble father's murdered', to which Malcolm replies in a line so apparently offhand that it is fraught with danger, 'O by whom?' Paul Scofield was playing Malcolm and was talking in my dressing room one evening when he missed his call for this scene. We suddenly heard shouts (this was before the installation of a Tannoy system) and the sound of running feet: I opened my door and saw an approaching stage manager shouting, 'Paul! Paul! You're off!' Paul went out of the room like a rocket, leapt down the stairs, arrived breathless on the stage and was informed, 'Your noble father's murdered.' Only when he tried to say 'O . . .' did he realise he had a cigarette in his mouth. He removed it, threw it to the floor, ground it with his foot, and continued, 'By whom?' Later it was pointed out that he had also failed to put on his wig.

It was the policy of the Memorial Theatre to include one play each season by one of Shakespeare's contemporaries. This year *Dr Faustus* by Christopher Marlowe was chosen, directed by the actor Walter Hudd. (Once, when watching a play, Hudd found himself sitting next to a man whose face he thought he knew. All through the first act he cast sidelong glances; he could not concentrate on the play; he was certain they had met, but where? Who was it? In the interval he went to the bar and there next to him again was the same man. There was nothing for it, he must face it out. 'Forgive me but don't I know you?' 'Yes,' said the man, 'I'm your agent.')

Robert Harris gave a beautiful performance as Faustus and Hugh Griffith was a wonderfully sinister Mephistopheles. Once again I had three small parts, a Knight, Pride in the Seven Deadly Sins sequence and the Second Student – not exactly exciting.

For the last production Sir Barry imported an American scholar, Frank McMullan from Yale, to direct *Measure for Measure*. We sometimes needed an interpreter: 'I want a couple of you in the corner pitchin' a woo.'

But now our future was our main concern. Each day we waited for a word from 'up there'. At last it came; fifteen of us out of a company of forty were invited back. Rehearsals for the 1947 season were to begin on 6th January.

5

WAS THIS THE FACE THAT LAUNCHED A THOUSAND SHIPS?

I was faced with three months' unemployment, but I had not done four and a half years of one night stands in MESA for nothing.

During the season John Harrison and I had become good friends and shared digs at the Rose and Crown (lunch was two shillings and sixpence), shared a dressing room at the theatre, had played several parallel parts, and with David O'Brien as our cox, had won an actors' rowing race on the River Avon — we shot the bridge a length ahead of Myles Eason and Anthony Groser. Having learnt a number of soliloquies and duologues — we had understudied many of the principal parts — we quickly learned a few more, such as the Brutus–Cassius quarrel scene from *Julius Caesar*, John hammered them all into an acceptable shape and, calling our entertainment *Curtain Up*, we went to stay with my parents in Ditchling. From there I telephoned around and booked a series of village halls, arranging for local shopkeepers to sell the seats in return for complimentary tickets. Our posters were printed by the Ditchling Press. We averaged two performances a week and on feeling that our local welcome had been exhausted, we set off for John's home town of Sidmouth in Devon, repeating the procedure while staying with his mother. We did not exactly make a profit, but at least we kept ourselves for twelve weeks, and the experience we gained was invaluable. And once again, what would we have done without our mothers?

MANOR HALL THEATRE, SIDMOUTH.

London and Avon Theatre Productions

present the personal appearance of

John Harrison, Donald Sinden

of the

1946 and 1947 STRATFORD-UPON-AVON FESTIVAL COMPANY

in

CURTAIN UP

A NON-STOP DRAMATIC RECITAL,

On FRIDAY, December 13

at 2.30 and 8. Doors open 2 and 7.30.

Seats, bookable at Culverwell's Fore Street. Numbered and Reserved, 5s.; 3s. 6d.; 2s. 6d. (inc. tax) At door, Is. 6d.

Culverwell, Printer, Sidmouth.

Contractually it is generally assumed that all actors live in London, so for the new season the Stratford management had booked a large warehouse off the Holloway Road in which to rehearse prior to going to Stratford-upon-Avon. Normally used by Donald Wolfit's company, it was here he stored his costumes.

The snow was falling heavily, so sporting an enormous scarf knitted by my sister in the black and yellow colours of the Brighton Tigers Ice Hockey Team, and in an old raincoat (I did not own an overcoat), I made my way there on 6th January (Twelfth Night). I carried my script for *Romeo and Juliet* ostentatiously. I felt sure people were saying, 'There goes a Shakespearian actor'. Travelling up by train from Hassocks station I had busied myself learning my lines and, as I looked up trying to remember a sentence, I saw another young man with a script on his knees engaged in the same chore. We smiled over the coincidence and introduced ourselves. He too was rehearsing a play in London, *Power Without Glory* by Michael Clayton Hutton, at the New Lindsey Theatre in Notting Hill Gate. His name was Dirk Bogarde.

Our company was now fifty strong and I was an old boy! I looked forward to seeing my old colleagues again and having 'in' jokes which the newcomers would not understand. And what were the newcomers like? Would they fit in?

I found my way into the hall and greeted Bobby Harris, 'Dickie' Hudd, Peter Brook, Paul Scofield and his wife Joy Parker, John Harrison, Duncan Ross and the other old hands. Peter introduced me to Beatrix Lehmann, whom I had long admired and who was to play the Nurse to Daphne Slater's Juliet and Laurence Payne's Romeo (whom I was to understudy as well as playing Paris). Dark and Italianate, Laurence was taking over the position occupied the previous year by David King-Wood as romantic lead. I then had time to look over the newcomers. On one side of the icy cold hall the girls were huddled around a coke stove with its flue rising up to the roof. The new boys formed an outer circle, among them John Warner, Julian Amyes, Ken Wynne, Leigh Crutchley, George Cooper, Douglas Seale, John Blatchley, Dudley Jones, Joss Ackland. Among the girls were Irene Sutcliffe, Helen Burns and Margaret Courtenay, but the one who caught my attention was a beautiful, dark-haired girl, tall with Grecian features. Incongruously dressed in these surroundings, she wore high-heeled shoes, a tailored suit with a cravat at the neck and – most incongruous of all – a hat! Fine for the West End, but strange for a Shakespearian company. And she talked of a Hunt Ball!

We were expected to enter our name on a list for lunch, so I asked hers: 'Diana Marney', I wrote. I was immediately corrected. 'No. *Marney*,' she said. 'I'm Irish and the correct pronunciation of M-A-H-O-N-Y is Mahrny.'

'Put your shoulders back,' I said. And she did!

Peter Brook approached nervously and led me away. 'Er, Paris . . . young Guards Officer I think – don't you?' With that simple but excellent guide line, we began rehearsals for *Romeo and Juliet*. The snow continued to fall and a few days later we started on *Measure for Measure*. A few more days of snow and work began on *Twelfth Night*.

The winter of 1946–47 is in the history books due to its severity and length. In the middle of February we travelled to Stratford to find the entire town under snow three feet deep. We had to walk from the station to our various digs. I had booked at the Winton Guest House in Chapel Street, and I discovered – to my surprise (!) – that the only other member of the company in residence was Diana Marney (sorry, Mahony). Should I admit that I had checked where she was staying while still in London? In fact there was one more occupant of Winton House, a commercial traveller from the Isle of Man, and the three of us had our meals together.

Here I must confess that I hate the mornings. I get up disgruntled and have my breakfast with my face buried in a newspaper. After that I ablute and become tolerable.

Why I cannot imagine, but for breakfast we three sat on one side of a large Victorian dining table – the commercial traveller on the left, Diana centre and me and my newspaper on the right – facing a large Victorian looking glass. Every time we looked up three sets of teeth could be seen chomping away. On our second morning we were given kippers – not the easiest dish to cope with through a newspaper. Diana, the most talkative of people I discovered, would natter away to the commercial traveller. Suddenly there was a silence of at least fifteen seconds which Diana felt it was her duty to fill. 'Isn't it frightening to look up and see yourself masturbating like that.' The commercial traveller snorted, I choked, ostensibly on a bone, and we both slid under the table. I couldn't wait to tell my friends in dressing room 6. From then on, each evening, they would ply me with 'What did she say today?'

I learned that she had just left the RADA and this was her first job. She revelled in it. Leaving our digs one morning with the sun bright on the pure white snow, Diana was wearing a knitted hat and sunglasses. Perkily she said, 'I feel so *theatrical* – with my sunglasses and little Dutch cap.' I climbed out of a snow drift and ran for dressing room 6 . . .

She was reading at the time *The Sun is my Undoing* by Marguerite Steen and in the crowded lounge of the Falcon Hotel during one of those silences that fall at twenty to or twenty past the hour she informed Bobby Harris in a loud voice, 'I'm reading a fascinating book – it's all about a cock fight in a bedroom.'

This girl needed someone to shield her from the world and I seemed to be the man for the job.

It had been impossible to clear the snow away, so deep channels were cut for Stratford's pedestrians – the roads were completely impassable. As April arrived so the snow melted and the poor River Avon, in consequence, burst its banks. The level of the floods rose and rose until the theatre became an island, the only way to reach it being by punt ferry boarded a hundred yards away up Chapel Lane. Would the waters subside in time for the opening of the season? Each day they receded a little more. God was on our side. Our first night was also the first occasion for weeks that it was possible to walk to the theatre with dry feet.

Romeo and Juliet had a mixed reception from the critics, but audiences, especially the young, loved it. The play opened with John Harrison clad in a long trailing cloak walking slowly across the front of the stage silhouetted against a deep blue sky. As he spoke the last lines of the Chorus, he disappeared into the wings . . . Whoosh! Every light on the stage came full on – the 'sun' beat down with a Mediterranean intensity. At the same moment a crowd erupted on to the stage. It was Verona in the rush hour. In this oppressive atmosphere it was perfectly natural for a fight to break out: 'For now, these hot days is the mad blood stirring.'

Although Ellen Terry once said that 'no actress can play Juliet until she is too old to do so', Daphne Slater really seemed to be fourteen at the beginning of the play and blossomed as it went on. Larry Payne had splendid attack as Romeo and Paul was quite the most memorable Mercutio I have seen. He was brought up in a village only three miles from Ditchling and a keen ear can detect in us both a slight Sussex accent in our pronunciation of words ending with OUND. I can still hear Paul saying 'I have it now, and *soundly* too'. I was rather good as a Guards Officer Paris.

Measure for Measure then rejoined the repertoire. All was well on the first night, until the final scene which lasts a good twenty minutes while all loose ends are cleverly tied by the author. (So many of Shakespeare's plays end in this way and they can be excruciatingly boring for the small-part actors who have to stand around looking interested and surprised at each revelation.) Half-way through, disaster struck – some pillars which were part of the scenery began to topple. Had it collapsed it would have brought down everything. One of the actors dived forward and succeeded in holding it, but only temporarily. Luckily the stage management had seen the imminent danger and four very large stage-hands crept on from the wings in full view of the audience and gripped the pillars from behind. The actors ploughed on manfully (and womanfully) pretending nothing had happened and willing the audience not to titter. But what nobody had foreseen was the last line of the play. On this night it got a stupendous laugh. 'What's yet behind, that's meet you all should know.'

In 1946 I had been in all eight production, but this year I had the luxury of a play 'out', *Twelfth Night*, which opened on 23rd April. I kept away from rehearsals – I didn't want to spoil my enjoyment of seeing this play for the first time. Duncan Ross (Fabian and another inmate of dressing room 6) said that he could never understand why one of his favourite lines, Malvolio's – 'These be her very C's, her U's and her T's – and thus makes she her great P's' – never got a laugh. I was determined that on the first night it should, so when Walter Hudd spoke the line, I let out a guffaw, but from the rest of the audience, however, there was silence. Walter Hudd was the only person who reacted: I think he recognised my laugh.

The play was dressed in the period of Charles the First and Diana looked absolutely stunning as a lady of Olivia's court, in a plain long black dress with a large white collar and cuffs, reminiscent of Henrietta Maria. After the performance we walked along the river side and on to a small footbridge below the weir. We stood talking. The situation was ridiculously idyllic with a full moon reflected in a glass-smooth river, rippling now and again as the white swans sailed past, and the spire of Holy Trinity Church dark against the stars . . . I asked her to marry me.

Unfortunately she had heard that I had been repeating her bon mots and was afraid that her answer would immediately be related to dressing room 6. She said no.

I tried again later under far less romantic circumstances and this time she agreed.

After *The Tempest* and *Love's Labour's Lost*, *Dr Faustus* rejoined the repertoire but this year Diana was playing Helen of Troy (that season she cornered the market in Goddesses – Diana in *Pericles* too). She entered wearing a diaphanous Grecian tunic and succeeded admirably in facing the daunting task of living up to Faustus's speech – one of the most famous in the language – Marlowe's mighty line,

> Was this the face that launched a thousand ships,
> And burned the topless towers of Ilium?
> Sweet Helen, make me immortal with a kiss.

At one performance a slight mental aberration caused Bobby Harris as Faustus to say, 'Was this the face that launched *ten* thousand ships . . .' In the audience, a large party from Diana's old school all naturally assumed that he was right and they had been wrong.

Many years later, my friends John and Gillian Cadell were at the Stratford first night when *Dr Faustus* was again produced and the asinine director caused Helen to appear stark naked in this scene. After Faustus spoke 'Was this the face that launched a thousand ships', Jill whispered, 'He must be the only man in the theatre looking at her *face*.'

John Harrison and I still shared dressing room 6 with six others, and we were often visited by one of the new boys, Joss Ackland, who had taken over from me the role of the company scapegoat. Joss was unbelievably clumsy. Twice I was about to go through a door when it was crashed open in my face: it had to be Joss on the other side. While making up I once dropped a stick of greasepaint on the floor, as I bent to pick it up a foot squashed it flat. It had to be Joss. It was.

Richard II was our next production, directed by Walter Hudd with splendid scenery designed by Hal Burton. Michael Redgrave once likened this play and its leading character to a violin concerto, and Bobby Harris gave our production a most musical soloist. I played Aumerle, Richard's cousin and closest friend: wherever Richard went Hal Burton ensured that I was at his side – in many more scenes than Shakespeare had intended. In the Flint Castle episode Richard, who is about to be deposed, says, 'Aumerle, thou weep'st – My tender-hearted cousin.' During rehearsals Bobby had said, 'If ever I catch you really crying, I will change parts with you.' From that moment, try as I may, I could not squeeze a single tear. For Richard's abdication in Westminster Hall a flight of steps led up to the throne and, after Richard had resigned the crown to the usurper Bolingbroke, and everyone had departed, I was left standing on the steps looking down at the Bishop of Carlisle and the Abbot of Westminster (who Aumerle thinks may join him in insurrection) and had to deliver the last line of the scene:

> 'You holy clergymen, is there no *plot*
> to rid the realm of this pernicious *blot*?'

There followed a pregnant silence and slowly, very slowly, the curtain came down for the interval. Every night after I had said these lines with all the portentousness I could muster, my holy colleagues, who had their backs to the audience, and unheard by anyone else, would indulge themselves: '*Wot*?' asked one, to which the other replied, 'Apparently *not*.' Now at one performance I could have coped with this, but night after night it became a near-insurmountable task to keep a straight face, especially as they varied the intonation behind their questions.

When Beerbohm Tree played Richard he invented a most cunning piece of stage 'business' in the death scene. In the centre of his dungeon was a massive Norman pillar made of wood and canvas but a large piece of real stone was set into the base. One of his murderer's assistants carried an axe which he swung at Richard, and hit the stone with a loud clang so that sparks flew. A scuffle ensued and Richard grabbed the axe which he then brought down on the assistant's head. The audience was horrified. What they did not know was that in the scuffle Richard had picked up an identical axe, but with a rubber blade.

Winton Guest House was proving rather expensive so John Harrison and I decided to look around for accommodation that we could share. In Sheep Street, not a hundred yards from the theatre, we found a beautiful sixteenth-century building called Shrives (Sheriff's) House, lived in by a Mrs Phillips who was prepared to rent us the first floor, which had two bedrooms and a sitting room all panelled in oak, a bathroom and kitchen. Neither of us had kept house before, so John agreed to do the cooking if I cleaned, and we split all costs. It occurred to us that buying in bulk was cheaper. We bought oranges by the crate and half went bad. We acquired a fourteen-pound tin of plum jam illegally (it should have been on the ration) from Mr Pilbeam, who owned the restaurant opposite and felt sorry for us, and were heartily sick of it less than halfway through. I bought a seven-pound tin of floor polish and never used any of it. When my mother came to stay she agreed to cook the lunch on Sunday if we bought the ingredients. John did the shopping, but was rehearsing on the Sunday morning. My mother started preparations and asked for the meat, which I found in the large refrigerator on the landing which we shared with downstairs. Peeling off the newspaper in which it was wrapped she disclosed an unappetising piece of pink flesh on to which the newsprint had transferred. She tactfully restrained herself from actually saying anything but I could see from her face that she was distressed by the conditions in which her son was living. She thoroughly washed the meat; soused it with vinegar and salt – I think she would have preferred Dettol – and put it in the oven. An hour later John returned and anxiously asked us if we had found the meat. 'I put it in the pantry this morning because I thought your mother would not want it frozen.' So what was in the oven? Enquiries proved it to be dinner for Mrs Phillips's dog.

Luckily for us both, John had fallen in love with Daphne Slater who had been at the RADA with Diana. Unashamedly we took advantage of them both. They took it in turns to do our catering which left John free to help me with the dusting. Diana and I were now besotted about each other although she got rather miffed one day when I asked her to go in a punt up the river. I was quite adept with the pole and we progressed further and further upstream and away from civilisation. Deserted fields lay on either side and the sun glittered on the water. A willow grew aslant a bend and there I turned the boat . . . I had failed to tell her that the willow was exactly one mile from Clopton Bridge and a group of us were competing for the fastest time over the distance. An independent observer had to be present to hold the stop watch. Surely she would not have wanted me to ask someone else to hold mine?

Richard II was followed by *The Merchant of Venice* in which I was to play Lorenzo opposite Joy Parker, Paul Scofield's enchanting wife. Joy had been in the company the previous year and as well as Jessica was now playing an interesting range of parts – the Queen in *Richard II*, Katherine in *Love's Labour's Lost* and she had taken over Ariel from David O'Brien. Lorenzo was the best part I had had at Stratford; he and Jessica have some of the most beautiful lines in the play, and it always amazed me that Shakespeare should have entrusted juveniles with lines like these until my friend Martin Holmes, who has written many books on the period, pointed out that, as we know, in Elizabethan times girls' parts were played by boys, and when their voices broke they graduated to playing young men. So the young actor playing Lorenzo had only recently graduated from appearing as Juliet and Cleopatra and knew exactly how to say

> Look how the floor of heaven
> Is thick inlaid with patines of bright gold:
> There's not the smallest orb which thou behold'st
> But in his motion like an angel sings,
> Still quiring to the young-ey'd cherubins, –
> Such harmony is in immortal souls,
> But whilst this muddy vesture of decay
> Doth grossly close it in, we cannot hear it.

People often ask why we don't get muddled when doing a repertory of plays. Although by the time we opened our ninth production, *Pericles*, we had dropped *Measure for Measure* and *Dr Faustus*; they were still in our heads but we could happily spend our days on the river or sightseeing in the Cotswolds until we came into the theatre in the evening where the wardrobe department had hung up the clothes for that performance. Only then did we look at them and say 'Ah! *Richard II*; and immediately we were 'in gear'. If the wrong costumes had been given us we would have given the wrong performance. In 1956 Richard Burton and John Neville alternated in the parts of Othello and Iago at the Old Vic: one evening two black Othellos came on to the stage – thanks to the wardrobe department.

When the season closed on 27th September the company embarked on a new venture: for the first time in its history the Stratford-upon-Avon Memorial Theatre Company was to give a season in London, with *Romeo and Juliet*, *Twelfth Night* and *Richard II* being presented at His Majesty's Theatre. It was to be another thirteen years before the Royal Shakespeare Company (as it was by then renamed) took the lease of the Aldwych Theatre.

When *Twelfth Night* – in which I had no part – was playing I returned to Ditchling. One evening I came home from Brighton to be informed that Laurence Payne was ill and I was to play Romeo the next day.

Such had been the pressure of work at Stratford that we were told at the beginning of the season what parts we were to understudy and from that moment we were on our own – there was no time for rehearsals, we had to learn our lines and watch our principals in rehearsal and from the wings to learn the moves. There were added complications: as Paris I had to return several times to the dressing room to change costumes, so while I was away I could not be checking Romeo's moves. But most dangerous was the fact that during the play Romeo is involved in several sword fights and these I had never done.

I stayed up all night refreshing the lines in my memory – the long speeches were easy enough but the short sentences in concerted scenes, where one had responsibility to others, were very tricky – and caught an early train to get me to the theatre by ten thirty. Again there was no time to rehearse any dialogue. I spent the entire day practising the fights with all the other actors who, in fear of their lives, had come in specially.

As is always the case, I, the understudy, was as cool as ice – no nerves at all – but the rest of the cast were on tenterhooks because they were the ones who had to adjust when I was in the wrong position.

By mischance Dame Sybil Thorndike had chosen this night to see the play and, enchantingly, she came to my dressing room to tell me that I was 'the best Romeo she had ever seen'. It can hardly have been true but for the rest of her life she always referred to me as 'my Romeo'. She always came to see whatever play I was in and sat on the edge of her seat in the front row with her wonderfully alert face brightly eager, and at the curtain calls applauded harder than anyone else (I always gave her a special bow which she used to acknowledge with an inclination of her head). Her optimism was infectious: after the death of Walter Hudd the students of the Central School of Drama gave a gala performance to raise funds to endow a scholarship in his name. We all arrived at its theatre (the old Embassy in Swiss Cottage) to learn that the chosen play was a fairly unknown Restoration piece called something like *The Beaux Belles – or She Would if She Wasn't*. Our hearts sank. Even the best of Restoration drama requires great expertise. Students should work at these plays but they shouldn't be seen doing it. Gloomily we stood around in the foyer until Sybil and her husband, Lewis

Casson, arrived and were greeted by the Principal, Gwynneth Thurburn. Sybil beamed and asked, 'What are we going to see?' Somewhat apologetically she was informed, '*The Beaux Belles* by Wychburgh'. Sybil's eyes brightened, her eyebrows raised, she clapped her hands, 'Oh, *GOOD*!!' she cried. She lifted the spirits of all who were there.

On the many nights we were playing at His Majesty's I stayed with Diana's parents who lived in a house with an enormous garden just north of London, which could easily be reached on the underground. I had met them both briefly at Stratford but the situation was now rather different – I had asked Diana to marry me but as she was still under twenty-one, parental consent was necessary. We confided in her mother who romantically thought it a good idea, but her father was a different matter altogether.

Daniel Mahony was the senior partner in Mahony, Taylor and Co., Chartered Accountants, with offices in London Wall to which he drove five mornings a week at eight thirty a.m. He specialised in liquidations. At the weekends, suitably garbed, he hunted otters or foxes – that is before *I* came on the scene. A very stern man, he had, as far as I could see, absolutely no sense of humour – indeed over the years I tried everything to find what tickled him, but without success. Certainly anything with a sexual innuendo – and I don't mean dirty jokes – found him a complete innocent. I sometimes wondered how Diana and her sister were conceived. During the war he had kept pullets in the garden to provide eggs; now with rationing nearly over he had been killing them off. We were seated once for Sunday lunch and we noticed tears welling in his eyes: he quietly laid down his knife and fork and said, 'I never thought I would see the day when we would sit around this table and eat my little red cock . . .' We all had to explain why we were simultaneously choking over bones.

He strongly disapproved of me, not only because I appeared to be the ring leader of the incessant chortling but also for being a 'damned actor' who was after his daughter whom he had earmarked for a duke. One night Diana had come into my bedroom and was sitting perfectly innocently talking to me. From below we heard his voice: 'Diana! Are you going to bed?' Two minutes later: 'Diana! Why don't you go to bed?' Then two minutes later: 'Diana!! Why aren't you going to bed?' And then in answer to Diana's reassurances: 'WELL GO TO BED THEN!'

As I was working every evening and didn't get back to the house until midnight or later and he left at eight thirty, I could never find the right relaxed moment to ask for his daughter's hand. I have already stated that I am not at my best in the mornings, but Diana and her mother devised a hideous plan that I should try to catch him before he left for the office. Unfortunately he seemed to sense why I wanted him. I was awakened at seven thirty and, having donned a dressing gown, made my tousled way from room to room in a comatose state in search of him, but the nearest I got was to see his bowler hat ducking under a window as he hurried to his car. At last I caught him but before I could think of the right phrase he said, 'Not now,' and left. It was another week before I managed to blurt out my intentions, et cetera. Very reluctantly he agreed – on condition that we were to be married in a registrar's office because 'It won't last'.

He hated me to introduce him as my father-in-law – 'It makes me so damned old'. He could never really accept me but about four times a year I was invited to lunch with him in the City, and these were miserable occasions. I would go to his office at twelve thirty and wait until he had finished doing something, and then, jamming on his bowler and swinging his umbrella, he strode out of the office with me in his wake. He always omitted to tell me where we were heading so I had to keep close on his tail to avoid losing him in the lunchtime City rush. With a screech of shoe leather we turned into a restaurant, sat down and, apart from a few pleasantries, ate lunch in silence followed by a quick trek back to the office before I departed on the tube. We both felt we had done our duty for another three months.

The car he was driving at this time was a pre-war Jaguar. When petrol rationing had started at the beginning of the war he drove it into his garage and closed the door. Four and a half years later he pumped up the deflated tyres, put in a gallon of petrol and drove it out. Most cars betray the occupational hazards of the driver: his had a large dent in the bodywork on the outside of the driver's door. This dent in turn was pitted with smaller dents. The cause of this was D.M.'s habit of opening the window and knocking his pipe out on the panel. In 1947 he decided to sell the car and buy a new one, but although he was insured for quite a large sum the dealers were only prepared to allow him £20 in part exchange.

Not long afterwards he was driving down a lonely Hertfordshire lane when to his delight the engine caught fire. He got out and sat on the grass bank to watch it burn, thinking only of the insurance. To

With my grandfather, Alfred Edward Sinden.

With my grandfather, Albert Emmanuel Fuller.

With my sister Joy and my younger brother Leon.

Overseeing 'The Power Unit'.

My mother and father (Mumps and Pop).

The Limes, High Street, Ditchling.

Me posing for Sir Frank Brangwyn as the boy Jesus.

Brangwyn mural in the Rockefeller Center, New York, featuring most of the Sinden family and other villagers.

I spent my days in Colman's factory (above) and my evenings entertaining the troops, here (below) in a typical fit-up performance of *The Normandy Story* (Winifred Shotter, Laurence O'Madden, me and David Ashe).

With my guru, Laurence O'Madden.

Charles F. Smith and H. Jack Keates.

Jack and Winifred Keates.

Diana.

With Joy and Paul Scofield at Stratford-upon-Avon, 1946.

The happy couple, May 3rd, 1948.

Daniel Mahony – D.M.

My first and last fish.

James Donald, me, Ralph Richardson, Peggy Ashcroft in *The Heiress*.

his horror a man appeared with a bucket of water and extinguished the flames. D.M. was beside himself with fury and for weeks regaled everyone with a diatribe against the unfortunate man: 'No, I didn't hit him – I only pushed him down.'

He was obsessed with maps and knew every road, lane, cart-track, bridle-path and footpath in Hertfordshire, but due to some extraordinary oversight someone omitted to tell him that the M1 motorway was being built. Driving along one day he found his turning barred by a NO ENTRY sign. This had to be wrong – he had used that route for years – so down he went only to find himself on the brand new M1 travelling against the on-coming traffic. He blasted his horn at all the 'damned fools who didn't realise they were on my side of the road'. Not only that, but he was going north and he wanted to go south, so he crossed the central reservation (there was no barrier then) and, still going against the stream, proceeded to the next exit.

Only the year before he had ordered a special pair of boots from a West End bootmaker, because when he was otter hunting it was frequently necessary to walk for long distances and to wade through streams and these boots, made to his own intricate design, would be totally waterproof, double welted and continuous tongue – not one drop of water could get in. He went to the workshop every day to see how they were progressing. At last they were ready and as the assistant was wrapping them he said, 'The only thing that worries me, Mr Mahony, is supposing you go through a stream that is deeper than the boots – they will fill with water and it will *never* come out.' 'Good God,' said D.M. 'Look – bore a couple of holes in each instep to let the water run out', and despite protestations ('Damned fool didn't understand') insisted it was done.

On one occasion only, D.M. pursuaded me to join him on a fishing expedition. The experiment was never repeated. It was the time of his annual trip to Scotland, and on discovering that I had never tried the sport before, he decided against fly-fishing and opted for the simpler trolling. He provided me with all the things I might need and off we set for the Killin Hotel, situated at the end of beautiful Loch Tay, where we arrived in time for dinner. The people staying at the hotel were men who were there only to fish for salmon – and there they sat in the dining room, singly or in pairs. Apparently one of the guests had caught a salmon that day and this information was whispered from table to table. Halfway through the soup the door opened and in proudly walked the man of the hour. Twenty-six pairs of eyes glistened as they watched him solemnly walk to his table, seat himself as if unaware that he was the focus of attention, and not until he dipped his spoon in his soup did the eyes return to their own cooling broth and the whispering resume.

The moment the other guests finished their dinner and began to leave the room they each found an excuse to pause at his table and idly mention, 'I hear you caught a salmon today.'
'Yes.'
'How much did it weigh?'
'Thirteen pounds.'
'Where did you catch it?'
'Just off Target Rock.'
'What were you using?'
'A yellow belly.'
The next day every one of them would be found just off Target Rock using a yellow belly in the fond hope that his salmon would have left a friend waiting there.

When I was awakened at the ghastly hour of seven a.m. I looked out of the window and saw rain pouring down – thank God, I thought, we can sit by the fire. Not at all. There was D.M. thundering on my door: 'Good God – aren't you up yet?' I hurriedly dressed, donned D.M.'s spare set of waterproof trousers, coat and sou'wester and we set off to the landing stage where a small rowing boat was tied up. The ghillie helped us in, took the oars and slowly rowed us up the loch. He was a monosyllabic man and for twenty minutes he and D.M. carried on an abortive conversation at cross purposes.

D.M.: Good day for fishing.
Ghillie: Noo.

D.M.: The spring is early this year.
Ghillie: Yes, much later.

D.M.: You look like having a good season.
Ghillie: Yes very bad.

D.M.: Target Rock should be a good spot.
Ghillie: Yes, avoid that.

D.M.: One was caught there yesterday.
Ghillie: Noo, not for three years.

D.M.: Mr Sinden is married to my daughter.
Ghillie: Noo.

D.M.: They should be rising now.
Ghillie: Yes, this afternoon.

D.M.: I suggest a yellow belly.
Ghillie: Noo, not this end of the loch.

Four lines were run out and the ghillie rowed slowly and deliberately up and down while the rain continued to pour. It beat into my face and I could feel it trickling down under my clothes. I was never more miserable and dejected. Absolutely no salvation was to hand. Suddenly one of the two lines which D.M. had designated as mine jumped: 'A bite – a bite!' D.M. and the ghillie were on their feet and the little boat rocked, 'Wind it in – wind it in!' 'No – No! Let it run!' 'Wind it in!' 'Let it out!' 'Hold on.' 'Let it go.' 'Keep the line clear.' 'Let it out!' 'Wind it in!' 'There it is!' A streak of silver surfaced and dived again.

D.M. was beside himself with frenzy – his damned fool of a son-in-law was likely to lose the fish and his rod as well. I must admit that the pull on the line was considerable, but I heaved away and tried to obey the conflicting instructions of D.M. and the ghillie. At long last the fish was brought alongside the boat, the ghillie leaned over, practically tipping us all overboard, and gaffed it. We stayed out for several more hours without further success and finally returned to the hotel where I was photographed holding my fish, which weighed fifteen pounds. We bathed and changed but as we reached the top of the stairs on our way down to dinner, D.M. held me back while he looked over the banisters. 'No, not yet – wait a few minutes,' he said. When all the other guests had gone in, D.M. said, 'Let's give them half a minute . . . all right – now,' and in we marched while twenty-six pairs of eyes glistened as they followed us to our table. Unfortunately I ruined the whole scene. When the first visitor stopped at our table and asked, 'I hear you caught a salmon – what were you using?' I could not resist saying, 'A bent pin on a piece of string.' The visitor said, 'This is no time to be facetious, young man,' and walked away. D.M. sternly reprimanded me and explained that to his certain knowledge some of these people had been coming to Killin for the past seven years and never caught anything. I must admit that I always believed that people only went fishing to catch fish. Why else?

D.M. was a leading member of the Enfield Chase Fox-Hounds and in the Season turned out in his immaculate pink coat, white breeches and top hat. One year a splendid photograph was taken, in which D.M. featured prominently, of the hunt meeting at Old Temple Bar which stands in Theobalds Park, Hertfordshire, and the following year it was used extensively on Christmas cards for general sale.

Out of the blue I received a peremptory summons to 'meet me for lunch on Thursday.' I arrived at the office and waited. Out he came, bowler hat square, umbrella at the attack. I trailed after him round corners, through alleys, across roads where cars were commanded to 'Wait!' and unexpectedly we turned into W. H. Smiths: crash went the door, shoppers gave way before us as he arrived at the counter where hundreds of Christmas cards were displayed. He rummaged through them, tossing this and that aside before suddenly picking one up and thrusting it into my face. 'WHAT DO YOU THINK OF THAT?' he roared. I focused on it: it was D.M. with the Enfield Chase at Temple Bar – but what was I supposed to say? I had seen it before but from his attitude and tone of voice something of importance was required. 'Ah. Well. It's a very fine photograph . . .' I began. 'LOOK AT THE COLOUR OF MY COAT!' he spluttered. Being colour-blind it looked perfectly normal to me. Luckily he continued, 'THEY'VE PRINTED IT ORANGE!' Angry letters were exchanged with the makers and he threatened to sue. But that day he forgot about lunch.

When our first son, Jeremy, was born he softened considerably and proudly displayed him to his friends: 'My grandson'. His daughter and son-in-law seemed to have had little to do with it. As a baby Jeremy refused to crawl on all fours and developed his own idiosyncratic way of moving about: sitting down, he leaned forward on to his hands and slid his bottom up to his hands. He could move quite rapidly in this fashion. Another phone call: 'Meet me for lunch on Wednesday' (it never occurred to D.M. that I might possibly have a previous engagement). The usual pattern was repeated. The office. The wait. The exit plus bowler and umbrella. The trek to the restaurant. Again we had lunch in almost total silence, but with the coffee came the unpredicted: 'Donald – you know the way Jeremy crawls?' 'Yes,' I agreed tentatively. 'Well, I don't mind admitting now that when I first saw that child crawling like that I was *terribly* worried – I thought that boy will never be able to ride a horse, but I have been making enquiries and I have discovered that the best horseman I know also crawled like that! So all is well.' Subject closed – home on the tube.

I must recount an anecdote concerning D.M. which is a bit near the mark – perhaps the innocent reader should turn on to Page 103.

In the 1960s I tried to reciprocate for the City lunches by taking D.M. to the Garrick Club on an occasional evening – but here I need to set the scene for you. When the Garrick is closed for staff holidays in August the members are made welcome at the Travellers Club, of which someone is reputed to have said – quite erroneously – that the only time laughter is heard in the bar of the Travellers is when the Garrick is closed. The two clubs, while having many similarities, are distinctly different. The Garrick dining room is dominated by one enormous table around which the members eat and talk. The Travellers dining room has many small tables at which individual members can eat and read a newspaper. Owing to the closure of the Garrick it was to the Travellers I took D.M. one evening. We made our way to the bar which was deserted but for two Garrick members, a Professor and a Surgeon. I introduced them to D.M. and they got on like a house on fire. They were all in their seventies and seemed to have much in common. We decided that we should all dine together, so up we went. The dining room was crowded and all the small tables were occupied by members with their lady guests. Only one table was free and this was in the very centre of the room. We ordered our meal and as the waiter left the Surgeon made a remark that had absolutely no bearing on our previous conversation. It was the kind of remark that Boswell quotes baldly as a cue for one of Dr Johnson's cataclysmic replies:

'Did you know that it was the secretary of the Travellers Club who wrote the *Dictionary of National Biography* entry on Rosa Lewis?'

This was received by an awed silence; we all pondered the remark. After some thought the Professor asked, 'Who was Rosa Lewis?'

'You knew Rosa Lewis,' said the worldly-wise Surgeon, 'she ran the Cavendish Hotel up in Jermyn Street.'

'Cavendish Hotel? I've never heard of it.'

'Of course you have. Not the one that is there now; they pulled the old one down – it was a famous knock-shop.'

D.M., who had been worrying the recesses of his mind trying to think if the name Rosa Lewis meant anything to him, suddenly reacted – he was losing the thread. 'A what?'

'A knock-shop. Cavendish Hotel – *famous* old knock-shop.'

You could see the wheels of D.M.'s mind turning – a hotel had been trading in some commodity of which he had never heard – and as a man of the City, indeed of the World, he should have heard, but should not admit that he hadn't.

The Professor, however, ploughed in: 'No. No, it can't have been. I knew every knock-shop in London in my time. Mind you, I did most of my f – ing in India.'

D.M. tried desperately to concentrate his mind – he was a man who could contribute to a conversation on any subject but now the subject had jumped to something done in India – perhaps one bought the equipment at the knock-shop: 'I beg your pardon . . .?' he ventured.

The Professor was more interested in disproving the credibility of the Surgeon. 'I said I did most of my f – ing in India.'

D.M. was a man who prided himself on knowing more about blood sports than most people. Perhaps this – this – whatever he said – was akin to pig-sticking, but he must clarify: 'I'm so sorry – *what* did you say?'

The Professor was now convinced that D.M. must be deaf and in the roar of a retired officer in the Indian Army he shouted, 'I SAID I DID MOST OF MY F – ING IN INDIA.'

From around the room there was a clatter as scores of knives and forks were dropped on plates.

Many years later when I went to the nursing home to visit a pathetic little crumpled figure, incontinent and hardly able to move as a result of a stroke; who sometimes could not remember who Diana was but could still recite the whole of Gray's *Elegy*, I could hardly believe that this was the man who could clear a five-barred gate with the best of 'em; whom I have seen look at a column of figures and add up the pounds, the shillings and the pence all at the same time; and who was the Master of the Worshipful Company of Innholders. He died in 1981.

6

THE MARRIED MAN

I did warn you didn't I? – I advised you to turn to this page. I fear I have digressed rather badly this time. Where was I? Oh, yes – at His Majesty's Theatre in 1947.

I continued to play Romeo for the rest of the Memorial Theatre's London season, as well as looking around for future work. Although asked to return to Stratford for another year, I felt the time had come to make a change. I had written ahead to make appointments, including one with a well-known casting director for a large film studio, who at the interview said that before she could cast me it was essential for her to see me doing something. 'You don't know how lucky you are!' I said. 'At this moment I am playing Romeo with the Memorial Theatre Company at His Majesty's Theatre!'

I was thoroughly dashed when she said, 'Oh, it's no use seeing people in Shakespeare.'

A miserable period of unemployment followed – more grist to D.M.'s anti-Sinden mill. Luckily, early in 1948 an offer of a television play turned up, adapted from a brilliantly funny book by Caryl Brahms, *A Bullet in the Ballet*. I was to play the important part of Inspector Quill. This production taught me many things – the first being never again to play a detective. The part is always difficult to learn. Most characters in plays are involved in conversation, which is comparatively easy to learn – any one line is usually a logical reaction to another – while a detective does nothing but initiate often random questions that have nothing to do with the previous answer. For instance, if a witness is asked, 'Is your name John Smith?' the witness has a fifty-fifty chance – either the answer is yes or no. But the poor detective has to be certain which question to ask – it could be 'Is your name John Smith?' or it might be 'Where were you on the night of the 14th?' or two hundred other possibilities.

It was a mammoth production with many complicated sets for which the BBC used their only two large studios at Alexandra Palace – A. & B. As this was before the days of video, the whole performance, involving an enormous cast of actors and an entire ballet company seen performing *Petrushka*, was broadcast live on a Sunday evening and repeated the following Thursday – with no extra rehearsals in between. On several occasions Inspector Quill was required to finish a scene on one set in studio A and to be at the opening of the next scene in studio B. To effect this the director would arrange for the camera to stay on the person to whom I was speaking while I stood up and moved quietly to the door, followed by a man with a microphone. I spoke my last lines out of vision and then had to run like a hare down the corridor – fifty yards or more – to studio B where another camera was already photographing another actor talking to an empty chair into which I slid as unobtrusively as possible, while trying to say my first line without sounding out of breath. The moment the director saw I was in position he cut the shot to me.

A Bullet in the Ballet was a hair-raising experience but an invaluable one and was the direct beginning of a long friendship with Caryl Brahms.

In the early days of television the decision was made that as a performance was continuous and live, the medium was more akin to the theatre than to the cinema – where actors were only required to sustain dialogue for a few seconds at a time. Thus stage actors were employed and suddenly expected to perform in a mechanical medium. New techniques had to be learned – sometimes to disguise a deficiency: when one actor forgot his lines, he continued, silently, to move his lips. This caused the control box to start twiddling knobs in panic, as they assumed the sound equipment had broken down. Another actor developed a villainous idea. The view finders on the first cameras showed the picture upside down, which meant that the operator, if he was to follow an actor walking from left to right, saw him apparently moving from right to left. As the operators never attended rehearsals – apart from sheets of instructions telling them what to expect, the first they actually saw of the action was on the day of the performance – there was frequently confusion. When the actor in question was involved in a duologue, with both actors in view, he waited until his first speech of any size and while speaking moved slowly backwards until they were too far apart for both to be held in frame. The safest thing, therefore, for the operator was to follow the actor who was speaking, with the result that the other actor remained out of shot for the rest of the scene.

As there was no way of deducing how many viewers a programme had – if any – how could fees be calculated? Someone came up with the bright idea that an actor's fee should be deemed to be three times his weekly salary in the theatre. It remained at this established rate for many years. For *A Bullet in the Ballet* I was paid thirty-six pounds for two performances on the whole television network.

I fondly imagined that with two seasons at Stratford and a passable performance of Romeo behind me (performances on television did not count) managers would now be clamouring for my services. But, sadly, this was not so. I hung around for weeks and then came the one and only offer. A long-running play called *Off the Record* by Ian Hay and Stephen King-Hall had recently transferred to the Piccadilly and, resulting from a cast reshuffle, I was asked to take over as walking understudy to nine parts. It was a large cast and with all the other parts understudied by people already in the play, the structure was such that had any one of the leading players been unable to appear everyone else moved up one and five understudies would have played – if *any* of the men were off I would be called on. With no alternative I accepted the job.

Heading the cast was Hugh Wakefield as a very irate Admiral. A master comedian, it was an object lesson to see him cope with the audience. In one particular sequence he pours himself a Scotch and is in the act of adding soda when a calamitous event is announced . . . the soda syphon squirts into the glass, sprays in all directions and his face quivers with apoplexy. That was what an audience at a bad matinee saw. But, varying in length, according to the quality of the laughter, he would then turn his attention to the carpet and 'rub out' the pool of soda in which he was standing. His feet being wet, he then moved to a drier part of the carpet on which he tried to dry his shoes, thereby making that part of the carpet wet; backing away he again trod in the first pool, and so on. With a splendid house I saw him thus complete a full circuit of the stage – and all the time remain completely believable.

Hugh was understudied by an actor named Roger Maxwell who would loom large later in my life. It was Roger who reported to Tom Gill – one of the actors I understudied – that in rehearsal I had changed one of his lines, possibly for the better. The part was a 'silly ass' who has learned on the telephone that the Admiral's car has been stolen and just driven through the gates: he asks, 'Who was driving it?' At rehearsal I had said, 'Was anyone driving it?' Tom purloined the line and got a beautiful laugh.

My 'guru' for this play was Jack Allen, a superb comedian from whom I learned an enormous amount. I sat with the audience for ninety-six consecutive performances of the play and each night Jack and I conducted a post-mortem on the actors and audiences. He quizzed me on why certain lines got a laugh – or didn't get a laugh. One line, we discovered, only worked when he crossed his legs on a certain syllable; if they were crossed on the previous or following syllable – nothing. In confidence we discussed the other actors and he encouraged me to speculate on where their faults lay.

From Jack I learned not to disclose all my 'cards' at once, but to play them deliberately one after the other. For reasons best known to the plot, Jack, playing an MP, has to pretend to be a naval officer arriving on his new ship, and we can be sure he will make a hash of it. The scene is the wardroom and we expect our hero to enter through a door in the centre of the back wall after arriving on the deck above. We hear the bosun's whistle and the stamping of feet as the crew come to attention – we start to giggle – a slight pause and then: dong – dong – dong as he misses his footing on the metal ladder just off stage – the laughter begins – and then . . . CRASH as he falls the last few steps – the laughter builds. Another slight pause and he is seen through the doorway trying to straighten himself before making his official entrance to his officers – even more laughter – at last he is ready. He steps forward, but has not seen the section of bulkhead across the bottom of the door . . . he trips and falls flat on his face – enormous laugh, during which he remains prostrate until it subsides, before painfully rising to his feet. But his sword belt is twisted and the sword is between his legs. We have seen it, but he has not and we know what will happen and begin to laugh again. He straightens his hat, his tie and his jacket. The laughter has almost stopped when, with his hand extended to greet his Number One, he steps forward and – of course – goes flat on his face again. We cannot believe our luck, we believe that only tonight has the sword got entangled and we are privileged to have seen it – we must applaud the occasion. The goodwill he has fostered will make us prepared to think that everything he says or does in the rest of the scene will be funny.

Another actor doing the above sequence might have run it all together, resulting in only one laugh.

Two days after signing my contract to understudy for at least three months, I received an offer from the Old Vic Company. The director, John Burrell, had seen me playing Romeo and as a result I was being asked to play Dunois in Shaw's *St Joan* with Celia Johnson. But my management justifiably refused to release me. It was a blow, but only a temporary one, because the Old Vic then suggested that I should join their other company at the Theatre Royal, Bristol, at the end of the three months. In fact it was not quite so simple. Rehearsals in Bristol started before I had finished with *Off the Record*, so for one week I rehearsed in Bristol during the day, caught a train back to London in time for the performance at the Piccadilly Theatre, and then raced to the station in time to catch the last train back to Bristol where I slept the rest of the night.

It was a classic season at Bristol. The company included Catherine Lacey, Robert Eddison, Paul Rogers, Elizabeth Sellars, Rolf Lefebvre, John Glen, Nuna Davey, Leslie Sands, Pauline Winter and Jane Wenham. The director was Hugh Hunt, with whom I suffered in the first production from a lack of communication. The play was Pinero's *The Second Mrs Tanqueray* in which the name part was played by Catherine Lacey, who had herself understudied the great Mrs Patrick Campbell in the same role. She was splendid as she paced the stage like a caged tigress. I had the small part of her daughter's lover, Hugh Ardale. Whenever Hugh Hunt suggested anything to me, I quite misunderstood him. I became nervous and tongue-tied, with the result that Hugh quite misunderstood my ideas. At the first performance I was like a stammering Zombie. The next day I was furious with everyone – myself in particular. I did what I often do – I went for a long walk and debated with myself: I had been so happy at the Piccadilly – why should I come to Bristol to be made miserable – life is too short – forget Hugh Hunt – forget the Bristol Old Vic – no – the part should be very easy – go on stage tonight and be true to myself – just do what I know I can do. So at the second performance that is what I did. When the final curtain fell I found Hugh waiting for me. 'That is *exactly* what I wanted!' he said ecstatically.

I was captivated by Bristol and the surrounding countryside. I loved to walk through the narrow streets of the old town and by the docks and on the Clifton Downs, where I was to discover a strange trait in myself: the most exciting, spiritual, elemental thing I have experienced is to stand in the middle of Brunel's bridge, suspended hundreds of feet above the Avon Gorge, during a thunder-storm, as it sways perilously from side to side, the rain beating down, blackness below and creaking irons and chains above. The story is told of a lady travelling in a train in the early part of the nineteenth century. An elderly gentleman companion stood up, opened the window, put his head out and stayed there for fifteen minutes with the rain beating into his face and the smoke from the engine blowing past. When he sank back into his seat, he remained for some time with his eyes closed. The lady, intrigued by his behaviour, did as he had done and leaned her head out of the window . . . a year later she went to the exhibition at the Royal Academy and joined a small group looking at Turner's impressionistic *Rain, Steam and Speed* in which is seen a train crossing a landscape lashed with rain. Someone mocked at the painting, 'It is ridiculous – who ever saw anything like that?' '*I* did!' she cried. Her elderly travelling companion had been Turner himself. My experience must have been akin to theirs. At the first sign of a stormy night I always rushed back to my chosen position on the bridge.

The Bristol Theatre Royal was (and is) a gem of a building. Built in 1766, it was still in my time basically unaltered – the narrow pit passage which led to the area, now the stalls, where the audience – the groundlings – had to stand; the gallery where were still to be found the rough wooden benches; and, most exciting of all, the shallow space between the ceiling of the auditorium and the roof which contained a fascinating relic, a 'thunder roll'. A long, narrow, slightly inclined trough of wood was attached at its lower end to a similar trough, which continued the incline back to a foot or two below the end of the first trough. An iron cannon ball placed at the top would slowly roll and bump down the trough, hit the wood at the end and roll back again ready to be lifted to repeat the operation. Placed strategically above the heads of the audience, it gave a wonderfully realistic impression of thunder – the building itself seemed to shake. A second cannon ball would double the decibels. It took hundreds of years before stereo matched the effect in cinemas.

The front of the stage had been pushed back five or six feet, but it was easy to imagine where it had been originally, with the side boxes on the stage itself, into which David Garrick confined the spectators. Previously they had been allowed to wander around the stage area, even, on occasion, participating in the performance!

Hugh Hunt had arranged for the company to visit Dublin and Belfast before appearing in London at the St James's Theatre in *Hamlet*. As I wanted Diana to join me, this seemed the ideal opportunity to marry. D.M. consented – we had given him the impression that otherwise Diana would accompany me unmarried, and that he would *not* countenance. Back in London, Diana had to make all the arrangements. The date was fixed for 3rd May as I was not needed for the forthcoming production of *Hedda Gabler* which opened on that date, but I had to be back in Bristol for rehearsals on 6th May (the birthday of Catherine Lacey, who was playing Hedda). As Diana's family are all Roman Catholic, D.M., still convinced that 'it would not last', would only agree to having the ceremony performed by a registrar (in D.M.'s eyes this really constituted no commitment at all) as far away from the family home as possible, and none of his friends were to be invited. We were helped out by the stage manager of *Off the Record*, Freddy Kerr, who lived in Shaftesbury Avenue and kindly agreed to allow Diana to establish residence there and thus qualify for the Holborn Registration Area.

Early on 3rd May, 1948, accompanied by my family, I set off from Ditchling for the registrar's office in Russell Square, where we found Diana's sister Sheila and D.M. Mrs Mahony had decided to accompany Diana as she feared that had D.M. been allowed to do the conventional thing, he would have abducted the bride. Diana arrived on time looking very beautiful in a yellow suit (being colour blind I had better check that . . . Yes, it was yellow) and yellow boater. We grinned stupidly at each other and were shown into the office where we stood self-consciously looking at the floor. As a voice started to intone the ceremonial 'Do you', etc., we looked up and discovered, with some surprise, that the registrar was a woman and she had a large black patch over one eye. It was too much. We both dissolved into fits of giggles.

The next day we set off for Bristol where Diana joined me in theatre digs run by Mr and Mrs Cousins. And vastly embarrassing it was. I had only to sit on one end of our rather ancient double bed to remove a sock, for John Glen, who had the room below ours, to be subjected to a noise equivalent to a tympanist dropping his entire collection of tubular bells from a great height.

The company then moved to Dublin, where we were extremely fortunate in having Hugh Hunt with us. Having been the director of the Abbey Theatre between 1935 and 1938, he organised tours around Trinity College, to the Abbey and Gate Theatres, and to St Michan's church where the first performance of Handel's *Messiah* had taken place and where the verger pointed out the wood carving on the organ loft 'done by the famous English firm of Grinling and Gibbons'. He then took us down to the crypt where some of the ancient coffins had broken open and we were encouraged to 'shake hands with a fifteenth-century nun'. In Ireland Diana, who had frequently found herself temperamentally at odds with the English, was in her element. Here was a whole nation who thought as inconsequentially as she did and who were delighted to 'meet a Mahony' and talk away the hours.

We had, however, overlooked one essential commodity – contraceptives, which were illegal in Eire. There was nothing for it: I telephoned my father to send by express post some Volpar Gels. Villainously, he sent a small crate! Being terrified that we might be arrested and deported, or at the least fined, if our dustbin was found to contain incriminating evidence, we did not throw away the empty bottles, but kept them secreted in our suitcases. The day came when we were to return to England and so did the idea that we would possibly have to open our cases for the Customs. What could we do with the damned things? But of course! Throw them overboard from the boat. Halfway between Dun Laoghaire and Holyhead, we appeared on deck carrying a large paper carrier, but the only part free from swarms of people was near the bow and from there, pretending that it contained potato peelings, we threw the carrier bag nonchalantly over the side. But disaster! As the bag hit the water it burst open – foolishly we had not removed any of the screw caps so not one of the bottles sank – dozens of them, proudly labelled VOLPAR, bobbed along past the electrified passengers.

Worse was yet to come. Eire had been neutral during the war and to our war-worn, newly-married eyes was a land of plenty. We stocked ourselves up with linen sheets and lengths of material and with meat, eggs, butter and cream – all of which were rationed in England. On a number of these we might be charged duty at the English Customs. 'Anything to declare?' we were asked. Trying not to quake I said, 'A hundred cigarettes, a bottle of wine and some handkerchiefs' (which was true) . . . I paused, hoping he would accept that much declaration. The officer was either kind, tired or busy and he just said, 'Right,' and chalked a cross on each of our suitcases. Now this was the first time Diana had been through the Customs and she misguidedly assumed that the cross exonerated us. I had a heavy suitcase in each hand halfway between counter and floor when she said, 'Well, we got away with that!' If only the ground could have opened for me. The officer was still there in front of us. I looked at him sheepishly. A few hours passed in as few seconds before a smile of sympathy and commiseration spread across his face. We said no word, we had no word to say . . . He turned to the next passenger.

In many of Shakespeare's plays it is almost impossible to differentiate between certain groups of characters: Bushy, Bagot and Green in *Richard II*; the Lords in *The Tempest*; Cambridge, Scroop and Grey in *Henry V*; Solanio and Salarino (known theatrically as the Salads) in *The Merchant of Venice*. In *Hamlet* there is the same problem with Rosencrantz and Guildenstern: memorable as the Bristol Old Vic production was, I have had to search out an old programme to discover that I played Rosencrantz. Robert Eddison was a superb Hamlet, his great sonorous voice making organ music of the verse. Every actor brings something new to the part. (Sometimes it is not worth bringing, as with one Hamlet I saw who spoke his wonderfully loaded first line as 'A – littel – mawer – thun – kin – 'nd – less – thun – koind' and stayed that way for the next three hours.) Eddison's and Gielgud's are the only two out of twenty-seven I have seen that wholly satisfied me.

My dear friend Joyce Carey told me that she accompanied Noël Coward to the first night of Leslie Howard's *Hamlet* in America. As Howard delicately spoke that same first line Noël clutched Joyce's arm. 'Beautiful – beautiful,' he whispered, but from then on nothing grew, the whole performance remained muted and impassive. At the end they went to Howard's dressing room and Joyce wondered what Noël could possibly say. Coward embraced Howard and said, 'Oh Leslie, you know how I hate over-acting – and you could never over-act – but please, please try.'

Russell Thorndike performed a Herculean task when he went to America with Ben Greet's company: at universities he played the bad quarto version of *Hamlet* in the mornings, the good quarto version in the afternoon and the complete folio version in the evenings.

The story is told of Henry Irving dining at the Garrick Club with Wilson Barratt shortly before the latter embarked on a tour of the USA. 'Tell me Barratt,' piped Irving, 'what repertoire are you taking to America?'

'My usual,' rumbled Barratt. '*The Sign of the Cross*, *The Silver King*, *The Manxman* – and of course – "The Dane".'

'Is that wise?' interjected Irving.

'What do you mean?'

'Well, I myself have achieved-mmmmmmmmm-some success – in the role of Hamlet in the United States.'

'You don't think you're the only actor who can play Hamlet, do you?'

'No,' replied Irving. 'But you are the only actor who can't.'

Max Beerbohm asked Henry James about William Poel's 'Elizabethan' production of the play with Esme Percy as Hamlet: 'It was like morning prayers in a workhouse.'

Probably the nicest story is of a young actor who was studying the psychology of the character and asked an old actor if he thought that Hamlet had actually been to bed with Ophelia. 'I don't know about the West End, laddie, but we always did on tour.'

For his production of *Hamlet* Hugh Hunt incorporated some ingenious effects. The stage at one point was divided halfway across by a wall: on the right was Claudius's chapel; on the left Gertrude's bedroom. Between the two was an enormous crucifix.

Preparing to pray Claudius removed his sword and placed it on the ground behind him. Hamlet entered, saw first the kneeling figure at the prie-dieu and then, seeing the sword, withdrew it silently from its scabbard and said, 'Now might I do it pat' (whom, irreverently, actors think of as Hamlet's Irish friend). Then, changing his mind and still carrying the sword, he continued to his mother's bedroom.

The King looks up and notices that the head of Christ on the crucifix is turned away.

My words fly up, my thoughts remain below,
Words without thought never to heaven go.

He then reaches to replace his sword: the scabbard is empty!
Someone has been in that chapel while he was kneeling unpro-
tected! The lights fade on the chapel and rise on the bedroom where
we see Polonius talking to Gertrude. On Hamlet's approach he
hides behind an arras. Hamlet enters still carrying Claudius's
sword. While talking to his mother he hears a sound behind the
arras and, thinking it to be the King, uses the sword to kill Polonius.

While saying 'Confess yourself to heaven; repent what's past', he
indicates the crucifix on which the head of Christ appears to be
gazing upon him compassionately. He then lugs the guts of Polonius to 'a neighbour room' leaving the bloodstained sword behind
on the floor. Claudius enters and seeing his own sword says. 'It had
been so with us, had we been there!'

The sword has come full cycle.

From Lichtenburg's letter to his friend Henrich, we can learn
much about eighteenth-century productions. Concerning *Hamlet*
he unintentionally remarks that when the ghost first appears 'he
stands motionless, clad from head to foot in armour, for which *a suit
of steel-blue satin did duty*'. How brilliant! The text tells us that the
ghost is dressed in armour but how do you dress an actor in armour
which does not 'clank' in a most un-ghostly fashion. The perfect
answer is to reproduce the armour in 'steel-blue satin'. The letters
are full of such fascinating clues.

Our production moved to London's St James's Theatre where in
1948 my Rosencrantz was quite unmemorable.

It was at the St James's, however, that the actor Douglas Quayle
had· a most frightening and memorable experience which he recounted to me. He was appearing in a play in which a line from
Macbeth was quoted – and no actor likes that. During the opening
performance everyone was too fraught to notice anything strange,
but by the end of the first week Quayle was convinced that he heard
an eerie 'laugh' after that line was spoken: the next night he
thought he heard it again . . . No – no – it must be his imagination
. . . but the next night there it was again. He confided in another
actor who admitted that he, too, thought he had heard something.
At the next performance they both awaited the line with some
trepidation. The play was forgotten, all they could think of was the

approaching line. They stiffened and cocked their ears. The line was spoken and sure enough they both heard a sort of sinister cackle coming from the cavernous fly tower above the stage. They speculated on the source of the 'laugh': perhaps some stagehand with a perverted sense of humour? Without telling anyone they arranged to stay behind at the end of the performance. The audience left the theatre, followed within half an hour by the other actors and stage staff. The night-watchman/fireman was at the stage door preparing to lock up. Without disclosing their intent the two actors asked if, in return for a couple of pints, they might accompany him on his rounds.

An empty theatre is a most ghostly place at the best of times – the only light was the night-watchman's torch as they groped their way through the pass door into the auditorium, up staircases and along passages which only a few knew to exist, as the fireman made his various checks. Into the gallery where another hidden doorway took them into the top of the fly tower. Ninety feet below them one naked light bulb lit the stage. An up draught caused the ropes around them to sway slightly and the wind creaked a shutter above their heads. Wooden ladders took them down to the fly rail (the platform where stagehands raised and lowered the scenery. In the days of gas lighting these stagehands were recruited from men who worked during the day in breweries because their trade caused them to be immune to rising gas fumes.) More ladders, and they were down to the stage. With absolutely no doubt that apart from the three of them, the theatre was deserted and no one had any foreknowledge that Quayle and his friend were to stay behind, the three stood in the centre of the stage. Quayle took an enormous breath and bellowed the offending line from *Macbeth*. Hardly a second's pause and from the blackness above came a hideous howl which evolved into a fiendish cackle! The three of them fled from the theatre. The night-watchman never returned, but the two actors had to continue the run of the play which was luckily (unluckily?) short.

My association with the St James's had a most unfortunate sequel. In 1957 it was proposed that this beautiful historic theatre should be demolished and an office block built in its place. (How often we have seen the destruction of buildings which either by their use or architectural delight enhance the quality of life, to be replaced by some cubicular mass to house more desks and filing cabinets used by people who then have to flee from the concrete jungle in search of the very qualities they have destroyed.)

A 'demonstration' was organised in which I joined many other actors, including Vivien Leigh and Laurence Olivier, to march through the West End carrying banners protesting against the proposed demolition. Some days later Vivien Leigh attracted far more publicity to the cause by throwing a kipper from the public gallery of the House of Lords. She was ejected and every newspaper carried the story. A day or so later on 17th August, 1957 the *Daily Mail* printed a letter on another subject which closed by saying '. . . then surely Miss Leigh is the last person who should condemn for this action', signed 'Donald Sinden, Westcliff-on-Sea'. I was shocked. A number of friends telephoned me, all of whom thought that I had written the letter. I had no idea that another Donald Sinden existed. I found his telephone number and called; sure enough he did exist. I consulted my solicitor who wrote to the editor of the *Mail* asking that they print a note to the effect that the letter was not from me. This they refused to do on the grounds that they never implied that it was D.S. the actor who had written. I tried to explain to Vivien, but it was too late, the damage was done. I cannot say she never forgave me, but a rift remained.

Perhaps, after all, it was a good thing they pulled down the St James's – the sight-lines were terrible.

Diana and I moved into a furnished one-room flat in Spring Street, Paddington and there a telephone call asked if I would join the Old Vic Company for the following season at the New Theatre after a short provincial tour. This coincided perfectly with the end of *Hamlet*. The company was to be headed by Edith Evans, as Lady Wishfort in Congreve's *The Way of the World* and Madame Ranevsky in Chekhov's *The Cherry Orchard* – and by Cedric Hard-wicke who was to play Dr Faustus, Gayev in *The Cherry Orchard* and Sir Toby Belch in *Twelfth Night*.

Having already done two years in *Dr Faustus* I asked for a change from my old parts of Second Student and Pride in the Seven Deadly Sins. Not very generously, I thought, they offered me First Student and Envy in the Seven Deadly Sins. After Robert Harris at Strat-ford, Cedric Hardwicke was a great disappointment: years of filming in Hollywood had made him lazy and he never really committed himself to the part. At one early rehearsal he said, 'Was this the face that launched the fish and chips . . .' We dutifully laughed, but he repeated the joke at every subsequent rehearsal,

until we began to wonder if he would say it during the performance. (He didn't.) But it was during a performance that he betrayed
his sang-froid. Addressing his two student companions, he is about
to tell them the horrific details of his diabolical pact with Mephistopheles and begins 'Ah gentlemen, hear me with patience and
tremble not at my speeches . . .' One night he got as far as '. . . hear
me with patience and . . . and . . . er . . . *worry* not at my . . . er . . .
(He looked at the two of us and a grin spread over his face) . . . well,
words will do.'

Before the first night of *The Cherry Orchard*, Edith Evans, having
spent her customary few hours mentally adjusting herself into the
character, was waiting in the wings ready for her first entrance with
Gayev. Her cue was only seconds away when Cedric slapped her on
the back and said, 'Good luck, Edie old girl – you're not a bad little
actress, you should go far!'

Cedric did, however, come into his own in *Twelfth Night*. He
played Sir Toby Belch with the *Sir* heavily underlined, his was the
most gentlemanly of Belches – a whisky-and-soda man. Robert
Eddison was an unusually melancholy Feste. The great joy of this
production of *Twelfth Night* was having the pleasure of working
with Alec Guinness, who directed it. I was cast as Sebastian,
because I had similar looks to the actress who was to play Viola and
for whom I could be mistaken, but this actress pulled out of the
production and was replaced by Jane Baxter. I did my best, but
could never succeed in looking as beautiful – and I was also six
inches taller.

Martin Holmes, in his book *Shakespeare and his Players*, points out
that at the time of the original production of *Twelfth Night* an
audience did not have programmes, and they could not have read
the play, indeed the only information given to them was from the
stage during the course of the play. At the beginning of *Twelfth
Night*, after a shipwreck, a young girl whose name we do not know
is cast ashore on an island; on being told that Duke Orsino reigns
there, she says that she will dress as a boy, call herself *Cesario* and
serve the Duke. From then on she is known to audience and players
as *Cesario*, until the last scene when, still dressed as a boy, she is
confronted by her supposedly drowned brother Sebastian. Neither
can believe their eyes. He says, 'I had a sister . . . I should . . . say
"thrice welcome drowned *Viola*".' They are the only two people to
whom the name *Viola* has any meaning. The audience should be
just as surprised as the players. But now the character is always

named in programmes and advertisements as 'Viola' and we are robbed of that element of discovery. Will our playhouses in future please state '*Cesario* played by . . .'?

It was as Sebastian that I had to speak a soliloquy for the first time. I was terrified. To be out on the stage quite alone and facing a thousand people! And one night it happened – I forgot my lines. I got as far as 'His counsel now might do me golden service . . .' and then my mind went blank! I could not even remember which *play* I was in. I looked in desperation at the prompt corner where the assistant stage manager was sitting, but she was busy talking to someone. The silence was deafening until it slowly dawned on her that all was not well; she looked at her script and whispered some lines to me, but they were ones I had already spoken. However they were something and I accepted them gratefully. Just like a horse that refuses a jump and the second time takes it beautifully, when I came to the fence it all came back and I sailed safely on. '. . . For though my soul disputes well with my sense . . .'

In *The Way of the World* our director was John Burrell, the man who had seen me as Romeo and had drawn me into the Old Vic companies. I understudied Harry Andrews as Mirabell and was therefore able to attend all the rehearsals and performances and watch Edith Evans creating her incomparable Lady Wishfort. (Many years before she had had an enormous success in the same play as Millament.) Hearing a knock at the door Lady Wishfort says, 'see who that is – set down the bottle first. Here, here under the table – what, would'st thou go with the bottle in thy hand like a tapster . . .' As Edith said 'set down the bottle first' she snatched it from the maid's hand and I was surprised that her next words (here under the table) were quite inaudible. I should have known! In performance her outrage on the first half of the line produced an enormous laugh. She stood there 'like an old peeled wall', and then hid the bottle *herself* under her dressing table. The second half of the line was obsolete.

Edith once said that if she could not think what to do with a line she spoke it as if it was obscene. One only has to think of her intonation on 'A Handbag!' in *The Importance of Being Earnest* to know what she meant. I once asked her if she had ever worked on eighteenth-century plays; 'No, my dear,' she said, 'I don't like the eighteenth century. Give me Restoration plays – I'm always game for a bit of bawdy.'

Walking down Shaftesbury Avenue one day I met Roger Maxwell, my old friend from *Off the Record*. In conversation I mentioned that, because we only had a three months' tenancy of our furnished flat in Paddington, Diana and I were in dire need of somewhere to live. Roger's eyes pierced me and in a matter of seconds apparently assessed my character as satisfactory. 'I have a house in Chelsea and there are some rooms vacant in the basement. Give me a ring tomorrow.'

Roger, whose real surname was Latham, was a 'gentleman of means', who looked and behaved like one too. He was a character. His head, always thrown back, was rather devoid of hair on top but an impressive ring of white encircled it. A bristling white moustache, brushed upwards, supported an impressive nose. As an actor he always played generals, brigadiers, Conservative MPs, or, conversely, butlers. His face was round and pink from exposure playing golf, to which he was addicted. (He had bought an old ambulance and fitted it out with an elegant bed, desk and dressing table and in this he would drive off to wherever a tournament was to be held. Nobody thought of preventing an ambulance from driving straight to the eighteenth green where Roger would camp out for the duration with a grandstand view.) He deeply resented being compelled to make National Insurance contributions and set himself the task of getting back as much as he paid in. The first minute he was not gainfully employed, he registered at the labour exchange. He would drive up in his sleek sports car, stride in and tolerate no inefficiency or incivility from the staff who were ordered to open up extra 'windows' if there was a queue. This scene was at its most colourful during Ascot week when Roger would appear resplendent in morning suit, top hat, binoculars and a bouquet of badges and passes. To add to the encounter he was rather deaf and his thunderous dialogue was laced with 'What? – WHAT?'

With his wife Ivy and son Andrew, he lived in a large house at the lower end of Tite Street – almost next door to the one that Godwin had designed for Whistler – and, on the death of his mother, he inherited a tall nineteenth-century house on five floors in Cheyne Gardens in which she had lived, one of the conditions being that the married couple who had been her chauffeur and maid should continue to be housed on the top two floors. The rest of the house was empty. Roger kept the large L-shaped room on the first floor as an office-cum-workroom, where he did his football pools, wrote his letters and tried his hand at upholstering and repairing valuable antique furniture – with a hammer and nails. He also played around with radios and electrical equipment. (After we had been in residence for a year a power point, used for the electric kettle, fused and in trying to discover the cause I found that the wire buried in the wall was only the smallest two-core flex which led to a light socket connected to a 15 amp fuse!) His mother's furniture he stored in two rooms on the ground floor; a third room at the back, now a bathroom, led via a conservatory to the walled garden beyond, at the end of which lay the large garden of Queens House in Cheyne Row where Rossetti and Swinburne once lived.

The basement comprised two large rooms with iron bars over the windows and a kitchen opening on to an 'area'. The rooms were connected by a wide corridor lined with great floor-to-ceiling cupboards, which previously held all the plate, crockery and pans for the whole house. At the front was a door leading to the coal holes under the pavement and a flight of steps up to the road. One of the rooms had a large black round boiler in the fireplace which fuelled the antiquated central heating system for the whole house. On condition we kept this going during the necessary months, Roger was prepared for Diana and me to move into the basement plus bathroom/conservatory at a rent of two pounds per week *inclusive* of gas, light, heat and boiler fuel – and the garden would be ours too! (Many years later Diana discovered the reason for his philanthropy: he thought he had detected in me something of the young Seymour Hicks, a great friend, and he felt that this should be nurtured.)

We had no furniture, but my mother gave us a bed; two orange boxes draped with material became bedside tables; we bought a fridge on the HP; the boiler room became our sitting room and the former kitchen dresser shelved our few books. Roger again came up trumps by lending us two beautiful sofa tables, a desk and an armchair.

Having finished a season in Dundee Repertory Company, Diana was now offered a tour of Germany, and happened to mention to the greengrocer that she was worried that I would be incapable of looking after the flat by myself. She was overheard by another customer who, because her son had just started going to school and her husband was out at work all day, found herself at a loose end and volunteered to be of assistance. By this chance meeting Joan Gooding came into our lives: after looking after us for six years in

Chelsea, she and her husband George have remained two of our best friends.

Chelsea seemed full of actors. Almost next door to the green-grocer lived Athene Seyler and her husband Nicholas Hannen, and round the corner Sybil Thorndike and her husband Lewis Casson. Every evening Lewis could be seen plodding up the road in his carpet slippers, crossing the busy Kings Road, buying his evening paper outside the cinema, and then, with his face buried in the centre pages, beginning his return journey by heading straight across the main road, traffic swerving and skidding around him, quite oblivious of the chaos.

They were blissful, happy and untrammelled days in Chelsea: walking by the river; in Battersea Park; exploring the old streets and decorating 'our own home'.

The Old Vic Company was housed at the New Theatre (now the Albery) in St Martin's Lane. This was the very theatre in which I had seen those scintillating seasons at the end of the war when, among others, Ralph Richardson had played Peer Gynt and Falstaff; Laurence Olivier, Richard III, Oedipus and Puff (in Sheridan's *The Critic*). Those of us who saw Olivier perform that incredible double bill of the towering drama of Oedipus followed by the joyous farce of Puff, were not aware that during the fifteen minute interval Olivier had to race against time to remove his blood-besmeared Grecian make-up, have a quick shower, and replace it with the round pink face with arched eyebrows and tip-tilted nose of Puff. And a change of wig. And a change of costume. He told me that on one occasion he was just stripping off his first costume when there was a knock at the door and in came the actor, George Curzon:

'Hello, Larry, I was just passing the theatre and thought I'd pop in to see you.'

'Help yourself to a drink.'

Nonchalantly George did so and draped himself on a settee. Larry hurried to the make-up table and began ripping off his 'nose' and slapping cream on his face, 'What are you up to, George?' (His dresser turned on the shower.)

'I'm rehearsing for *Peter Pan* – giving my Captain Hook – any ice?'

Larry hopped into the shower and, as he lathered away the sweat, grime and wet-white of Thebes, said, 'I hope you are also playing Mr Darling – it's essential that the same actor should do both.'

(The dresser gave George his ice and handed a towel to Larry.) 'Yes I am, Larry – but you can have no idea how exhausting it is to play two parts in one evening.'

When Olivier made the film of *Richard III*, I was delighted to find that he had incorporated the line written by Colley Cibber when he 'adapted' the play in the early eighteenth century – 'Off with his head; so much for Buckingham', because this line has been the cause of so many theatrical stories.

Perhaps it is not necessary for me to explain that for more than a century after the Restoration the plays of Shakespeare were freely adapted by other authors (indeed in our own time Bernard Shaw wrote a new last act to *Cymbeline*). *King Lear* and *Romeo and Juliet* were given happy endings and many others were altered considerably. In the Cibber version of *Richard III*, which held the stage for 150 years and was used by actors such as David Garrick and Edmund Kean, Catesby rushes on to the stage and announces, 'My liege, the Duke of Buckingham is taken.' To which Richard replies, 'Off with his head; so much for Buckingham.'

In a provincial company in the early nineteenth century a young actor nearly ruined the scene by racing on and proudly announcing, 'My Liege, the Duke of Buckingham is taken – *and we've cut his head off*!' Poor Richard was left aghast and open-mouthed. This story eventually reached the metropolis where Edmund Kean, who was playing Richard at Drury Lane, had a reputation that *nothing* would make him falter in a performance. Someone bribed his Catesby to deliver this same line to Kean. The next night the young actor ran on and stuttered, 'My Liege, the Duke of Buckingham is taken – AND WE'VE CUT HIS HEAD OFF!' Kean wheeled on him, pierced him with his eyes and, remaining in perfect iambic pentameter, said, 'THEN BURY HIM – so much for Buckingham!'

A famous provincial manager, Tate Wilkinson, had inaugurated the system of booking seats in advance at an extra charge of a shilling. Prior to his time a seat could only be bought at the time of performance. While seated in his office one day, a distraught box-office clerk rushed in to say that an irate customer was stamping about and shouting that a dire mistake had been made in his ticket. 'To hell with him,' said Tate, ' – off with his bob, so much for booking 'em.'

One of my fondest memories of the New Theatre was after a performance of *Twelfth Night* when Ralph Richardson, who was still a director of the company and had just returned from America, visited us in our respective dressing rooms. Our dresser was an ex-chorus boy of uncertain age with permed hair and a pinched-bottom walk. He pranced up to Richardson and lisped, 'Oh, Mr Coward, we haven't met since we were together in *Bitter Sweet*!' Richardson's eyes widened and he paused before saying, 'Ah! Yes – I remember.' But more of the redoubtable Richardson shortly.

7

AZILON-AZI-AZIL-AZ-AZILON

The Old Vic season was drawing to a close when I received a call from H. M. Tennent who were then, and had been for twenty years, the leading West End management.

It is difficult today to envisage the West End scene as it was in the Forties. Each management had their 'favourites' – you were either 'in' or 'out'. As there was nothing colder than being 'out', every young actor tried to get 'in'.

H. M. Tennent had their offices on the top floors over the entrance of the Globe Theatre in Shaftesbury Avenue, approached by the world's smallest lift, which could just hold one large person or two thin ones pressed close together. The firm was headed by Hugh (Binkie) Beaumont, assisted by his great friend John Perry, with Bernard (Barney) Gordon as General Manager, Daphne Rye in charge of casting and Vivienne Byerley as press representative. Kitty Black ran their Company of Four at the Lyric Theatre, Hammersmith.

A young contemporary of mine had eventually succeeded in getting an interview with Daphne Rye. Feeling he had acquitted himself well, and rather elated, he entered the lift, the gate was closing when suddenly a hand pulled it back. Into the confined space stepped Binkie. My friend flattened himself against the wall and the lift slowly – oh, so slowly – ground its way downwards. The great man smiled at him. He smiled back. As the lift stopped my friend tried ineffectually to reach around Binkie to open the gate, he then squeezed ahead to open the door into the foyer, but failed to notice a step and tripped up. Apologetically and nervously he overtook the man who dominated the theatre world and succeeded in holding open the door on to the street. A chauffeur was holding open the door of a car at the kerbside and just before entering Binkie turned and said, 'Can I give you a lift anywhere?' My friend was so wrought-up that he could only stammer: 'N-no thank you – but that is unkindly common of you.'

The meeting place for the leaders of the profession in those days was the Ivy, a restaurant built on a triangular site appropriately opposite two theatres, the St Martin's and the Ambassadors, off Charing Cross Road. Inside the Ivy, the confined apex of the triangle was known as the Royal Circle, where Ivor Novello, Noël Coward, John Clements and Kay Hammond, John Gielgud, Henry Sherek, Douglas Byng, Laurence Olivier, Henry Kendall, Lilian Braithwaite, Emlyn Williams, Hermione Gingold, Diana Wynyard and James Agate each had a permanent table when in London. Through this luminous assembly all others had to pass to reach the main body of the restaurant. We young actors would save up to eat there in the fond hope of receiving a smile from one of the circle – or better still, stopping to exchange a brief word – and having passed through, it was akin to Sir Peter Teazle's exit in *The School for Scandal*, 'I leave my character behind me'. It was a red-letter day when Henry Kendall allowed Diana and me to use his table to celebrate our engagement – he didn't pay for the lunch; the loan of the table was enough.

It was in this Royal Circle that Alan Dent sat waiting for his host, James Agate, who was delayed. He decided to while away the time by catching up on some writing. Suddenly he became aware of a figure standing looking over his shoulder. It was Agate: 'What are you doing – writing my obituary?'

'As a matter of fact, I am,' admitted Dent.

Agate insisted on seeing the 'copy' and the lunch was spent discussing the details.

Here, too, sat Douglas Byng entertaining lavishly and always complaining about the bill: his famous twitch jerked his head from left to right, taking his jaw nearly round to his shoulder (caused, it was said, by sitting too often with his back to the Ivy's door). 'This is quite exorbitant – there must be a mistake. Bring me the head waiter.' The head waiter checked the bill and could find no fault. 'But this is disgraceful – nobody can be expected to pay a bill of this size – it's outrageous! Send for Mario!' Mario appeared. 'What are you doing to me? For a very simple lunch I am presented with this *enormous* bill – I may never come here again!' Mario tried to mollify him and explained that after all he had entertained five guests; they had consumed six bottles of wine; brandy and liqueurs; and the asparagus was out of season. Byng's twitch became more violent and he trumpeted: 'In which case I demand to see Ivy herself!'

Ivor Novello, who had supplied the theatre with a series of

romantic musicals, was then living in a sumptuous flat above the Strand Theatre and it was a minor accolade to be invited to one of his parties. Margaret Rutherford received an invitation following her first success in a play called *Spring Meeting*. Nervously she rang the bell and there to greet her star-struck eyes stood Ivor, and, beyond him, sitting or standing, a galaxy of Ivor's friends framed in the exotic decor of the room. 'Oh Ivor!' gaped Miss Rutherford, and her pendulous jaw quivered. 'It's fairyland!'

When Novello died in 1951, the cremation took place at Golders Green, where a lilac tree was later planted in the Memorial Garden recalling his famous song, 'We'll Gather Lilacs'. His friend of many years, Robert (Bobbie) Andrews, was distraught, but, nevertheless, had to make the arrangements for the funeral as well as coping with several mildly hysterical phone calls from the actress Ivy St Helier who was one of Ivor's charmed circle of friends.

'Bobbie darling, I'm *so* upset. I know if I go I am sure to break down – what should I do?'

'I know I *ought* to go, Bobbie, but it would be too awful if I were to create a scene – what should I do?'

'It's no good, Bobbie – I *can't* go – I can't stop crying – but I feel I *should* go – what should I do?'

Bobbie, having made soothing noises, could stand it no longer. 'Ivy darling, only you can decide. Ivor wouldn't be going himself unless he had to.'

Ivor left behind him a whole troupe of actors and singers who had rarely worked for anyone else. Some years later an anthology of his works was put together and went on tour under the title, *The World and Music of Ivor Novello*, the leading part played by Barry Sinclair, who had succeeded Ivor in most of his roles during the long runs. Barry told me that after a matinee at the Golders Green Hippodrome who should appear in his dressing room but Olive Gilbert (who had sung so frequently with Ivor), Bobbie Andrews and Fred Allen (Ivor's personal business manager). The only place to get tea was at the Express Dairy, opposite, and there the four sat reminiscing about the great days of Novello musicals. Barry said to Bobbie how enchanted he was that the three of them should take the trouble to come out and see his performance . . . 'No, I must tell you what happened,' answered Bobbie. 'Some time ago Fred said to Olive, "You must bring Bobbie up to lunch at my little house in Highgate", so it was arranged that we should go to his little house in Highgate today. After a lovely lunch Fred said, "What shall we do now?" and Olive said, "Let's go down to the crematorium and look at Ivor's lilac tree." So we all went down and looked at Ivor's lilac tree. Then Olive said, "What shall we do now?" and Fred said, "Let's go and look at Kenneth Kent's Urn." So we all went to look at Kenneth Kent's Urn. Then Fred said, "What shall we do now?" and I said, "We might just as well go and look at Barry's matinee" – that's why we're here.'

One day in Charing Cross Road I saw Bobbie, who trotted across the road, saying as he approached, 'Donald, my dear, I hardly recognised you – you're looking so young and beautiful – for a moment I thought you were Bobbie Andrews.'

They were exotic, hot-house days. But where was I? Oh yes. A call from H. M. Tennent offering – yes offering, not asking me to go for an audition, but actually offering – me a part in their next production, *The Heiress*, dramatised by Ruth and Augustus Goetz from Henry James's novel *Washington Square*, to be directed by John Burrell (so that is why I got the part!). I was to play Arthur Townsend, a small but significant part with only seven lines. My first West End play.

Dr Sloper (Ralph Richardson), a wealthy widower, lives with his daughter (Peggy Ashcroft) and sister/companion (Gillian Lind). One evening his sister (Madge Compton) visits the house in order to introduce Arthur Townsend, the fiancé of her daughter (Gillian Howell). Arthur brings with him his cousin Morris (James Donald) who then sets about the seduction of the doctor's heiress daughter. Also in the house is the maid (Pauline Jameson).

I had sat enthralled on so many occasions watching Ashcroft and Richardson on stage, and here I was working with them and it was fascinating to watch them rehearse. Richardson built up his characterisation day by day. Today there would be a raise of an eyebrow, the lifting of a hand, the tilt of the head, that was not there yesterday, while Ashcroft simplified each day, fining down and down until only the bare essentials remained.

I noticed that Richardson was perturbed if he did not have the first line as he entered and the last as he exited. At the opening of the play, with the maid, Maria, on stage, we hear the front door close and then the doctor enters: she says, 'Good evening, Doctor', to which he answers, 'Good evening, Maria'. Later in the play as he left he said, 'Good night, Maria', and she answered, 'Good night, Doctor'. The second time we ran the scene, Richardson had already solved his problem. He came on to the stage, registered surprise at seeing Maria, raised his eyebrows and uttered, 'Ah!' – 'Good evening, Doctor', 'Good evening, Maria.' Later, as he left, we had 'Good night, Maria', 'Good night, Doctor' and his bowed shoulders turned slowly, as he gazed at Maria with a wealth of meaning in his eyes ('If only you knew.' 'If you were not a menial I could tell you.' 'I am likely to have a terrible night', and so on) as he plaintively said, 'Ahh . . .'

While all seemed to be well to us lesser mortals, in the corridors of power all was *not* well. Clandestine meetings and phone calls had taken place. The first we knew was at the end of the third week of rehearsals when the whole cast was called together and John Burrell made a prepared speech to the effect that he was leaving the production owing to disagreements and that John Gielgud would be taking over as director on Monday morning. There was a stunned silence. We each felt that someone should say, 'Oh dear' or 'Oh no', but nobody did. John Burrell left the theatre and went to America.

That weekend we regaled our wives and husbands with the astonishing news and on Monday we re-formed for rehearsal. We were due to open in one week's time! John Gielgud entered and made a faltering speech that – he was in rather an embarrassing position – he hoped it would not distress the cast – he only wanted to help us – *he did not want to change anything* – would we please run the play as we had been doing it.

Two and a half hours later, we gathered on stage. John had a quiet word with Peggy and Ralph and then addressed us all, 'Yes. Well. Let us start at the beginning.'

He then changed *everything*. Every move; practically every 'reading' of a line; the scenery which had been cream was repainted an olive green; entirely different furniture was brought in and the following Monday, in January 1949, a virtually different play opened at the Theatre Royal, Brighton.

Rehearsals continued, John encouraging me to inject as much comedy as possible into my seven lines – a dangerous thing to do – and on 1st February we opened at the Theatre Royal, Haymarket.

It must be every actor's ambition to play in this magnificent theatre. Although the auditorium has been altered considerably and redecorated many times, it is still the same theatre, designed by Nash to be a focal point in his remodelling of London, and first opened in 1821. Cyril Maude, who was its last actor/manager, appropriated the magnificent dressing rooms on the first floor as his

office and when he left in 1905 the rooms remained as offices with
the result that today any leading man has to climb several more
flights of stairs to a similar suite of rooms, still with the original
fireplace, on the second floor. This was where Ralph held court.
(The leading lady usually uses the original green room, on the
ground floor, from which she has access to the sumptuous royal
loo. And here reigned Peggy.) The rest of the dressing rooms were
on two floors up even more stairs, *above* the stage. Gillian Howell,
Pauline Jameson and I were at the very top and at the back, with
semi-circular windows overlooking Suffolk Street. Having received our calls from the call-boy, who was actually in his sixties,
we had to set off many minutes before being required so as to reach
the stage in time.

With this play I heard, for the first time, the ominous but
thrilling buzz of a West End first night audience: if the play is to be a
great success, they want to be there at the moment of decision; if it is
to be a great disaster, they want to be there to make that decision. As
at a prize fight, they are hoping for a knock-out. Nothing compares
with that sound which actors hear through the lowered curtain. The
story is told of a young actor – it wasn't me but it could have
been – who has done his time in the provinces and is about to open
in the West End, playing a big part. Having been fairly nervous all
day he arrives on the stage and hears that frightening 'buzz' for the
first time: beads of perspiration break out on his forehead, his throat
is dry, his diaphragm seizes up and his knees begin to shake. What
can he do? In desperation he kneels down and begins to pray. An old
actor passes him and says, 'Don't rely on Him in the second act,
dear boy – He's helping me with a quick change!'

The Heiress was an enormous success. It was a glittering first
night; 'everybody' who was 'anybody' was there – Binkie had a
genius for 'dressing' his first nights – and the final curtain fell to
thunderous applause. Elated, we climbed to our dressing rooms.
Of course Peggy and Ralph knew scores of people who had been
'out front' and who now descended (or rather ascended) on them,
but I knew only Diana, who had come with D.M. (who had spent
the evening grumbling about the bad breath of a person sitting on
his other side). Awaiting their arrival I heard a knock at my door
and there stood an elderly gentleman. 'I felt I must come up to tell
you how much I enjoyed your performance – I know it's small, but
you have made a real character out of it. You won't know me but
my name is Gerald Lawrence.'

My computer flicked into action: I peered at him: No – No – he must be dead – could it be? I stammered out a stupid remark, 'Forgive me, but are you *the* Gerald Lawrence?'

Bemused, he said, 'What do you mean by that?'

'Is it possible that you are Irving's last juvenile and were with him the night he died?' Tears welled in his eyes and his arms reached out to me: 'I am – I am.'

From that encounter developed a friendship. He had first been married to Lilian Braithwaite and delightful, mischievous Joyce Carey is their daughter. He subsequently married Madge Compton who was playing my prospective mother-in-law in *The Heiress*.

Gerald hero-worshipped Irving and had been in his company for several years. He had also worked with most of the great actors of that period; Forbes-Robertson, Benson, Martin-Harvey and especially Beerbohm Tree.

Next door to his theatre (Her Majesty's) stood the Carlton Hotel where Tree regularly patronised the Grill Room. Coming out of his theatre one night, Tree hailed a hansom cab and ordered the driver: 'Drive like hell to the Carlton.'

Walking up Lower Regent Street with Gerald, Tree turned into the post office, advanced on the counter and ordered an astonished assistant, 'Show me some penny stamps.' Uncomprehendingly the young man slid a whole sheet of stamps across the counter. Tree spent some minutes examining them closely and then pointed at one right in the middle, 'I'll have *that* one.'

Hailing a cab on another occasion he abstractedly said: 'Drive me home.'

'Where do you live, sir?' said the cabby.

Tree came to with a jolt and exploded, 'Do you think I am going to tell you where my beautiful wife is!' – and got out, slamming the door behind him.

But enough of that – back to *The Heiress* and the Haymarket where we settled in for a long run.

When the lessee, Frederick Harrison, died in 1926, he bequeathed his shares to his manager, Horace Watson, and his stage manager, Charles La Trobe. By 1949 Watson's son was now the manager, but La Trobe, who had joined the company in 1908, was still the stage director, where he ruled supreme. Many other members of the stage staff had been there for decades. The Haymarket was unusual in still having an orchestra – not that one could see it. Palm leaves had been laid on wire netting stretched over the orchestra pit, thereby hiding Leslie Bridgewater and his musicians, who as a result did not have to wear evening dress. In a long run it is the usual practice for the final curtain call to be taken only by those actors who appear in the last scene, but for *The Heiress* this would have meant that only four members of the cast would be there, so La Trobe decreed that the *whole* cast should remain on the stage at the end of every performance and, with the audience, stand to attention as the National Anthem was played. One night the musicians came to the high notes of '. . . send him victorious', when from below we heard the most extraordinary squeaking. It got worse and more frenetic. We cast sidelong glances at each other. What could it be? We could see the faces of the audience breaking into smiles. Our own faces began to crease. Most unloyal laughter ran around the theatre. When the curtain was finally lowered, La Trobe stormed on to the stage and demanded an explanation. It transpired that in the absence of the first violin a substitute had taken his place who, as a staunch monarchist, had stood up to play the Anthem, his bow had caught in the wire netting and, in trying to extricate it, he continued in his panic to scrape away on the E string.

The stage door keeper was a delightful old character known as Bibby who in 1949 was ninety years old and had been at the Haymarket for as long as anyone could remember. He was quite hopeless at relaying messages – the one received had almost no relevance to the one sent. For instance, George Bishop, theatre correspondent of *The Daily Telegraph*, and Charles La Trobe had appropriated the task of arranging practically all theatrical memorial services, which traditionally took place at St Paul's, Covent Garden or St Martin-in-the-Fields. After the death of James Agate, Bishop telephoned La Trobe with news of the final arrangements. Bibby took the message, which reached La Trobe as follows: 'MR A. GATE WILL BE AT ST MARTIN FIELDS AT 11.30 AND WOULD LIKE YOU TO JOIN HIM.'

Between 1853 and 1878 the Haymarket was under the successful management of J. B. Buckstone and his ghost is supposed to haunt the theatre. Supposed? No it *does* – I have seen it! One evening Gillian Howell and I received our call and as usual we started to walk down the stairs together. As we rounded the corner on to the landing outside Ralph's dressing room, we saw Ralph dressed in his costume of 1860 period, deep in thought with his back to us, looking out of the window. We both said, 'Good Evening'. The fact that we received no reply did not worry us: we were used to

Ralph's idiosyncratic individuality. We passed within two feet of him and continued on our way still gossiping. A flight and a half down we both stopped in our tracks and clutched each other. Ralph at that moment was on the stage in the middle of his first scene! I raced back up the stairs, but the figure had gone. There was no other member of the cast who could have been there – let alone in the period costume.

Gillian and her husband, John Cadell, son of the marvellous actress Jean Cadell, became our great friends. Many years later when he started as a theatrical agent I joined him and he has looked after my business affairs ever since.

Having played my small scene each night – I was on and off within twenty minutes – I then had to find ways of occupying the rest of the evening. There were certain scenes that I never missed watching from the wings – one in particular when Peggy was awaiting the arrival of the 'suitor' who jilts her. She played this poignant scene so beautifully that even at the end of a year, having seen it at every performance, it was all I could do to stop myself rushing on to the stage to cradle Peggy in my arms and say, 'My darling, don't weep – it is only a play.'

I also understudied James Donald with whom, for another part of the evening, I played two-handed pontoon in his dressing room during his longest break. I got there two or three minutes before he arrived, shuffled the cards, dealt two for him and two for myself; I was always the 'bank'. James arrived, took off his jacket, sat down and, invariably, we played in complete silence. The price of a card was fixed at a penny. To buy, he just threw a penny towards me; to 'twist' was illustrated by an almost imperceptible twist of the wrist. If he 'stuck' he placed his cards face down. If he 'bust' he turned them over. This procedure was repeated eight times a week until James left the cast nine months later. I kept a tally and at the end of our marathon I was forty-three pennies down – I never have been good at card games.

With Thurston's Snooker Hall in Leicester Square round the corner, and having done my short scene, I would often slip an overcoat over my costume and, after informing everyone where I was going – in case I was required in a hurry as James Donald's understudy – I would sit enthralled watching Joe Davis and other masters of the game. And it was always at the most exciting moments that I had to return in time to take the curtain call.

I worked hard at my seven lines and before long I was getting nine laughs – on six of the lines and on two pieces of 'business' – but I was not satisfied. Wouldn't it be splendid to say that in one part I got a laugh on *every* line! But there was still one that defeated me. To do myself justice, 'How do you do, Miss Sloper?' is not exactly funny, but I worked at it and on one glorious occasion I got a beautiful laugh (I have to admit that it involved tripping on the hearthrug and clutching Peggy Ashcroft's outstretched hand to prevent myself falling). I danced back to my dressing room, but at the end of the performance received a message that 'Sir Ralph would like to see you'. Ralph, who was removing his make-up as I entered, looked up and said, 'Congratulations, Donald! – I've seen you working for that laugh and you've done it – congratulations', and then, almost apologetically, continued: 'But I don't think we really need it, do we?' I had to agree – but at least at one perform-ance I did get a laugh a line.

I wish I could say I learned a lot from Richardson but I didn't – he is such an original actor. I have watched countless numbers of his performances, but I have never discovered 'how' he does it. At the time he drove an enormous Rolls-Royce and one evening he offered me a lift. How lovely, I thought, but ten minutes later found myself on the pillion seat of a 1275cc Harley-Davidson motor cycle, clutching at Ralph's belt as we raced up the Haymarket. I should have remembered his predilection for motor cycles: stationed in Sussex with the Fleet Air Arm during the war, he was riding along the straight stretch of road towards Ditchling, got into a speed-wobble and was thrown off and carted to hospital. My father, then serving as a war-reserve policeman, was given the task of pushing the mammoth machine into the village garage.

A story is told – untrue, I suspect – about Ralph approaching a man on a railway station and saying, 'My dear Robertson! How you've changed! You look so much younger – your face is round – you've got a good colour – you've shaved off your moustache – my, how you've changed!'

Bewildered, the man said, 'But my name isn't Robertson.'

Ralph started back, 'What! Changed your name too?!'

When Richardson, Laurence Olivier and John Burrell were fel-low directors of the Old Vic and were heavily engaged in rehearsals, something cropped up of momentous importance concerning the future policy of the company. The only time to discuss it was during the one-hour lunch break at a public house in St Martin's Lane. As they entered, a man caught Ralph by the arm and said something. The other two continued to a table and waited – and waited – and waited. Twenty minutes out of the precious hour had gone before Ralph apologetically joined the now very irate others.

'Who the hell was he?' snorted Olivier.

'I don't know, Larry,' replied Ralph. 'He thought he had seen us somewhere before, and I was trying to help him remember where.'

Ralph had given instructions to *The Heiress* stage management that on no account was he ever to be prompted – he would always get out of any difficulty. But the results could be confusing. One of his lines should have been, 'Consider how he has behaved with money – he "enlarged his capacities in Europe" '. Without a pause or the flicker of an eyelid this once came out as, 'Consider how he has behaved with money – he "enlarged his experiences in Africa" '. As Europe had everything to do with the plot and Africa absolutely nothing, the audience were understandably bemused. But worse was yet to come: to another character who says, 'He admits he has been wild, Austin, but he has paid for it', he should have replied, 'So that accounts for his impoverishment', but actually said, 'So that accounts for his impotence'. That really did confuse the plot!

With me ensconced at the Haymarket, Diana went off to join the repertory company in Lichfield, where a young man just down from Oxford was beginning his career as the director: his name was Kenneth Tynan. In order that Diana and I could be together I used to catch a train late on Saturday night and meet her in Lichfield. We both felt that the time had come to start a family, so on 3rd September our first baby was conceived in Diana's digs at No 20, Beacon Street.

At the end of a year Peggy and Ralph left the cast, to be succeeded by Wendy Hiller and Godfrey Tearle (Ralph Michael had already replaced James Donald). I had idolised Wendy since seeing her in *Pygmalion*, *Major Barbara* and other films and now here I was saying to her, 'How do you do, Miss Sloper'. Godfrey was one of the most charming men I have ever met, a representative of that breed of matinee idol, including Owen Nares and Leslie Faber, now extinct (Oh dear! My mind races off at tangents: I am immediately reminded of a Leslie Faber story.)

Tall, handsome, with a splendid profile topped by dark wavy hair, Leslie Faber was quite the opposite of a young actor by the name of Robertson (Bunny) Hare who was very short. Bunny hero-worshipped the magnificent Faber who was everything that Bunny was not or ever could be. An incongruous friendship sprang up between them. One day as they entered The Volunteer, a public house in Baker Street, a youngish, ill-kempt man with pale face and hollow cheeks, and wearing a crumpled raincoat was leaning on the bar; his eyes suddenly glazed and uttering a strangulated cry he collapsed to the ground. In complete control of the situation, Faber said, 'Stand back' and, demanding a glass of water from the barmaid, he filled his mouth and 'squirted' it into the man's face. With a shudder the man revived, and Faber, taking his lapels in one hand, lifted him to his feet. With the other hand Faber extracted his wallet, peeled off a pound note and gave it to the unsteady man saying, 'There you are – if you have any sense you'll eat with it. If you haven't you'll drink with it. Get out into the fresh air!'

Bunny stood gaping with admiration at his hero – the aplomb, the wisdom, the sheer strength of this man. He never forgot it.

On holiday in Budleigh Salterton many years later, Bunny had just reached the bottom of a zig-zag staircase that led from the top of the cliffs to the beach below, when his wife said that she would like a box of chocolates. 'Very well, my dear – I'll get you some', and he started back up the steps. Halfway up a panting Bunny arrived at a small landing, to find an ill-kempt man with a pale face and hollow cheeks wearing a crumpled raincoat, leaning on the balustrade. As he passed, the man uttered a strangulated cry and with glazed eyes collapsed to the ground . . . Bunny's experience of his youth leaped to his mind – this would be his moment of triumph. He had to stop three passers-by before one agreed to search for water. Eventually some arrived and Bunny echoed Faber's command: 'Stand back.' Taking a mouthful of water, he 'squirted' it in the man's face. But even using two hands he failed to lift him without asistance. He fumbled for his wallet, remembering the pound note and the advice that went with it, but the man had already revived – shaking the water from his face, he glowered at Bunny and his eyes widened. 'You dirty rotten bastard,' he said and chased poor Bunny up the steps.

But back to Godfrey Tearle. I was at the stage door one evening when a dishevelled man appeared and asked for Mr Tearle, who had yet to arrive. He introduced himself to me and immediately I recognised his name: he was a playwright who in 1932 had written an incredibly successful play which had run for years in the West

End and was subsequently performed all over the world (I had done it in rep). We chatted and at last Godfrey came through the door, took one look at the playwright and, saying fiercely, 'Get out! I don't want to see you here ever again', he rushed on up the stairs. This was so unlike Godfrey. During the evening he asked if I knew the man. 'Don't get caught,' he advised me in his fatherly tone. 'That man has ruined his life through drink and now sponges on people. Last week I gave him a fiver before the performance and he came back at the end, drunk as a newt, and asked for more.'

Hidden away in Godfrey's entry in *Who's Who in the Theatre* is the most delightful sequence. Between 1904 and 1906 he toured in *his own* company playing Hamlet, Othello, Shylock, Brutus, Romeo and Sir Peter Teazle. Years later at His Majesty's Theatre he is playing Marcellus in *Hamlet*, Ludovico in *Othello*, Lorenzo in *The Merchant*, Octavius in *Julius Caesar* and Trip in *The School for Scandal*. Big fish in little ponds to little fish in big ponds.

He told me that in *Antony and Cleopatra* in 1946 at the Piccadilly Theatre, the young actor playing his servant Eros was suddenly taken ill and an unprepared replacement was pushed on at the last minute to assist in removing Antony's armour. Godfrey spoke: 'Unarm, Eros; the long day's task is done. Off, pluck off.' The young replacement looked aghast. 'I'm so sorry,' he said and retired from the scene.

Still *The Heiress* continued. Diana had now got a new job as understudy to Margaret Leighton in Henry Sherek's production of Philip Barry's play *Philadelphia Story* which suffered a disastrous first night. One actor was so unduly nervous that he took some tranquillising pills which flattened him so much that he gave himself a large brandy. The combination caused him to pass out in the dressing room. Black coffee was administered, and he went through this bright comedy in a daze, with his performance getting slower and slower. In the last scene he had to carry a large tray of fully charged champagne glasses: the poor fellow dropped the lot! With Diana getting larger and larger each day, it was fortunate that the play did not have a long run. She had registered at Queen Charlotte's Maternity Hospital and in the middle of one night I was awakened, 'It's on the way'. I was so sleepy that Diana had to call her own ambulance in which we both went with her pre-packed suitcase. At the hospital I was told to take her other clothes, even her underwear, return home and await a telephone call. Not expecting this, I had nothing to put the clothes in so rolled them in a bundle, tucked them under my arm, and started to walk home from Hammersmith to Chelsea. It was three a.m. Halfway I was stopped by a patrolling police car and had great difficulty in explaining away the female attire! But it was all a false alarm and we had to wait for another week, when halfway through a matinee I was told that Diana had gone to hospital again. Between performances I raced off to Queen Charlotte's to find Diana in the labour ward right in the middle of a particularly painful spasm. She took one look at me and said, 'Go away!' She actually meant 'for a few minutes', so that I wouldn't be upset but I assumed that my presence was not required and returned, rather crestfallen, to the theatre. That evening, on 14th June, 1950, I was informed that we were now the proud parents of a baby boy. We had been thinking for some time of a name: with no boys in Diana's family, we had decided his middle name should be Mahony, and Winifred Keates had insisted that he be given a saint's name: I had always been intrigued by St Jerome, but someone was perturbed by the thought that for anyone who did not know the correct pronunciation of Mahony the poor little thing might be known as Jeromee Mahonee Sinden, so we settled for the spelling of Jeremy.

Gillian Howell (Cadell) had already left the cast of *The Heiress* to give birth to her first baby, Simon. Shortly after this I went to a matinee performance of Ralph Richardson's new play *Home at Seven* and afterwards in his dressing room we gossiped. '. . . And how is the old team?' he asked. I gave him various pieces of news, adding, 'By the way, Gillian has had a baby boy.' Poor Ralph was a little confused by the fact that she had played my fiancée in the play; he held out his hand: 'Ah! Congratulations, my dear fellow!'

Dear, wonderful Roger Maxwell had again come to our rescue and placed the rear room on the ground floor of the house in Cheyne Gardens, at our disposal. We had been hard at work decorating it and making curtains for which we had found some gay (in the correct and only use of that delightful word) printed material. I made the grave mistake of cutting it by using the pattern as a guide, only to find that it had been printed skew-whiff: they always looked as if the pattern were running downhill. Within no time Jeremy was installed in the best of our rooms with a view of the garden.

And still *The Heiress* continued. We passed the previous record for the longest run for any play at the Haymarket Theatre and only two members of the cast had not missed a single performance – Ann Wilton and myself. We cosseted ourselves. We were doubly careful every time we crossed a road. We took vitamin tablets. We avoided anyone with infectious colds or coughs. We gargled morning and night. The end of the run was announced in the press and then, ten days before we closed, poor Ann slipped when getting off a train and broke her ankle. I was delighted! But I still had ten days to go. I have never been so nervous, but I made it.

On behalf of the Haymarket Management, Charles La Trobe presented me with an engraved silver ashtray: 'For Donald Sinden. 644 performances non-stop 1949–50.' I had given more consecutive performances at the Theatre Royal, Haymarket, than any other actor since it opened in 1821. My father took full advantage of the newsworthiness of the story and every Sussex newspaper and several national ones printed articles which he supplied.

Fortunately for me, to relieve the boredom of a long run, there existed several societies, such as the Repertory Players, who on Sunday nights presented single performances of new plays. For these, actors received no fee, but they were a wonderful shop window because they were seen by managements and agents. During the run of *The Heiress* I did five of these and, in one way or another, benefited from all of them.

At the Bristol Old Vic, Hugh Hunt had been succeeded by Denis Carey who now asked me to return to the company. This meant leaving Diana and Jeremy in London – at least for the time being. Denis had assembled a talented team for the new season – John Phillips, Donald Pleasence, Joan White, Pamela Allan, John Neville, Hugh Manning, Newton Blick, Gudrun Ure and Stuart Burge – and we opened on 4th September, 1950 in Christopher Fry's *The Lady's not for Burning*.

I had seen the play twice before in London: first with Alec Clunes at the Arts Theatre and later when he was succeeded by John Gielgud, in the only performance of his which disappointed me. John Phillips now played that role. I threw myself into the part of Nicholas: for nineteen months I had behaved sedately in Victorian evening dress, but now I could let myself go. In one scene I was to rush in, kneel and propose to my loved one, Alizon Eliot, who was seated in the middle of the stage. Of course I overdid it. Out of sight I crouched in a sprinter's starting position and on cue came through the archway like a rocket, skidding to a stop, kneeling, and blurted out my line which began, 'Alizon Eliot . . .'

One night I catapulted myself on to the stage, slithered to a halt at her feet and started, 'Azilon. – Azi Azil – Az – Azilon – Azil –

Azi – Az Azilazillazil . . .' I couldn't stop myself. Poor Gudrun Ure, as Alizon, began with astonishment, then through giggles to near hysteria. Of course I blamed Christopher Fry – who but a poet would have thought of spelling Alison 'Alizon'?

It has taken me many years to cure my impetuosity. If something is amiss, stop; take a deep breath; think; and only then continue – I always used to plough on regardless.

My first leading part followed: Mr Honeywood – Goldsmith's *Good Natured Man*. This was my first experience of eighteenth-century dialogue – and I wasn't very good; barely adequate. My only memory of the production is of a scene in which John Neville as Leontine had to accuse me – unjustifiably – of some wrong-doing and, drawing his sword, try to provoke me into a duel. By the third performance I was convinced that John was barely suppressing something that was amusing him. Were my flies undone? – always an actor's first thought – no they weren't. The next night the same 'smirk' was there. An answering smile spread across my face. The night after, the same thing again except that when I smiled his face now broke into a grin. It got worse and worse. I asked John later what had caused him to smile: he retaliated by saying that it was because I was smiling. We agreed it had to stop. Only then did I discover that when John tries to look vicious his face betrays an underlying humour and the two expressions become almost identical.

The succession of plays that followed included *The Merry Wives of Windsor*, in which I played Pistol, Denis Johnston's *Blind Man's Bluff* and Pinero's *The Magistrate*, in which Newton Blick gave a virtuoso performance of the name part. (I played his son.) What a comedian that man was! It is so difficult to describe a comedian – his art is so contemporary and ephemeral. Learned books are written on the art of tragedians and on how their styles come in or out of fashion, from the 'Classical' of Betterton to the 'Mercurial' of Garrick, and then from the 'Classical' of Kemble to the 'Mercurial' of Kean. But a comedian is always immediate, as Viola/Cesario says,

> This fellow is wise enough to play the fool;
> And to do that well craves a kind of wit.
> He must observe their mood on whom he jests,
> The quality of persons, and the time;
> . . . this is a practice
> As full of labour as a wise man's art.

I will, nevertheless, try to describe Newton Blick in a performance of *The Two Gentlemen of Verona*. In this play there are two parts for comedians: Launce, who has some splendid comic dialogue and is always accompanied by a dog which causes endless trouble, and Speed, who, alas, is not nearly so well served by Shakespeare – and if you were to cut out all the dull bits practically nothing would be left – and for this production Newty was lumbered with Speed. The character is given a long soliloquy which might have been hilarious when it was first written in 1594, but raises hardly a titter in the twentieth century. Newty, however, was an exceptional actor. He was standing and at the beginning of this speech he took a knife from one pocket and an apple from another, and began to peel it. We all know how difficult it is to prevent the spiral of peel from breaking and as we watched, fascinated, the peel dropped lower and lower, and as the speech went on and on so the peel got longer and longer. Newty seemed unaware that we were watching the peel, but appeared rather hurt as we were not listening to what he was saying, and began to speak as if to a child. But still our attention was fixed on the loop of peel which now dangled around his knees. He timed it so accurately that he finished the speech at exactly the same moment as he finished his peeling, whereupon he threw away the apple and *ate the peel*, feeding it into his mouth like spaghetti. He received a round of applause and no one had listened to a word he said.

It was now Christmas and John Phillips wrote us a pantomime based on *Puss in Boots* – and what enormous fun it was! We still remember it fondly. Donald Pleasence and I played the Ugly Brothers involved in endless knock-about routines – and the cornier the gags the more the audience laughed. Indeed we learned a basic theatrical fact: give the audience what they expect and enjoyment is tripled. The moment a character lifts a custard pie the audience know immediately that it will finish on someone's face – the question is *whose*, and the artistry is in withholding that information for as long as possible.

For reasons best known to the plot, we were being chased by the Ogre's men and Denis Carey suggested that we might lead them over the orchestra pit and out into the auditorium. We were given three minutes before returning to the stage . . . Oh the anarchy! Donald and I had water pistols with which to hold the villains at bay and – quite accidentally, of course! – our aim was so bad that most of the water hit members of the audience. We replenished our pistols at each fire bucket. We found that in those three minutes we could cover all parts of the house, including the gallery, and get back to the stage where we finally evaded the Ogre by climbing ropes suspended from the Flies, taking the ends up with us. (We must have been fit!) One Saturday night, unbeknown to us, students from Bristol University had booked the entire front two rows of the stalls and when Donald and I made our way over the orchestra pit we were met by a cloudburst: every student was armed with a water pistol! A veritable battle ensued, we were hopelessly out-numbered and finished up wet through. We expected further trouble at the final curtain call because it was customary for Donald and me, when we took our joint bow, again to shoot our pistols at the audience. Sure enough, as we ran down from the back of the stage, the front two rows stood up and discharged their guns at us. But we were prepared! We had hidden our secret weapon in the wings: we raced off and returned with a stirrup pump and two buckets of water and while I pumped, Donald aimed the hose. The chaos! What neither side had foreseen was that between us lay the Netherlands of the orchestra and they bore the full brunt of the attack. Violins and cellos were hastily passed out of range. Thank-fully no damage was done.

The Ogre was played by Hugh Manning wearing six-inch lifts to add to his already considerable height. One evening for a gag, after drinking from his salad bowl 'cup', he smacked his lips and said, 'Ah! Bristol Cream!' By sheer luck some directors of Harveys were in the audience and next day Hugh was presented with a case – a case! – of Harveys Bristol Cream. That was too much for the rest of us. At subsequent performances we put in scores of local gags – Wills' cigarettes, Fry's chocolates, Bristol Aircraft Corporation – but nothing, nothing.

This was my first and only pantomime – and if anyone is in-terested, I can't wait to do another!

I now made an error of judgement.

I received a call from Denis Arundell, who had directed me in one of my Sunday night performances, asking me to go on a fifteen-week tour of a revival of *Froufrou* by Meilhac and Halévy, playing opposite Jean Kent, then at the height of her film fame. What a problem. I was idyllically happy at Bristol and professionally it was just what I should be doing, but I was being paid sixteen pounds a week, with a wife and child to keep in a flat (albeit cheap) in London as well as my own digs in Bristol. And nothing in the bank. The tour could be lucrative. What should I do? The problem seemed insuperable. Integrity told me that I should stay in Bristol – but . . . Oh, dear!

The new manager asked what salary I required, so in a panic I doubled my Bristol salary and said boldly, 'Thirty-five pounds a week.'

'That's fine,' he said. Immediately I felt a fool – I should have asked for one hundred and thirty-five.

I tried to retrieve the situation '. . . but the problem is that I have been stuck in Bristol for twenty-six weeks and my wife will be furious if I am away for a further fifteen . . .'

'Is she an actress?'

'Yes.'

'Well, I'm sure we can find a part for her too.'

I had no answer: I was committed. With a sinking heart I handed in my resignation to the Old Vic. We found a Nanny for Jeremy, who then went to stay with Diana's parents, and we began rehearsals. Diana was to play the quite important 'maid' and I the 'romantic suitor' of the leading lady – a jolly good part, but of course the billing on the posters showed Jean Kent's name at the top in type even larger than the title of the play (quite rightly, of course, as her name alone could ensure a full house) and everyone else was lumped together at the bottom in very small print.

I am reminded of a story told me by William Armstrong who, as a twenty-year-old actor, was employed by Beerbohm Tree, with his name right at the bottom of the list of also-rans. After a year with the company his mother suggested that he should talk to Tree and have his billing improved. Tentatively he approached his boss. 'Would you mind coming outside for a moment?' and at the front of the theatre Armstrong continued, 'You see, my name is at the very bottom . . .'

Unhelpfully Tree said, 'Yes.'

'Well, er um . . . do you think it could possibly be er um elevated . . . a little . . .?' Tree made no answer. 'Or if not,' bravely Armstrong went on, 'could it read, so and so, so and so, so and so, AND William Armstrong?'

Tree ruminated for a while. 'Ye-es – why not BUT?'

Froufrou opened in Leeds. Going up in the train Jean Kent travelled First Class and the rest of us Third. She stayed at the splendid

Queen's Hotel where a hired Rolls-Royce ferried her to and from the theatre – and quite rightly too; the public was clamouring for a sight of her and the appurtenances reinforced their expectations. This was how a film star should live.

At the end of the week, when Diana and I went to say goodbye to our landlady, we found a child tucked up in a small bed in their living room. 'Is she ill?' asked Diana and held the child's hand.

'Nothing to worry about – she's got the chicken-pox.'

Ten days later, in Aberdeen, Diana woke up covered in spots. I had to telephone my mother to find, thank goodness, that I had already had it ('You've had *everything* – except diphtheria'). Diana had to be carted off to the local isolation hospital. In those days actors worked on a 'no play – no pay' contract. Managements were also entitled to terminate a contract if one missed two consecutive weeks and we were very grateful to ours for not doing so in Diana's case: she was incapacitated for three weeks. The tour continued and Diana was left languishing in Aberdeen.

In Sheffield a local landlord decided to give a party in his pub after the performance to which the entire company, including Jean, was invited. At one o'clock in the morning there was a hammering at the door and in burst several policemen who took our names and addresses. They refused to believe it was a private party and we were all charged with consuming intoxicating liquor on licensed premises after hours – the case to be heard in three months' time. I was for the high jump. I came from a long line of teetotallers who would be shocked and there was I drinking, with my poor wife ill in Aberdeen. And I promise you – my entire consumption between eleven p.m. and one a.m. was one glass of Guinness. D.M. was the only one whose reactions were divided. On one side I was letting down the family by being involved in a court case, on the other at last I had taken to the bottle – he had always been disturbed that I often refrained from joining him in a glass.

Diana rejoined the company at the time that Jean Kent was beginning to discover that her rarefied existence was a very lonely one – all the fun and camaraderie seemed to go on below stairs. By rights, I, as her leading man, should have squired her, but for two good reasons I couldn't: I had my wife with me and anyway I couldn't afford the hotels. She therefore suggested that she might join us in digs. It so happened that Diana and I were the only ones who had booked ahead for all the fifteen weeks and I was asked if I would write to the various landladies asking if they could take one extra. We began sharing in Manchester where we were accommodated by the Misses Flynn – three Roman Catholic ladies, known to us as the Holy Trinity – who were slightly shaken by the Rolls-Royce which arrived to take Jean to the theatre.

Theatrical digs are now few and far between, but for years they were an institution and all actors have had their experiences – good and bad: each actor kept his own jealously guarded list and it was advisable to write well in advance to secure good accommodation.

At the fall of the final curtain on a Saturday night the play's scenery would be dismantled and stacked on horse-drawn drays (which gave rise to the fascinating and enigmatic entry in theatrical account books, 'Get-out and cartage'). The speed at which this could be accomplished was astonishing: stage hands encircled the set, which was held together by rope 'lines' laced around 'cleats', and during the last fifteen minutes of a play everything extraneous would be removed – as a door closed for the last time the 'flats' outside disappeared – and then the principal 'lines' were thrown so that finally the whole set was being held up by hand and within thirty minutes of the end of the performance the stage was bare. Woe betide any actor who loitered on the stage – he would have been trampled under foot, if he had avoided being struck by falling scenery. This of course was before the time when stage hands were recruited into a union which decreed that double time should be paid after midnight . . .

On Sunday morning actors and scenery would meet at the railway station ready to set off for the next 'date', which invariably involved changing trains at Crewe and it was here, on windswept platforms, that we had many joyful reunions with other companies as our journeys intersected. Arriving in the new city, we found the way to our digs, to be greeted by a landlady, friendly or otherwise. (I was once shown up to my room and told, 'Remember, dear, this is your home while you're in Bournemouth – and mind – no messing up the sheets!') These landladies specialised in 'theatricals' and at their best provided better food and more comfort than most first-class hotels – and they were by no means expensive: An old actor, Edward Petley, told me in 1945 that he had never paid more than thirty shillings a week for full board. Meals were arranged to suit the peculiar hours lived by actors – breakfast at ten thirty a.m., lunch at two p.m. and supper after the performance whatever time the curtain fell. Over almost every dining room fireplace I seem to recall a reproduction of Landseer's *Monarch of the Glen* and every landlady kept her Visitors' Book filled with strange and exotic comments. Many of these stalwart ladies handed on the business to their daughters or daughters-in-law and with it went the Visitors' Book, which by then had acquired antiquarian interest.

When with two other actors I first stayed with Mrs Simmonds in Newcastle she proudly showed us her large leatherbound book as we arrived. Dutifully we thumbed through it: the first entry was for 1886 and Frank Tyars of Henry Irving's company had written, 'You must try Mrs Simmonds' Lemon Pudding'; some time later a member of Tree's company had entered, 'Mrs Simmonds' Lemon Pudding is amazing'; later a Bensonian actor had implored, 'Don't leave without trying Mrs Simmonds' Lemon Pudding'; from Fred Terry's company, 'Mrs Simmonds' Lemon Pudding is a master-piece'; every few months an entry asked, 'Have you sampled Mrs Simmonds' Lemon Pudding?' Thus when Mrs Simmonds (the daughter-in-law of the original Mrs Simmonds) re-entered the room we asked if we might partake of her renowned speciality: her face glowed with pride and she cooed, 'I hoped you would ask – Thursday evening.' We could hardly wait. On Thursday we raced back from the theatre and guzzled our way through the main course, the plates were removed and shortly Mrs S. came back carrying a large dish in the attitude of a portly eighteenth-century chef bearing a flaming Christmas pudding to the assembled guests in a timbered inn. She placed it in the centre of the table. On the dish was an inverted white pudding basin which she removed with a theatrical flourish, held it aloft and with 'I *know* you'll enjoy it' she left us alone. Facing us was a pure white mound of wet, sticky suet. Disenchanted, someone took a knife and, sticking it in, struck something solid . . . he cut around it and disclosed a whole lemon – skin and all. We could not disappoint her so we ate what we could of the suet on which we poured sugar and lemon juice.

Obviously, when a young housekeeper, the first Mrs Simmonds had been asked to prepare a Lemon Pudding – she had used her imagination to the apparent approval of her guests and had im-parted her recipe to her daughter-in-law. When we left on the following Sunday we could write only one thing: 'Whatever you do, you must try Mrs Simmonds' Lemon Pudding!'

Ba Holloway told me that at the turn of the century an actor arrived at his digs and in a declamatory voice informed his landlady, 'On Monday I wish you to prepare a steak for my lunch – *under*

cooked – after which I will lie down to rest on your – no doubt –
excellent bed. You will then call me with a cup of tea – no sugar –
at *five* o'clock. This will give me time to make my way to the
theatre, unpack my skip, costumes and make-up and be ready for
the performance. Is that understood?' His landlady served his steak,
went out shopping, and completely forgot about calling him until
she returned home at *six fifteen*. He leapt from his bed and shouting
'You're a bloody fool, woman,' raced from the house and ran to the
theatre. As he mounted the stairs to his dressing room he roared out
for the callboy, then tore open his skip, found his cigar box, and
started feverishly to slap on his make-up. A few moments passed
and a young man arrived panting: between applications of greasepaint the actor said, 'Inform the stage manager. Hold the curtain –
I'll be as quick as I can – bloody fool of a landlady forgot to call
me.'

The young man said, 'It's all right, sir – don't panic – the performance has been cancelled.'

'What do you mean? – Just because I'm a little late!'

'No, sir. Queen Victoria died today, sir, and performances all
over the country have been cancelled.'

The actor's blood pressure dropped as slowly he removed his
make-up and then made his way to the pub next door where he
joined other members of the company. 'Good evening, gentlemen – Guinness, please – terrible news, gentlemen, terrible.
Sixty years a Queen! – Sixty Glorious Years – and to die – like
that . . . mind you, it's a damned good job she did – I'd have been
off!'

During the last war the stage director Ronald Giffen had digs in a
street of little terraced houses, each with a long, walled backyard at
the end of which were two doors, one leading into the street behind
and one to the small, and only, lavatory. In the middle of the night
Giffen needed to 'go' – and urgently: he must have eaten something. Putting an overcoat over his pyjamas, he groped his way
downstairs and felt his way along the wall. He opened the door and
was presented with two problems: there was nowhere to hang his
coat and he didn't relish the idea of sitting on that particular
seat – he had seen it during the day and it was not exactly pleasant.
He threw the back of his coat upwards over his head and dropped
his pyjama trousers, then, taking the strain on his knees, he lowered
his backside to a position that just avoided contact with the seat . . .
At that moment, his half shrouded, half naked, crooked figure was

picked out by the headlamps of a police car. He had used the wrong door and was suspended over the gutter.

I do digress, don't I? – I do apologise.

By the end of the *Froufrou* tour we had managed to save some money and this seemed a perfect moment to take Diana to Paris for our first holiday. On the Left Bank we found a small hotel with an uncomfortable bed and continental breakfast for only fifteen shillings a night. This meant we could extend our stay. Walking down the Champs Elysées we saw a London *Evening Standard* for sale; we bought it and, having settled down with some coffee, my eye was immediately caught by a headline: JEAN KENT GIVEN FIVE YEARS.

We had almost succeeded in forgetting the Sheffield court case. Like the other defendants, I had been advised to plead guilty by letter to the charge of drinking after hours rather than contest the case and thereby incur the extra costs of having to attend the court when the outcome was unpredictable anyway.

Oh God! *Five years*. It might be better never to return to England than face five years in gaol! With trembling hands we read on. It transpired that the sentence was not nearly so bad. We had all been fined three pounds, but at the hearing Jean's age had been given as five years older than she, in fact, was.

We returned to Ditchling for a brief stay and my dear mother took me out for a walk. In the middle of a country lane – and with no one else about – she stopped and took from her handbag a little wad of newspaper cuttings referring to the court case, handed them to me and said that she could perfectly understand why I had taken my young wife to Paris rather than expose her to the unpleasant publicity.

We heard later that the poor landlord, because of his conviction, was likely to lose his licence and we were all asked to appeal, which two months later we did. I had never before been in a court of law, and I found the appeal hearing rather intimidating. I had (by then) to get back to London in time for a performance so our (collective) defence counsel, who was to us a magnificent man, in the mould of Leslie Faber – tall, elegant and with a good honest profile – asked if my evidence might be given earlier and out of sequence. That did not endear me to the court. Handed a card on which the oath was printed, I waived it aside and in a ringing voice proclaimed, '. . . The evidence I shall give shall be the truth, the whole truth and nothing but the truth – so help me God.' Everyone from the judge downwards glowered at me. (I was told later that 'so help me God' is not used in English courts – I had picked it up from American films! Not a good start.)

The prosecuting counsel uncoiled from his seat. To me the villain of the piece, I saw him as a singularly unpleasant, oily man with a wig several sizes too small perched on his head. He spoke in a whining voice: 'Is your name Donald Sinden?'

'Yes.'

He looked from me to the judge implying that I had told my first lie. 'And do you live at . . .' His voice carried the implication that every house in Cheyne Gardens was the haunt of thieves and rapists.

'Yes' – my second 'lie'.

He consulted his papers – 'With which question shall I deliver the coup de grâce?' – mumbled a sound that could have been yes – yes – yes or no – no – no, and then, with his back to me, asked, triumphantly, 'In what capacity did you attend this "party"?'

I was totally bemused as well as nervous. I tried to work out the question . . . seconds ticked by . . . I failed and said, 'I'm so sorry – would you repeat the question.'

He gave a look of utter disdain – 'Am I to spend the entire day questioning ill-educated thespians?' – and flashed a glance of apology towards the judge. 'In – what – capacity – did – you – attend – this – "party"?' he repeated, as if to a foreigner.

I could imagine only one answer and gave it: 'In a perfectly sober one.' I was not trying to be funny, but it got a laugh and silence was called for.

The prosecuting counsel was enraged and belaboured me with, 'Do you think it is funny to be here today!?' and 'Will you give a serious answer to . . .' and 'I hope you are not going to waste His Lordship's time with any more "jokes".'

Our hero, the counsel for the defence, rose, smiled at me and in a beautifully modulated voice said: 'Mr Sinden; I understand you were a guest at this party?'

'Yes.'

'Did you pay for any drinks?'

'No.'

'Thank you, Mr Sinden.'

A policeman was called and in evidence stated that he was on the pavement outside the saloon bar and heard among other things a voice (*my* voice) say, 'And I'll have a Guinness.'

Defence counsel was on his feet again: 'In your evidence at the lower court you said . . . (and here he quoted) but today you say . . . (and he quoted again).'

The difference was minimal – only a question of an 'if' or a 'but'. The officer stammered that he could not explain the difference.

'*But which is correct*?' demanded the D.C.

'What I said today – I have it written down.'

'Then how do you account for the discrepancy?' pressed the D.C.

'I can only imagine that it was taken down incorrectly at the magistrates' court – perhaps the shorthand stenographer mis-heard what I said.'

That was just what our noble St George was waiting for! 'And how far away from you was the stenographer sitting?'

'About twelve feet.'

' "About! *About*!" You claim to be a police officer and you cannot be more accurate? Come, come – how far away was the stenographer sitting?'

'I would say twelve feet,' the officer feebly replied.

'So you are stating that a stenographer sitting – "you would say" – twelve feet away from you "perhaps mis-heard what you said" in a quiet room, with no distractions – but you do not doubt what you say you heard through *a plate glass window*!'

The case was as good as ours and our appeal was allowed.

But this was in the future. Diana and I returned from Paris having spent our all (not very much) and I was faced with the bleak prospect of unemployment. I had reneged on the Bristol Old Vic and this was my come-uppance. Each day I sat by the telephone waiting and the telephone stared back at me. The only pleasure was meeting Roger Maxwell in the dole queue . . .

Financially we were in dire straits. Nobly Diana helped out. It was the time of the Festival of Britain and she got herself a job as a barmaid at the International Trade Club. She was paid only eight pounds a week but when offered a drink in lieu of a tip she learned from her colleagues the art of accepting the offer and pouring herself a glass of water, with ice and a slice of lemon to make it look like a gin; she could then pocket the money. We could just keep our heads above water but not above gin.

At last a call came – would I play the part I had understudied in *The Heiress*?

8

360° FOR THE FOURTH TIME ROUND

Near the north end of Kew Bridge stood the Q Theatre run by Beatrice (Beattie) de Leon whose husband Jack was a West End impresario. This little theatre by the River Thames saw the first productions of many new plays that were later to transfer to the West End and was a wonderful shop window for actors. It did not have a regular company: each play was cast separately and, after one week's rehearsal, played for one week. The top pay for actors was ten pounds and as one was not paid for rehearsals, this meant an average of five pounds a week – uneconomic unless one could do more plays consecutively.

Beattie, knowing that I had understudied James Donald in *The Heiress*, asked me to play his part in her forthcoming production. During rehearsals she asked me to stay on for the following play which would be rehearsed the week we played *The Heiress* – twenty pounds for three weeks: the average was going up. I seemed to have my foot in the door because, while apologising for having nothing to offer in the following play (*Two Dozen Red Roses*), she asked if I would stay for the next but one. A week off pay; down would go my average.

'Is there nothing for me in *Two Dozen Red Roses*?'

'Sorry, dear, only a very small part of an Italian.'

'Couldn't I play that?'

'Yes, but I am only paying eight pounds – it's a very small part.'

Eight pounds being better than nothing, I agreed to stay on.

I had never played a foreigner before – nor, for that matter, any part that required an accent: I think the one I assumed owed a considerable debt to Charles Boyer. Being colour blind caused some problems but with a liberal use of greasepaint (Leichner No 8b, a sort of olive, I was told) my make-up passed without comment – and so did the entire production. The only thing I now remember is that in this part I invented the 'noise' – what I can only describe as a wolf growl – which I used whenever a pretty girl passed by. Years later I was to make much greater use of it as Benskin in the 'Doctor' Films.

I worked for ten weeks at the Q Theatre and then found myself unemployed again. I haunted the offices of managements and agents but always the same depressing, 'Nothing at the moment but keep in touch'. I was by now a member of the Green Room Club, for which Gerald Lawrence had proposed me, and also the Buckstone, of which I had been a founder member when Oscar Quitak and Hazel Vincent Wallace had started it in a basement opposite the stage door of the Haymarket Theatre. It was then known as the Under Thirty Club because all members had to be under thirty years old; later when the original members topped thirty, we changed the name – and the rules. In both these clubs actors foregathered and gossiped and we could learn if this or that management was auditioning for a play.

Auditions themselves are not exactly calculated to raise ones spirits. Actors queue at a stage door and one by one are summoned to the stage by an indifferent stage manager who calls out your name – frequently incorrectly – to an invisible group of individuals sitting in the auditorium. You bravely step forward and announce your prepared 'piece', which those in front have probably heard several times already that morning. Your mouth is dry, your diaphragm is tight, your stomach is empty and your thoughts are predominantly on the fact that possibly your entire future depends on the next five minutes: to eat or to starve. You do your piece, at the best adequately. A ghastly pause follows. All you can hear are a few grunts and hisses. A shadowy figure may move across the aisle and lean on the shoulder of a seated figure. You tremble as you think of your wife and children. And then a bored voice says, 'Thank you – we will let you know.' As you leave the stage you ask the equally bored stage manager, 'Was that all right?' (We need some comfort.) 'Yes – next, please – name?' With luck you may go through this twice a week. Stuart Burge told me that as a young actor he once did quite a good audition for the Old Vic and was asked to come back with a selected few to again audition for the hierarchy. Again he felt that he acquitted himself well, but a week later learnt that his services were not required. Another week later he was asked to audition at the same place for the Bristol Old Vic Company. (Why couldn't it all be done at the same time?) Again he was unsuccessful. Yet another week later he was called to audition for the Old Vic's touring company. This is ridiculous, he thought, but again he turned up at the theatre. As he waited his turn he began to fume at the injustice of it all; his indignation grew to the point that when he stepped on to the stage and was asked what his 'piece' was, he said through clenched teeth, 'Just this!' He then stood on his head and recited, 'You are old Father William . . .' He barely finished before a voice said, 'Well done – can you start work on Monday?' They were casting the part of a clown who was expected to stand on his head!

A story is told of an actress who after months of auditioning unsuccessfully was finally offered a job. She stammered, 'I don't think I can accept – I only do auditions.'

Being a resilient breed, actors have tried to turn unemployment into a joke. Traditionally actors keep their make-up in old cigar boxes and one day an actor saw a friend walking down the road with his cigar box under his arm.

'Hello,' he called out. 'Working?'

'No,' came the reply. 'Just moving.'

'Oh, the romance of the theatre!' said an actor. 'One minute you're down and out, no prospect of work, you don't know where the next meal is coming from, it is six o'clock in the evening, it is pouring with rain and you are slouching along Shaftesbury Avenue with one foot in the gutter. Suddenly along comes Lord Grade in his Rolls-Royce and *there you are*! – covered in mud.'

One of the saddest stories concerns a husband and wife music-hall comedy team. They had been out of work for months and months and when at last a job turned up the wife was seven months pregnant. They had to take it and opened at the Grand Theatre, Brighton. In the middle of their routine the wife, who was wearing a long, voluminous skirt to hide her condition, whispered to her husband 'Jack – Jack – it's happened! – the waters have broken! – what shall I do?'

The husband hissed, 'Stand back – and wait for the laugh.'

There used to be a rule that an actor's contract could be terminated at any time during the first two weeks of rehearsal and to all actors these weeks were nerve-racking. One particular actor had been unemployed for a long time, he now had a job, and for the fourteen days he was terrified. All seemed to be well until he returned home from rehearsal on the fourteenth day and his wife, shaking, handed him a telegram. He turned ashen and with trembling hands ripped it open and read it. 'Oh, thank God!' he breathed, 'Mother's dead.'

One day at the Buckstone I saw dear old Harry Pease who was the permanent stage manager of the Haymarket Theatre, and with whom I had worked during *The Heiress*. He told me that the understudy to Owen Holder was leaving the current production, *Waters of the Moon*, in two weeks' time. I raced off to H. M. Tennent's office to see Barney Gordon. 'I hear there is an understudy going at the Haymarket.'

Barney was slightly incredulous. 'Surely you won't want to do that; I thought you were well on the way up the ladder.'

'I need the job,' I said.

Barney, always the most delightfully courteous of men, put it beautifully: 'Look, Donald, I would not dream of offering it to you, but if you want it the job is yours.' And the following week I was back at the Haymarket, but several steps back down the ladder.

N. C. Hunter's *Waters of the Moon* had already been running for months with Edith Evans, Sybil Thorndike and Wendy Hiller in the cast, all of whom were extremely kind and never for one moment made me conscious of my lowly position. Sybil greeted me with 'My Romeo'; Wendy was as ever delightful and Edith, who was always a slightly aloof figure in the theatre, would call out to me from her dressing room, 'Donald, come in and make me laugh' – I only once heard her make a remark that could be described as disparaging. I was standing beside her in the wings as she waited for her entrance while on the stage an actress who had a large private income and for whom Edith had little professional regard, was performing. Edith watched her and said quietly to me, 'It must be lovely to have her money and just *play* at it.' Edith's clothes in the play were made by Balmain and during my time Binkie Beaumont suggested that it was about time they were replaced by new ones: Edith would only agree, 'if Sybil has a new cardigan.'

Edith was at this time looking for a new house and I mentioned that I knew of a charming one near Diana's parents in Hertford-shire. 'Oh, my dear,' she said. 'That's much too far out.'

'Do you mean somewhere like Chelsea or Hampstead?'

'Oh no, dear. I've never lived further away than Hyde Park Corner.'

Regrettably, as Owen Holder never missed a performance, I didn't have an opportunity to appear but he and I began a friendship with the result that our two families have remained very close ever since.

To our great relief Diana was then offered the understudy to Judy Campbell in Noël Coward's new play, *Relative Values*, which after a six-week tour began a run of fourteen months at the Savoy Theatre. She had several opportunities to appear, and received an additional one pound per performance which also helped to balance our books.

After ten weeks with *Waters of the Moon* I was sent by my agent, Frederick Joachim (who had signed me up on the strength of my work at the 'Q'), to see Jack de Leon who was about to put on a play called *Red Letter Day* with a cast headed by Fay Compton, Hugh (Tam) Williams, Dorothy (Dot) Dickson and Nora Swinburne. I arrived for my appointment at three thirty, only to be met by Jack who said, 'What a pity, we cast Terence Longden as the juvenile this morning.' Dejected I turned to leave, when he suddenly called after me, 'Didn't you play an Italian at 'Q' for my wife Beattie?'

'Yes.'

'Well, there's a Brazilian in this play – would you do it?'

So again with the help of Charles Boyer and Leichner No 8b, I opened on tour, heading for London in my second West End play.

The leading players were enchanting to me. In Manchester, Tam took Fay, Dot and me to the races where, at the invitation of Caroline Ramsden, the secretary of the course, we were given lunch in the stewards' dining room and then watched the races from their enclosure. At least this protected me from the thieves, pickpockets and razor gangs who, as a result of my sheltered upbringing, I felt certain peopled a racecourse. Stealthily I placed bets, but only on the Tote, yet I won on four races out of five; better than all the others. On the way back to the theatre in the car Dot said, 'Well, I am thirty-two pounds three shillings up on the day.' Fay had made twenty-seven pounds and four shillings, Tam admitted to fifteen pounds – 'And what about you?' he asked. I felt somewhat foolish and unsophisticated as I said, 'Twelve shillings and sixpence.'

The play opened its West End run at the Garrick Theatre, but was hardly a resounding success – it eventually ran for three months – but I did get some encouraging personal notices in the press. Charles Frend, then casting for his next film, *The Cruel Sea*, saw one performance and asked me to do a test at Ealing Studios for the leading part. In a subsequent interview Frend said that during the performance he had observed that no Brazilian has blue eyes, I was therefore an actor and not a native.

I had yet to read *The Cruel Sea*, Nicholas Monsarrat's best-selling novel, but luckily, walking down the Kings Road in Chelsea, I bumped into Esmond Knight – the husband of Nora Swinburne – and because I never like to mention a job until the contract is signed, I said not a word about my forthcoming test, but merely asked if he had a copy of the book. We walked back to his house where he loaned me his.

It seemed that every actor aged between twenty-five and forty-five was tested for the part. At the studio I was put in a Naval uniform, seated on a chair and faced to the front, to the left and to the right while Frend talked to me from behind the camera. Two days later I was called back and had to learn a short part of the dialogue which was then filmed with two or three other actors. Several days of silence followed. Diana and I hardly dared speak to each other. Another call to the studio; this time a second dialogue scene, but in a more dramatic situation. A further week of silence and then a telephone call from Charles Frend apologising profusely for wasting my time but the studio felt that they could not possibly risk using a totally unknown actor in the leading role. Diana and I consoled ourselves. We were no worse off. No better off, but no worse off. Back to the treadmill.

A week later came another telephone call. The studio had failed to find anyone else. I later discovered that although Ealing's head, Michael Balcon, was against taking the enormous risk, the producer, Leslie Norman, was convinced that I could do it; I should be given another chance. This time much more care was given to my clothes, my hair was carefully cut and set, the head make-up man was put to work. I was to do a scene with Jack Hawkins. Both Leslie Norman and Charles Frend cosseted me – nothing was too much trouble. The result must have been fairly good because two days later I was called back yet again to try my hand at a love scene with Virginia McKenna, who had just been cast in the part of Julie.

Two sleepless nights followed. Everywhere we went we left a telephone number with my agent. We went to lunch with Nigel Davenport and at one fifteen came a telephone call . . . it was Charles Frend . . . When I returned to the dining room someone said, 'Well?'

I could not speak. Diana said, 'Have you got it?'

'Yes.'

We all embraced. Nigel rushed out and returned five minutes later with a bottle of champagne.

Will I ever experience the thrill of such a moment again?

I have since advised all young actors not to pick and choose, but to take whatever job is offered. If I had not played an Italian for Beattie at 'Q' for eight pounds I would not have landed *The Cruel Sea*.

Esmond Knight presented me with his own copy of Nicholas Monsarrat's book, suitably inscribed. Although written as a novel, it was in fact a largely autobiographical story of the author's life in the Royal Navy during the war. I was to play Keith Lockhart, a thinly disguised portrait of Monsarrat himself, rising from a green sub-lieutenant at the beginning of the story, to the rank of lieutenant commander at the end. As Ericson, his captain throughout this period, Ealing Studios cast Jack Hawkins, a brilliant choice, who had already made a name for himself and was therefore naturally given top billing, and whose part became the 'lead'.

Freddy Joachim negotiated my contract. I had never made a film before so I had no accepted fee. My contract stipulated that my work for Ealing should be for seventeen weeks for a fee of £1,250 and that the Rank Organisation, who distributed all Ealing films, reserved the right to put me under a seven-year contract, the option to be exercised after seeing the first rough cut of *The Cruel Sea*.

On one glorious day the fact that I had landed the part appeared in all the newspapers – I had hitherto been sworn to secrecy, and apart from Diana and Nigel Davenport, I told only my parents. That evening we went to the Buckstone Club. In the bar I was greeted by an actor colleague, 'Donald, what wonderful news! There's hope for us all – if it can happen to *you*, it can happen to *anyone*!'

I knew what he meant, but it didn't sound quite right.

The pace of my life suddenly accelerated. Costume fittings at Bermans, interviews with the press and I still had a short post-London tour of *Red Letter Day* to do. The film schedule was exceedingly unhelpful, overlapping the last week of the tour, and, unfortunately, I found that I had to pay the rehearsal expenses of my successor in the play. Then off to Plymouth where we were to stay – all expenses paid by someone else for the first time in my life – while filming on board ship, sailing each day from Devonport.

The film required a class of ship, already obsolete, called a Corvette. But at the end of the war one had been sold to the Greek Navy. Now decrepit, it had been on its way to be broken up at Sunderland, until Ealing Studios stepped in and postponed its demise for five weeks. Originally *Coreopsis*, then renamed by the Greeks, Ealing re-registered her as Monsarrat's *Compass Rose*.

As naval adviser the studio secured the services of a retired naval captain, Jackie Broome, a submariner, sometime captain of the battleship *Ramillies*, on which Prince Philip trained, and author of *Make a Signal*. He had now been given the responsibility of making the Corvette seaworthy, no mean task. Broome contacted a number of his old colleagues – some retired, some on leave – with the result that almost the entire crew were commissioned officers who for the fun of it took on ordinary seamen's duties. The decks were scrubbed, the brass polished, a broken boiler repaired, actors and a film crew taken on board and after two weeks everything was ready for the first day's shooting.

Living and working with the Navy was an enormous help to the actors. By the end of the first day we had ceased to say 'upstairs' and 'downstairs' and 'corridors'. I suppose it took about two days to come down a ladder forwards instead of backwards and in only one more day we learned to slide down on the hand rail. The 'regulars' watched over the filming with an eagle eye; we were criticised for our saluting, our dress, our phrasing, our terminology.

For one scene we had to set off a pattern of depth charges to blow up a supposed submarine. Under war conditions the ship would steam full speed ahead preferably along the length of the submarine. One depth charge would be dropped off the stern of the ship, then two fired broadside, one from each side of the ship, then another two, and finally one dropped off the stern to make a pattern of six. The charges would be set to explode at the estimated depth of the enemy submarine, but never less than a hundred feet.

All was ready; three cameras were primed. Actors were drilled in the correct procedure – ostensibly we gave the orders but the real crew actually fired the lethal charges. Jackie Broome, first making sure we had a good head of steam, ordered 'Full speed ahead'. The director shouted, 'Action!' and over the side went the charges set at a hundred feet. We waited . . . a shudder ran through the ship and from a distance six volcanoes of water shot upwards. A conference was held; apparently when seen through the camera the plumes of water were so far away that they looked small and undramatic.

What could be done? The only way to improve the shot was to steam at half speed and set off the charges at a depth of fifty feet. We had infinite faith in Jackie. Steam up. 'Half speed ahead.' 'Action! . . .'

I would not wish to live through that moment again. Hardly had the last charge dropped over the stern before the first exploded. Poor old retired and battered *Compass Rose* seemed to be lifted out of the sea like a toy, and dropped back again. We were all thrown off our feet. Some time later the first lieutenant showed us his pocket watch which he had left hanging on a hook; it was still on the hook but the inside was a tangled mass of cogs.

For another scene I was in charge of the fo'c'sle gun which had to be fired in a scene shot at night. We were provided with regulation earplugs and anti-flash helmets. The camera and director were on the bridge looking down on us. I had to be looking ahead through binoculars and when I heard 'Action!' I was to say, 'Fire', the leading gunner relayed the order by saying 'Shoot', and off should go the four-inch gun. Everything seemed ready and we were considerably nervous. I had no previous experience of standing that close to a gun – and the gun had not been used for some years . . . 'Action!'. He had to shout it twice before I could hear it through my earplugs: 'FIRE', 'SHOOT'. There followed a noise no louder than a 5th November banger and out from the muzzle fell a wad of burning cotton wool! Obviously we would have to do it again and I thought I could assist communication if I removed my earplugs; unbeknown to me the director and Jackie decided to use a live round. As I awaited my cue I peered through my binoculars and spied a light on the horizon. Suddenly 'ACTION!' 'FIRE', 'SHOOT', and my eardrums were nearly ruptured as a live round whistled off. A flashing Aldis lamp in the distance informed us that we had missed a cargo ship by about a hundred feet! I felt that it would not assist matters if I admitted I had seen the other ship.

As a goodwill gesture some of the actors agreed to attend the WRNS tennis tournament. I found myself sitting next to the gym instructress, a tall, massive lady with short-cropped, iron-grey hair and a moustache. She was wearing 'plain clothes', a thick tweed suit, thick-knit stockings and heavy brogue shoes. She had a powerful contralto bark. Tea was to be taken in the wardroom and our way lay through the gymnasium. As we entered, she suddenly clouted me on the back and roared, 'Race-you up a rope.' I have never felt more effeminate in my life. Diana and I have made a collection of catch phrases over the years. 'Race you up a rope' is certainly in it.

On this location I had my first experience of that unbelievably brave – or unbelievably stupid – breed without whom no action film could be made: stunt men. All young actors want to do their own so-called stunts – and where is the line to be drawn? Is running after and jumping on a moving bus a 'stunt'? Is driving a car at speed a 'stunt'? It is all a question of insurance. If a leading actor is incapacitated, shooting may be held up for days, weeks, or months. Thus film producers insure against this possibility which otherwise could cost hundreds of thousands of pounds. It is much safer and cheaper for them to put the clothes of the leading actor on a stunt man and let him run after the bus.

In *The Cruel Sea* all the stunts were done by Frankie Howerd (no, not *that* one). In one scene a British ship has been sunk by a submarine and the survivors are swimming around in the oily water. The captain of *Compass Rose* is faced with a Solomon type of decision; shall he pick up the survivors or blow up the enemy submarine which he suspects is lying immediately beneath them, thereby preventing it from destroying more ships. He decides to blow up the submarine. He steams straight towards the exhausted swimmers who think he is going to save them . . . This scene had to be done in a series of cuts, one showing the men in the water, another (shot from the stern of a tug) showing the bows of *Compass Rose* getting nearer and nearer, and finally a third showing the bows ploughing into the doomed men. For this a 'cradle' was slung over the side of the ship, two feet above the water, on which were placed the camera and its operator, Chic Masterson. Through the lens the knife edge of the bows could be seen cutting through the water at full speed. A number of lifelike dummies had been placed in the water and Frankie was seen swimming amongst them, then at the very last second he used his hand to push himself away from the prow of the ship, to be carried off on the bow wave under the camera! I tried to watch this scene from our deck, but had to turn away. What a way to earn a living!

For about a week we actors were aware of a major crisis brewing. Each evening at the hotel the producer and director met with the production manager; voices were raised, hands struck foreheads, carpets were paced. Slowly the news filtered through; Alan Webb had been engaged to play the admiral and in the scene to be filmed the day after tomorrow he was to come alongside in the admiral's barge. The film company had been negotiating with the Admiralty for the use of a barge, but it had proved impossible to secure one – each admiral has his own and there are no spares. By chance Jackie Broome heard of this impending calamity which, unless solved, could necessitate a script re-write and possibly costly re-scheduling. 'Why didn't you ask me?' he roared and picked up the telephone. 'Get me the Admiral Superintendent.' A pause. 'Captain Jack Broome' – a pause – 'Hello, Pinkie, Jackie here; look, could we borrow the barge on Thursday? – Very good of you, thanks.' Weeks of correspondence went out of the window. The old-boy network had saved the day.

Jackie excelled himself on another occasion. *Compass Rose* had to return to her home port of Liverpool. One dockyard is very like another so Devonport became Liverpool. We were to steam up the Tamar/Mersey, make a sharp turn to starboard into a closed harbour (for the unitiated this is a man-made enclosure with a narrow entrance, where ships may be parked) and pull up alongside a ship already moored at the quayside (double parking). This other ship – nothing to do with our film – was one of Her Majesty's destroyers.

Jack Hawkins was apparently in command on the bridge, but in fact Jackie Broome was giving the orders while kneeling down and peering through two peepholes specially bored in the bulkhead. My job was to be in charge of the fo'c'sle party of real sailors, who, on my command 'Stand by your wires and fenders', prepared to drop the fenders over the side to prevent one ship scratching the other and to pay out the hawsers which would secure us alongside. Again three cameras were to film this arrival, one on board our ship, one secreted on the quayside and another on the top of a crane to get an 'aerial' view. Under Jackie's orders *Compass Rose* came up the river at five knots, turned to starboard; my order 'Stand by your wires and fenders' was immediately executed and as a result of Jackie's 'Port 15', 'Slow ahead', 'Steady as you go', 'Full astern both', we came to rest nine inches away from the destroyer exactly on the spot required.

A perfect piece of parking.

We all gathered round Jackie to congratulate him. 'How do you do it?' someone asked. 'Experience,' replied Jackie. Unfortunately two of the cameras had failed to capture this masterpiece. We had to do it again, so back down the river we went, turned round and waited for 'Action!' Now nobody could accuse Jackie of conceit but our adulation had made him rather pleased with himself. This time he took us up the river at nine knots, we turned to starboard, on cue I said, 'Stand by your wires and fenders' but to my astonishment I found the crew were already doing it. I noticed the sea was rushing past us . . . suddenly the whole ship heaved, as our anchor, protruding from the side of the bows, tore a hole nine feet long and ten inches wide in the side of Her Majesty's destroyer! And there was Jack Hawkins in full view on the bridge – Jackie kept out of sight . . . From the wheelhouse of the destroyer emerged an officer, who, with perfect RN understatement, surveyed the damage and said, 'Who the flipping hell's driving your boat – Errol Flynn?'

The shot which appeared in the final film was taken from the top of the crane – the next time you see it look carefully, you can see the bows heave quite clearly.

In the story *Compass Rose* is sunk (this sequence was to be filmed in the studio). Ericson and Lockhart survive and continue their association in a new ship, a Castle class frigate. To film this sequence the unit moved to Portland harbour where Ealing Studios had been 'loaned' a frigate, HMS *Porchester Castle*, by the Royal Navy, under the command of its regular captain. Although they could not have been more helpful I doubt if the ship's crew ever really came to terms with the requirements of a film unit. By this time we actors had been so indoctrinated that we were indistinguishable from the genuine article; we were saluted wherever we went – we realised of course that it was the uniform that was being respected – and to avoid embarrassment we invariably returned the salute.

The ship's captain was required to take the ship out to sea and out of sight of land because all the scenes due to be filmed were exteriors (the interiors could be done later in the studio). The 'quality' of light has to be consistent throughout and many hours were spent waiting for clouds to pass (as Cedric Hardwicke once said, 'Filming is ninety-five per cent boredom, five per cent panic'). Then suddenly the captain and his crew had to produce 'Full steam ahead'.

Now if a duologue were to be shot the sun was expected to maintain its position on an actor's face for several minutes. This required an extremely accurate course to be steered. Once the shot on one actor was completed, the whole ship had to be turned around to produce equivalent light on actor number two. This operation can take some time. The ship is then required to steer an equally accurate course in the reverse direction.

One day some colleagues and I were keeping out of sight by hiding in the wheelhouse while a scene not involving us was filmed on the bridge. The coxswain was a large, florid, clean-shaven man with an apparent ability to forestall and pre-empt his captain's orders. He regaled us with splendid anecdotes of life in the Navy. Halfway through a sentence the captain's voice echoed down the voice pipe, 'Starboard fifteen'. Before the word fifteen had been completed the coxswain was already spinning his wheel as he repeated, 'Starboard fifteen – fifteen of starboard wheel on, sir'; he then completed the anecdote with no pause for breath. We all continued to chat away, each anecdote engendering another as the ship's engines thundered away at Full Speed Ahead. Some time later we were interrupted by the captain, screaming dementedly down the voice pipe, 'WHAT COURSE ARE YOU STEERING?!!' Quite unperturbed and in the calmest of voice, the coxswain replied, '360° for the fourth time round, sir.'

His was not to reason why.

While working at Portland we were accommodated in a hotel in Dorchester. Each evening when we returned from our day's work, Jack Hawkins would telephone his wife Doreen whom he had left in charge of decorating their new house at Roehampton, before joining Charlie Frend, Leslie Norman and me for dinner, when he would recount the latest developments, which usually involved, much to Jack's consternation, the spending of large sums of money. One Friday night Jack approached the table as white as a sheet, sank into a chair and moaned, 'Oh God, I've just lost my temper with Doreen. She burst into tears and said, "I suppose you've forgotten what today is? – it's my birthday!" What can I do? It's too late to send flowers – I'll never live it down!'

Callously we other three found this very funny and could hardly wait for Monday morning to tell our colleagues. While waiting on the quayside as equipment was loaded on the frigate I embarked on my version of the story. I got as far as 'I suppose you've forgotten what today is' when to my horror I realised that today – today – was *my* wife's birthday! Within minutes we would be out to sea with no possibility of doing anything about it. Panic. To my relief, I spotted Charlie's wife Sonja, who had come down in the car with him.

'Are you returning to Dorchester?'

'Yes.'

'Then will you do me a great favour. Promise me that you will send some flowers to my wife, but they must be there today.'

'What sort?'

'Red roses.'

All day I was in a cold sweat. When we docked that evening I was in the first car bound for Dorchester. I sought out Sonja, 'Did you succeed?'

'It's all right – relax – the florist assured me they would be delivered before mid-day.'

'Bless you, Sonja – you've saved my life. How much do I owe you?'

'Fifteen pounds.'

How much would fifteen pounds in 1952 be worth today? Diana said that she had never seen so many roses – nor will she ever again!

Our location work finished, we returned to Ealing Studios to begin work on the 'sinking' sequence. A replica of *Compass Rose* had been built, mounted on a hydraulic jack so that every movement of the ship could be reproduced at will. All the exterior fittings from the real *Compass Rose* had been removed and reinstalled on the replica.

For one particular shot I was leading my team in an effort to launch a lifeboat which had become jammed because of the 'list'. The deck, at a considerable angle, was some twenty feet above the studio floor. Various machines went into action; 'steam' hissed from every crevice; a hose pipe fired water at a fan the size of an aeroplane propeller, which then blew the heavy spray at us. With levers and brute strength we tried to launch the real lifeboat over the side of the tubular scaffolding and hardboard ship. Suddenly the unexpected happened – the lifeboat shifted and went over the side; I had been exerting considerable pressure; my gum boots slid on the wet deck and I followed the lifeboat. I grabbed at a rope and hung suspended by one hand. Everyone expected the entire structure to collapse on me, but at last I was hauled back to safety. A press photographer happened to be on the set and managed to take three photographs of the drama. This was my first, but by no means my last, experience of the dangers of filming.

Now that we were installed in the studio I found myself subjected to the full power of the Rank Organisation's publicity machine. During the first week a press reception was given in the studio, which I was virtually ordered to attend. I asked the publicity director for advice. 'Talk about yourself, the film and the Rank

Organisation – in that order,' he said, so with some trepidation I entered the room. Nobody turned a head – they were far too busy with their drinks. I looked around and chose the prettiest girl in the room – I introduced myself and talked about myself for a good twelve minutes, then about the film for eight minutes, then the Rank Organisation for four minutes. As I ground to a halt I asked my beautiful companion what paper she represented. 'I'm from the Rank Organisation publicity department,' she said.

On another occasion the publicity man came on to the set and asked me to meet one of the senior officers of the WRNS, who was seated some distance behind the camera. In the comparative darkness I extended my hand and sat beside her. I thought I would tell her my gym instructress story. I got as far as 'short-cropped iron-grey hair'; my eyes were getting used to the dim light and I saw that she too had short-cropped iron-grey hair . . . I continued, 'She was wearing tweeds and thick knit stockings . . .' To my horror I saw that she was dressed identically. But I could not stop now. I got to the tag line, 'Race you up a rope'. The officer turned to a companion whom I now noticed for the first time – she too was identical. The first slapped the second on the back and roaring with laughter, cried, 'That must have been Basher Gibson!'

One day I was called to the office of Leslie Norman, the producer. He asked me to sit down. 'Now look here, Donald, you are not behaving like a star. We are making you one, but you have to behave like one. You are letting yourself be pushed around.' (He was quite right of course. In the theatre one operated within a very small group, the hierarchy of which was long established. But in the film world everyone seemed very important. Rolls-Royces were everywhere. I could not work out the pecking order.) 'You've got to tell other people what to do . . .' He then lectured me on the responsibilities, the creating and maintaining of an image and so on. 'Remember, you're a star – behave like one! Think big!'

Leaving his office I felt ten feet tall. 'I'm a STAR.' I walked back to the set, convinced of my own importance. There was my chair with DONALD SINDEN emblazoned on it and I placed it in a prominent position and sat down like a Pharaoh. Two electricians wanted to lay a cable just where I was sitting. (Now, Sinden, start the way you mean to go on! Think big!) 'You can lay it over there,' I said imperiously. 'F – you,' he answered. I stopped thinking of myself as a star from that moment.

In the novel Monsarrat wrote a chapter about Lockhart and his girl friend Julie spending a month's leave in Scotland where the only action was copulation, but in 1952 film censorship was still very stringent; none of this chapter could be filmed. However Charlie Frend wanted to compensate by shooting a scene between the two of us standing under a lamp post and our prolonged kiss was to symbolise the sexual act as two people suffered the privations of wartime.

I seemed to provide Charlie with what he required, but Virginia McKenna had problems; she was very innocent; on what should she base her re-enactment? We did the scene again and again with Charlie growing more and more explicit in his directions, but to no avail. At long last he took me aside. 'You realise the problem, don't you? Well I am quite prepared to put this scene off until tomorrow . . .but for the sake of the film one of us ought to do something about it.'

Unfortunately both our wives were expecting us home.

As the nights grew longer, the unit moved to the open air tank at Denham Studios. At least an acre in size, it had an enormous sky-cloth erected at the far end and another replica of *Compass Rose* running away diagonally from right to left. This was 'hinged' at the side of the tank so that it could be 'sunk' at an angle as many times as necessary.

The evacuation of the ship was the first scene to be shot. The whole crew were to jump over the side – the stunt man from the top of the superstructure. The first assistant director came to me and asked, 'Can you swim?'

'No,' I said.

'OK – you jump from there,' and he showed me a position furthest from the bank. Now the tank was ten feet deep – five feet more than I would find acceptable. I was somewhat worried until I reasoned that there was possibly a shallow end.

Two giant wave machines were put into action. One was a massive sheet of iron which was dropped at an angle into the water and sent a giant wave across the tank. It was then hauled up and the operation repeated. By now the first wave was making its return journey. The other machine was like a great mangle with fins attached to the cylinders which revolved upon themselves and churned up the surface of the water. A hose once more played into the aeroplane propeller and 'steam' again hissed from the ship. Why, you might ask, was this scene not shot on location? Because, I was told, the camera had to be on a fixed point. Had it been on another boat the relative motion of the two could cancel out the effect – and you can only sink a real ship once.

The night was cold; cast and crew shivered as we waited for the 'sea' to become rough enough; and then 'ACTION!' I ran to the side, climbed up and as I jumped flexed my knees expecting to land in three feet of water. Down I went – glug, glug, glug. From my school days I tried to remember how to do a breast stroke but I couldn't make headway against the wave machines; every time I surfaced I seemed to be in the same place. All the others arrived safely at the bank and, thank God, Jack Hawkins heard someone ask, 'Where's Donald?' He dived in again and pulled me out just in time. It transpired that the first assistant thought I had been joking when I said I couldn't swim!

For another shot the leading players were required to swim past the camera in 'close up'. 'ACTION!'

First Jack Hawkins swam past, then a gap, and then Denholm Elliott . . .

'Donald, we didn't see you, let's do it again.'

Jack Hawkins – a gap – Denholm Elliott . . .

Suffering, as I discovered later, from negative buoyancy, I was certainly swimming past, but under water. The only answer was for Frankie Howerd to take an enormous breath and swim breast stroke under the surface with me lying on his back simulating a crawl. It looks quite good in the finished film.

At the press showing of the completed film I was detained and entered the cinema after the film had begun. I was so bemused at seeing myself on the screen that I could remember nothing of it. A week or so later Diana and I attended the gala premiere at the Odeon, Leicester Square. The excitement! The crowds, the lights, the film cameras and flashlights. We took our places. The house lights dimmed. Bombardier Billy Wells struck the Rank gong and on to the screen in enormous letters came 'JACK HAWKINS and DONALD SINDEN in . . .' I was so overcome I can remember nothing more of that performance, either.

Not until it came to my 'local' did I see *The Cruel Sea* with a cool head and critical eye.

9

WOULD ANYONE CARE TO LOOK AT AFRICA BY NIGHT?

News travels speedily in the film industry: a new young actor was starring in *The Cruel Sea*. I was the flavour of the month. Eight weeks before the end of our filming an enquiry came from MGM in Hollywood – would I test for a projected film? Unfortunately I was too heavily involved in the schedule, but most generously Sir Michael Balcon, Leslie Norman and Charles Frend arranged for various clips of scenes in which I featured to be linked together and the reel sent off to Hollywood. This was most unusual – the footage of a new film is always jealously guarded – and only from Ealing Studios could such treatment be expected. Within days I was offered the part.

The Rank Organisation moved with equal speed. My contract with Ealing Studios included the clause giving the Rank Organisation the option of putting me under long-term contract, such option to be exercised before a given date. Of course, the moment they heard of the MGM offer they took up the option. This meant that my salary would now be paid each week by the Rank Organisation on an annually rising scale for seven years; my services could be sub-let to any other film studio (e.g. MGM) and I would receive 'half the profits after deduction of expenses and idle weeks' (whatever that might mean).

It was beyond comprehension. *Seven* years. Seven *years*! We could look ahead, think ahead, plan ahead – for seven years. More important – we could eat for seven years. Instead of living from week to week we had security – for SEVEN YEARS. I have to admit that I did not notice the clause which said that the contract was 'reviewable' at the end of each year; the immediate excitement was the MGM film.

My friends at Ealing were delighted at the news and demanded to know all the details. The film was called *Mogambo*; it would be made in East Africa, and its two stars were Clark Gable and Ava Gardner. I was to play the English husband of a promising and quickly rising new actress by the name of Grace Kelly. And the director? I admitted I had never asked, so they had to wait until the next day when I told them, 'Someone called John Ford.' Actually I had never heard of him, but my friends seemed mightily impressed.

Two weeks later I had a telephone call from Irene Howard, casting director of MGM's British studios at Elstree, who had been responsible for putting forward my name in the first place, and had negotiated my contract with Rank: 'John Ford is in London and wants to meet you. I suggest that you come out to Elstree and join me for lunch at one o'clock in the studio restaurant and Mr Ford will see you at two thirty.' By the time I had arrived – at twelve thirty and wearing my best suit – I had been fully briefed by my friends: John Ford had entered the film industry in 1917, made nearly 200 films including such classics as *The Informer*, *The Plough and the Stars*, *Stagecoach*, *The Young Mr Lincoln*, *Drums along the Mohawk*, *The Grapes of Wrath*, *How Green was My Valley*, *Rio Grande*, *The Quiet Man* – none of which I had seen! – and had won two Oscars. Indeed Ford was one of the Great Names in the Film World and I was to meet him at two thirty.

I made my way to the restaurant and found Irene – the sister of the acting Howard brothers, Leslie and Arthur – who was charming and considerate. I reeled off the information I had gathered about John Ford, all of which, I was intrigued and slightly disappointed to learn, she already knew. We nattered away and at one fifty-five p.m. a tall, gangling figure wearing very crumpled denims over very dirty shoes, a bush jacket and a khaki cap with a long peak, rose from a nearby table and on his way out paused at our table and growled, 'Hi, Irene.'

'Oh, Mr Ford – this is Donald Sinden.'

I leaped to my feet. I gazed at the great John Ford. His face was as crumpled as his denims, he wore dark glasses which made it impossible to see his eyes and he was chewing one corner of a very dirty handkerchief which he tugged at with his hand. The black lenses bore into me and moved slowly down to my feet and up again and focused on my face. He said nothing. Time passed and suddenly I was ordered to 'Sid-down'. Again he peered at me. 'Whad de yer think of yer part?'

I suppose I could just have said 'Splendid' and left it at that, but I felt that more was required. I could at least prove that I had studied the script in detail so I embarked on a long, fairly intelligent dissertation. He listened without moving his lenses from my eyes but continued to chew hungrily on the handkerchief. I ground on. Suddenly he turned to Irene: 'Who the hell's this?!'

Irene jumped to my defence, 'Donald takes his work very seriously . . .'

'Does he,' said Ford ominously. 'We'll soon knock the hell out of that!' And for the next six months he proceeded to do just that. I found him the most dislikeable person I have ever met. I know now that the cause of the trouble was the fact that I was (am) pro-British and Ford was pro-American and pro-Irish. His was a romanticised American view of Ireland and he blamed me personally for all her troubles.

First I had to be fitted for my wardrobe. For some scenes I needed either a suit or a white evening jacket and black trousers, but most of the time merely a bush jacket to be worn with either long trousers or shorts. I was taken by the designer to Hawes and Curtis, the tailors of Dover Street (it appeared that film companies did not believe in off-the-peg) to have all these made. I felt it was rather extravagant to have tailored bush jackets and shorts – six sets of them – but mine was not to reason why. Shoes and four pairs of boots (all hand-made) followed. I was concerned about the boots, being made of magnificent suede, because in some of the scenes I would have to wade through water up to my knees. When I wore my outfit for Ford's inspection I tentatively asked, 'What will happen to these when I go in the water?' Back came the curt reply, 'They'll get wet!'

It was with some relief that I returned to *The Cruel Sea*, while Ford departed for Kenya to prepare the locations, but two weeks before the end of filming, Ealing received an urgent telegram: 'Sinden required in Nairobi next Sunday.' Again Leslie Norman and Charles Frend were magnificent. They rearranged their schedule so that I could finish my scenes first and after some frantic packing I caught a plane on the Saturday morning, leaving poor Diana and Jeremy to fend for themselves. But not before we indulged in one luxury – our first car. Dear Charles Frend was buying a new one and for £200 I bought his two-year-old Ford V-8 which was built like a tank – Diana had a licence, but I had never learned to drive. Africa would change that.

What excitement! – I could still hardly believe it. A Hollywood motion picture to be made in the African bush with a star-studded cast . . . The plane touched down at Nairobi airport where I was met by Ford's first assistant and whisked off in an enormous limousine to the New Stanley Hotel, where I was introduced to the film's producer, Sam Zimbalist. I asked what time I would be needed tomorrow.

'Oh, we don't start shooting for another two weeks,' said Zimbalist. 'Jack doesn't want anyone to use make-up so we've got you all out so you can get a good sun-tan. Enjoy yourself!' 'Jack' was John Ford and for a sun-tan Leslie Norman, Charles Frend and Ealing Studios had fallen over backwards to help me!

My suite was enormous. Not now a tiny room on the Left Bank at fifteen shillings a night B. & B. but a large bedroom, a sitting room and a palatial bathroom – and it wasn't costing me a penny. I turned on *all* the lights. I opened the windows and the warm evening air flooded in. I ordered an enormous breakfast from the lavish menu, to be served in bed, and for two weeks I had three baths a day with the bath filled to the brim – at someone else's expense. Everything was paid for by MGM. We were expected to eat in the hotel dining room, but in the basement was a magnificently sumptuous Grill Room and there, it had been agreed, each member of the unit could have one meal a week at MGM's expense. The actors soon discovered that other members of the unit were not interested in taking advantage of the offer so by clever manipulation we ate there every evening and chalked the bill up to different room numbers. In two weeks I put on seven pounds in weight! But on my first evening I had not yet discovered that trick and I ate my dinner quite alone in the dining room.

The next morning I reported to the unit office and was just being introduced to Robert Surtees, the cameraman – or 'cinematographer' as they are called in America – when in walked Clark Gable.

'Clark, this is Donald Sinden.'

'Hi, Don – join us for dinner tonight,' and the famous lips twisted into a smile.

Surely it is unnecessary to describe Clark Gable?

Taller than I had expected – about six feet two inches – he wore bush jacket and shorts (not so well cut as Hawes and Curtis') and long socks. His legs were like tree trunks, tapering slowly from large thighs to thick ankles, and wherever he stood it looked as if he had taken root. Only later did I discover the insight of Ava Gardner's remark when someone asked her what Gable was like: 'Clark? He's the sort of guy – if you say, "Hiya, Clark, how are ya?" – he's stuck for an answer.'

That evening, having spent the day on the hotel roof garden, I made my way to the Grill Room. There was Gable sitting with a ravishing blonde. My immediate thought was that my presence was not required, so I just paused at his table – 'Hi, Don.'

'Good evening, Mr Gable.'

'Hey – to hell with that – *Clark* – siddown – this is Grace Kelly – Don Sinden.'

Demure and amazingly pretty, Grace flashed me a smile – an unguarded smile as when acknowledging a colleague. Actors are strange people: the nature of our work makes us extremely vulnerable and it is necessary for us to erect different defensive barriers. Each actor I know has several smiles: the professional one that can be turned on during performance in a play or film; the one used when being accosted unexpectedly by a fan; the more genuine one when they hear a joke or anecdote well told (they don't laugh at the joke itself – only at the expertise in the telling of it); the one they use when trying to convince a director they are right for a part; the special one reserved for a loved one; the private one used only in the bosom of their family; but most telling is the very special one of professional understanding, acknowledgment and recognition used only between actors. This was the smile that Grace and I exchanged. She had arrived in Nairobi that day and, like me, was meeting Mr Gable – sorry, Clark – for the first time.

Our waiter was a Kikuyu and Grace proceeded to astonish Clark and me by ordering the entire meal for the three of us in Swahili. From the moment she first heard that the film would be made in Kenya she had swotted up on the language. Having served the coffee the waiter was just moving away when Grace called after him, '*Lete ndizi, tafadhali.*'

By then we had learned that '*lete*' meant 'bring' and '*tafadhali*' meant 'please', but Clark, with some incredulousness, asked her, 'What's an *ndizi*?'

Before she could reply, the waiter had turned and in a bored American accent answered, 'It's a banana,' and wearily made his way.

Apart from Grace none of us made much headway with Swahili except to learn a limerick (all the reader needs to know is that a *kibuyu* is a gourd and *ni huhu* means 'this one here'):

There was a young lady, a Kikuyu
Whose tummy was like a kibuyu
When she was asked who
Has done this to you
She replied ni huhu, ni huhu, ni huhu.

A number of Swahili words begin with an 'M' or an 'N' which are pronounced quite simply as mmm or nnn – thus *Ngoro-Ngoro* has a most beautiful sound. The Kikuyu were the only people who could make a single word of MGM.

The following day we three sunbathed on Clark's balcony and in the evening we dined together. The same procedure the next day and the next day, but that evening, when we foregathered for an early dinner, I happened to ask when Ava Gardner was due to arrive and Clark said, 'She's been here all along – in fact she arrived the day before me.'

'Where is she?' enquired Grace.

'Oh, she keeps herself to herself – she hasn't been out of her suite yet, she has all her meals sent up.'

'How very unfriendly,' I said. 'She should at least say hello.'

'Not Ava,' said Clark.

'But it's very anti-social – I've a good mind to go and bring her down for dinner.'

Clark's face creased into a smile; 'That'll get you no place – she won't come.'

'At least I can try.'

'You're wasting your time.'

But I was adamant and off I went.

I found my way to her room and knocked on the door. Beyond that door was someone who had already been voted 'the most beautiful woman in the world', whose face and most of whose body were known throughout the world, who had first been married to Mickey Rooney, then to Artie Shaw and currently to a singer called Frank Sinatra (whose career was then in the doldrums). Silence. I knocked again. A long pause and a quiet voice said, 'Who's that?' The sound came through the keyhole.

How absurd, I thought, to have to introduce myself in this way. I bent down and through the keyhole I said, 'My name is Donald Sinden. We are supposed to be working together: I've come to take you down to dinner.'

Another long pause and the keyhole quietly said, 'Wait there a minute.' I waited. The sound of a key being inserted and turned, the gentle rattle of a safety chain and eventually the door slowly opened to disclose the legendary figure in the process of wrapping a diaphanous dressing gown around a body which, unbeknown to her, was silhouetted against the light. Her beautiful dark eyes sized me up and came to rest locked on mine.

'Come in,' she murmured, and the door closed behind me . . . She circled me in silence, but I was not to be intimidated.

'I think it is rather discourteous of you not to join the rest of your colleagues – I've come to bring you down to dinner.'

Never taking her eyes off me, and after another pregnant pause she said, 'OK – I'll take a quick bath – help yourself to a drink,' and she disappeared into the bathroom.

The bath was not exactly a quick one and my imagination ran rife as I heard the splashings coming round the door which she had left slightly ajar. Suddenly she reappeared and on barefooted tiptoes floated around the room picking out various pieces of clothing. Carrying them she disappeared into the bathroom, from which she emerged a few seconds later fully dressed, one hand assertively posed high up on the door frame, lips moistened, eyes sparkling, head thrown back, awaiting the flash of an imaginary camera. 'OK? – come on let's go.'

We entered the Grill Room and all eyes turned in our direction – the first they had seen of Ava Gardner. And it was an eyeful. The head waiter scurried across and we were shown to a table in the middle of the room. At a side table Clark and Grace sat looking across with some admiration – Clark's smile developed into a smirk and he telegraphed an enormous wink.

Ava studied the massive menu in detail and after much thought said, 'Bring me a hamburger.' Rashly I ordered something like caviare and lobster thermidor. Our conversation was not exactly scintillating – merely filling in our personal and professional curricula vitae. After barely tasting her hamburger she pushed it away, swung round one of the spare chairs and put her feet on it.

'Please don't do that,' I said pompously. 'It's so inelegant.'

She looked as if she was about to argue, but smiled instead and removed her feet. She then leaned across and started to pick pieces of choice meat from my plate.

'I'm sorry,' I said, 'but I object very strongly to that – if you don't like your own dish and refuse an alternative, don't pick at mine.'

Can I have been the first person to thwart her? But from that moment I could do no wrong – she looked at me with new respect. And then we started to talk. I discovered she was deeply in love with Sinatra and was missing him dreadfully.

My shoulder became hers to cry on.

Any sign of a tantrum and I was sent for to placate her.

From then on four of us sunbathed on Clark's balcony.

Ten days later we were flown to our main location, 700 miles away in Uganda, where, in the middle of the African bush, beside the Kagera river which flows into Lake Victoria, and hundreds of miles from anywhere, MGM (or 'Mgm' as we began to call it, following the Kikuyu lead) had bulldozed an airstrip long enough for a Dakota DC3 to land. (Typically of MGM this aircraft was under exclusive contract for the duration of filming, but most days its only work was to fly in each morning with supplies – fresh milk, etc., and the mail, and return to Nairobi each evening with the day's rushes for processing.) After landing we were whisked off, in strict order of billing, by jeeps to our camp set up on a piece of land which was practically an island created by the river turning back upon itself. This promontory, which stood 200 feet above the river like a medieval fortress, was joined to the 'mainland' by a narrow neck of land and here Askari guards were permanently on duty and bonfires were lit at night, to protect us from the very real danger of wild animals. The unit comprised 150 of us 'foreigners' and 300 especially recruited local black people. Under the eagle eye of 'Bunny' Allen, the camp manager, tents had been erected in serried ranks and a strict order of hierarchy: the front-row tents each had only one occupant (from left to right, in the front row: John Ford, Clark Gable, Ava Gardner, Grace Kelly, me, the cameraman, the production manager and Colonel Wingate-Smith – Ford's brother-in-law and personal assistant), but each row behind had two per tent. Someone observed that but for a belt of trees facing the tents we in the front row could see right across the opposite bank of the wide river. No sooner said than done. Within days the trees were removed, presenting us with one of the most impressive views in the world – as far as the eye could see were miles and miles of uninhabited virgin African bush.

Our tents were rectangular in plan with the entrance at one end under a canopy. They contained a bed on one side, a desk and chair on the other and through a flap at the rear a semi-circular extension with a full-length canvas bath, for which hot water was provided morning and night. With the nights so hot it was necessary to roll up the lower flaps to allow some passage of air. To each tent was allotted a black servant who, better than any valet, took care of all our needs: clothes were whisked away each night and returned fully laundered next morning; shoes were cleaned; beds made. Two enormous marquees offered games such as table tennis, darts and cards, and a cinema with twin 16mm projectors on which a different film was shown every night – all MGM's, of course. Instead of one large mess tent, Bunny – the camp manager – had the bright idea of erecting twelve separate and smaller ones, thus creating a much more intimate atmosphere. But none of this would have been possible, but for an enormous generator which also supplied electricity for the radio transmitter to keep us in touch with the outside world; for the wardrobe tent's electric washing machines and irons; for the make-up department's electric hair-dryers and for the portable hospital's X-ray machine. You will appreciate the hideously primitive conditions under which we were to live for three months.

Ten White Hunters were seconded to our unit for our protection and to provide fresh meat. Among them were Viscount Mandeville (now the Duke of Manchester) and Lord Wallscourt, a delightful man whom Ford treated abysmally – sometimes quite sadistically. In Ford's eyes the poor man could do nothing right and was continually being bawled out (in some ways he took the heat off me). None of us could understand the reason for this appalling treatment, which the dear kind man in no way deserved. He himself was quite at a loss. Several weeks later we discovered the cause from Ford's brother-in-law: before emigrating to America, Ford's grandfather had been a labourer on the estate in Ireland of the then Lord Wallscourt: Ford was now getting his own back at his descendant. Not a charming sight.

I was called for my first day's work. In the film a British scientist (me) and his wife (Grace) arrive in Africa to study gorillas (which, incidentally, cannot be found in Kenya or Uganda). They engage the services of a White Hunter (Clark) to take them on safari; he falls in love with the wife. Matters are complicated by the arrival of a 'good-time' girl (Ava) who has been stranded in the bush.

The first scene to be filmed was the arrival down the river, by boat, of the scientist and his wife. Grace and I appeared in our costumes and were vetted by the cameraman who was horrified to find that because of our intensive hours in the sun we were now indistinguishable from the natives – especially as this scene was supposed to be our arrival in Africa. The make-up man who had thought that he was redundant was hurriedly sent for and our complexions were restored to an English pallor. Before leaving camp that morning I had been asked to report to the hair-dressing department, where I had found the make-up man armed with electric clippers: 'I have to remove the hair from your chest.'

'Whatever for?'

'Orders.'

It transpired that Clark, whose chest was completely devoid of hair, had insisted that no other actor should appear on film exposing a hirsute breast. There was no point in arguing – it only involved a trim once a week.

On the bank of the river a landing stage had been built and at it was moored a river steamer. The film crew and the camera were positioned on the bank and without a single word from Ford, Grace and I were bundled on to the boat which set off upstream. With us came the second assistant who established walkie-talkie communication with the unit. Round the bend of the river the boat stopped and turned about. We waited. No one had been given any instructions. We had had no rehearsal; the script merely indicated: 'The boat arrives and the scientist and his wife get off.' Over the walkie-talkie we heard, 'Roll 'em. Action', and the boat started to chug forward. Suddenly Ford's voice screamed over a loud-hailer: 'Grace – Donald – get below. OK. Donald – come on deck. Look around at the scenery. Call Grace. Put your arm around her. Point out a giraffe over on your right. Get your camera out – *quickly*. Photograph it – the giraffe. Smile at him, Grace. Grace – look at that hippopotamus on your left. Get Donald to photograph it. A crocodile slides into the water. You're scared. Grace – you're scared. OK. You're coming into the pier. Look around. What's in store for you? Natives are running down to meet you. OK. OK. Cut. Print it.'

And that was our baptism of being directed by Ford: exactly what he had done in the days of silent films.

Unit managers and designers had spent months searching out possible locations before we arrived. At one of these we arrived by jeep: Ford clambered out, a cigar sticking from his teeth, stood on one spot and turned round quite quickly peering at 360 degrees of magnificent scenery. 'OK – stick your camera here,' and he indicated the exact direction. In a matter of seconds Ford's expert eye pinpointed the perfect 'frame' for his next shot. I have no doubt that anyone else would have spent hours searching for the same effect.

On another occasion Grace and Clark (who was known to the unit as 'King' – King of Hollywood; John Wayne was always called 'Duke') were to play a scene on the brink of the escarpment that towers above the Rift Valley – again a perfect frame. Again they were subjected to the silent film technique: 'Action. Walk towards that tree. King, lift those leaves out of Grace's hair. Stop. Turn to Grace. Move back . . .' But at that moment, disaster: Clark disappeared over the edge of the escarpment! Oh God! He must have fallen hundreds of feet. Was he dead? Mercifully he had slithered and fallen to a ledge about fifteen feet down and a small sapling had prevented him from dropping further. Ropes were brought, someone was lowered and the two were brought safely up. People gathered around.

Only then did we notice that Ford had not moved from his position beside the camera. He sat impassively: 'Come on! Come on!' he snapped. 'King, you OK?'

'Yep.'

'Then get on with it. Action. Walk towards that tree . . .'

Without ever committing himself, Ford was always 'one-up'. I remember a group asking him if he would join them in a game of Canasta, then a popular card game.

'Do you play Three or Five Canastas?' he asked.

'Three.'

'I only play Five,' he replied and continued on his way. And I knew that had they said, 'Five' he would have answered, 'I only play Three'. On another occasion I was telling a small group some anecdotes of *The Cruel Sea* when Ford joined us: I referred to the presence of an American fleet in the English Channel and said, 'Their largest battleship the *Missouri* was anchored in Portland Harbour . . .'

Ford interjected: 'You said *the Missouri* – you never say *the* when referring to a ship.'

'You're quite right,' I said, and continued to the end of my story. Ford then embarked on a naval anecdote and himself said '*the Missouri*'. I could not let that go unchallenged: 'Aha! – You said *the Missouri!*'

'In the States we say *the Missouri*.' He played perfect one-upmanship.

The generator at the camp made so much noise that it had to be

With Newton Blick in *The Magistrate*, 1950.

Carrying Donald Pleasence in *Puss in Boots*, 1950.

'Envy' in *The Seven Deadly Sins*, 1948.

With Virginia McKenna in *The Cruel Sea* and below with the author, Nicholas Monsarrat and my 'Captain', Jack Hawkins.

MGM camp on the Kagera River.

John Ford.

The view from my tent.

Above: En route to Entebbe with Grace Kelly, Ava Gardner, Clark Gable and Frank Sinatra.

Left: 'What do you think...?'

With Akim Tamiroff.

How to carry a live alligator.

Four depressed medical students: Donald Houston, me, Kenneth More and Dirk Bogarde.

Rankery contract artists, 1954. Standing, left to right: Lyndon Brook, Peter Finch, Terence Morgan, Diana Dors, Jack Hawkins, Michael Craig, George Baker, John Gregson, me. Sitting, anti-clockwise from left: Eunice Gayson, Diane Cilento, Jill Adams, Belinda Lee, Sarah Lawson, Susan Stephen.

Above Us The Waves. Standing, left to right: William Russell, Anthony Newley, Lee Patterson, William Franklyn, Michael Medwin, Anthony Wager, Harry Towb and me. Sitting, left to right: John Gregson, James Kenney, John Mills and Lyndon Brook.

Right: The Venice film
festival: Belinda Lee, John and
Thea Gregson, me, Diana,
Doreen and Jack Hawkins
at the British Consulate.

Below: Royal Command film
performance 1954. From the
right: Peter Ustinov, Shelley
Winters, Rudy Vallee, me,
Ronald Shiner.

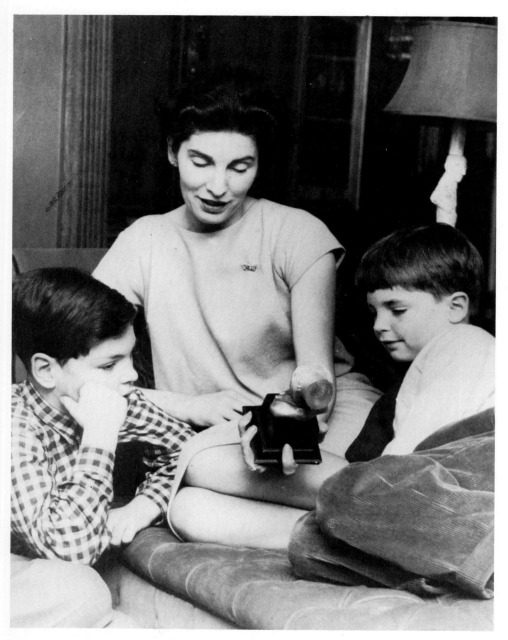

Jeremy, Diana and Marc in 1960 with my Variety Club award – 'the actor who made most progress in 1954'.

turned off at ten p.m. Thus, late one evening I was sitting at the table in my tent writing a letter by the light of a kerosene lamp when I thought I saw something out of the corner of my eye – something like a chiffon ghost – flit past the entrance. Warily I stood up and peeped round the side . . . But there was nothing, so I returned and picked up my pen . . . But there it went again – a white, silent ghost floated past. Again I peered out, but again, nothing. I had just seated myself when the 'ghost' appeared round the entrance to my tent. It was Ava in a white nightdress: 'Donald, have you seen Grace?'

'Well, I saw something white a few seconds ago – unless you've been past twice.'

'She's very upset,' continued Ava. 'She was very homesick and came to my tent; I gave her a drink, she burst into tears and rushed out. Help me to find her.'

I grabbed my torch, Ava got hers, and we set off in opposite directions. I quietly called, 'Grace . . . Grace . . .' as I shone my torch around and moved further and further away from the tents. Suddenly the beam picked up something white behind a bush . . . I approached cautiously . . . there, sobbing uncontrollably, was Grace in her nightdress.

I put my arm around her and lifted her up. I did my best to mollify her and slowly led her back some distance to the camp.

She was still sobbing as we passed Ford's tent when out he shot in his pyjamas: 'Donald! What have you been doing to Grace?!'

I should have known I would get the blame.

Although one section of the film concerned the capture of a rare black panther, no one seemed disturbed that black panthers are only to be found in South America. For the purpose of the shot one was hired, sight unseen, from an American zoo, but on delivery it proved very old and nearly bald on its back. The make-up department was therefore required to spend hours sticking on false hair. Even then it refused to snarl. This we attributed to it probably being toothless.

MGM also discovered rather late in the day that the Kenyans and Ugandans are not water-going people, but as the plot called for some canoes with appropriate crews three boats and sixty oarsmen had to be flown in from the Belgian Congo. (The whole film should really have been made in the Congo – what with the gorillas and everything.) On the Kagera river they looked magnificent – each canoe hewn out of a solid tree trunk, and under the command of a chieftain resplendent in head-dress and necklaces of lions' claws. (Through an interpreter I asked one of the chiefs if he had himself killed the lions; his reply destroyed all such romantic notions: 'I bought the necklace in the local market.') The sixty Congolese natives were in the care of a French Roman Catholic priest who outraged the equally Roman Catholic John Ford by insisting that transport should be arranged each week to enable his charges to visit the nearest brothel, some fifty miles away in a native village: unless they were accorded this facility they would not work. Ford had to agree.

When Ava and Grace saw these long, narrow, shallow canoes in which they were supposed to be transported they were considerably frightened. 'What's wrong?' demanded Ford. Plaintively they pleaded that it was possible the canoes might overturn, that they would be thrown into the river which everyone knew was infested with crocodiles and hippopotomi, and that, after all, there were two stunt girls attached to the unit . . . Ford chewed on his pipe and glowered at them through his dark glasses. He didn't say a word, merely turned, went down to the river and, fully dressed, walked straight in until the water came up to his chest; he then turned and waded out. Passing Ava and Grace as he made his way back to the camera, he said, 'Get in the boat!' They did with no further discussion.

Marcus (Lord Wallscourt) and I teamed up. We were the odd men out and we could commiserate together. He also taught me to drive in his jeep. That it had a left-hand drive produced many problems when later I had to face London traffic, but for the moment my learning took place on pot-holed African dust tracks that did service as roads. He insisted that I spent half our lessons driving in reverse and varying my vision by looking only over my left shoulder or over my right or using only the mirror – a splendid idea as reversing is now as simple for me as going forwards.

With Christmas and New Year approaching we were informed that MGM intended laying on a banquet in the games marquee. Marcus and I decided that we would be very British and wear dinner jackets – in the middle of the African bush! As Ava had to pay a flying visit to London, she kindly agreed to return with a 'mystery' parcel containing my outfit.

Frank Sinatra flew out to join the unit: hitherto Ava had contrived a novel way of keeping in touch with him. Twice a week she would leave the camp in a jeep driven by one of the White Hunters, and head off into the bush for a spot fifteen miles away, where, in the middle of nowhere, a small shed the size of an outdoor privy had been erected. Inside was a solitary telephone and there Ava would talk for half an hour to Frank in Hollywood. MGM had obtained permission to tap the overhead cables which ran across the African continent at that point.

Turkeys, Christmas puddings and champagne were flown in to provide the traditional fare. Marcus and I, resplendent in our dinner jackets, were the cynosure of all eyes and after dinner various members of the unit displayed unsuspected talents for our entertainment on a makeshift stage. Sadly the sound equipment broke down when Frank Sinatra, as the star turn of the cabaret, made his appearance and without his accustomed microphone hardly a sound could be heard of the famous voice.

Around an enormous camp fire the Congolese natives entertained with tribal dances, followed by a form of community singing involving the entire unit, most of whom were well and truly tiddly-pushed. We heard later that around three o'clock in the morning, when two native guards met on their patrol, one remarked, 'The Whites are restless tonight.'

One evening later on Marcus probably saved my life. It was dark when he and I decided to walk out of the camp and along the road. That day John Ford had gone too far and I was trying to pacify him and dissuade him from actually shooting Ford in return for his latest sadistic attack. Suddenly Marcus gripped my arm and hissed, 'Quiet! Stand still!' For a few seconds I hardly breathed. 'Give me your torch!' I passed it to him unlit. He aimed it at a bush about twenty feet away and turned it on. The reflection of two large cat's eyes flashed at us. 'Walk very slowly backward to the camp!' Slowly, slowly we retraced out steps as Marcus kept the beam focused on the receding eyes. Not until we reached the safety of the camp did he explain that it was a lion who might easily have attacked, but for being blinded by the light and not being sure of what lay behind it. It was then that I came out in a cold sweat.

On many occasions I accompanied the White Hunters when they went out to shoot the animals that we were later to eat. Having had no experience with a gun, I was not permitted to shoot – every shot must tell or many hours would be wasted. We drove off into the bush with a native guide who had eyes like a hawk. He could detect the smallest movement of an animal that was otherwise perfectly camouflaged. From the ground the terrain appeared to be heavily wooded, although from the air the trees were few and I was vastly intrigued to observe the technique of self-preservation used by a herd of impala. If one of them detected our presence the whole herd suddenly raced off at great speed to the far side of the nearest tree, which might be no more than twelve inches in diameter. I expected them to appear on the other side of the tree – a herd of fifty could not possibly hide behind one tree – but they just disappeared. Each animal had effected a perfect right-angled turn and in single file had raced off keeping only the trunk of the tree between them and danger. I also witnessed the incredible sight of running an impala to death: eight natives, spaced some distance apart, started to run after a herd of impala which can achieve amazing bursts of speed, but have no staying power. The herd took fright and raced off for a quarter of a mile. The natives kept on running towards them. The herd stopped and looked around. The natives kept on running. The herd then raced off again. The natives continued to run, keeping up a regular pace as in a 10,000 metre track event. The herd stopped again for a breather and then shot off again, but they were slowly tiring. The natives continued to run. The weakest of the herd began to trail behind. This was immediately spotted by the natives and the weakest became the quarry. Stopping and starting, the impala were now visibly tiring, but the natives continued relentlessly. At last, after about three miles one of the impala dropped to the ground exhausted, to be easily picked up and despatched by its pursuers. The hare and the tortoise.

Clark was an expert shot and had brought his own collection of guns with him – and what beautiful things they were, each worth thousands of dollars. I had not see them all together before, until one day when I came out of my tent I found him busy cleaning them at a table. 'Hi, Don' was usually the sum of his conversation for the day, but on this occasion I paused and admired the beautifully chiselled stocks and I asked him about the particular gun on which he was working. The flood gates opened! He waxed poetical for at least fifteen minutes on the virtues of that one gun . . . and then silence as he placed it back on the table.

'Tell me about that one,' I encouraged and pointed to another masterpiece. Again the words flooded out for another fifteen minutes. I followed with another enquiry and yet another. He talked solidly for an hour and a half until he ran out of guns and conversation. An embarrassed silence followed before I said, 'Well, I must be off – see you, Clark.'

'Yup.'

Our next location was on the Northern Frontier in Turkhana. Bunny Allen and his team had already gone ahead to build an identical camp – no question of striking our tents and re-erecting them somewhere else: this was MGM; a perfect replica was built while we were in residence in the original and the entire unit was ferried across in the Dakota.

We worked for some time on an amazing animal farm run by Carr Hartley, where he caught and bred animals for sale to zoos all over the world. In the film this was to be the farm owned by the character that Clark played. Ford's eye was immediately caught by a baby elephant in a stockade: 'We can use it. Ava, get in there with it.' She was given a handful of food as bait and immediately the baby elephant, which stood about three feet high, became her best friend and appeared to be quite playful. The camera just kept turning. When the food was exhausted the elephant became rather annoyed and kept nudging Ava, who began to back away and failed to notice that she was moving towards a muddy pool. Someone made to warn her, but Ford barked, 'Shut up!' Ava slipped and fell backwards into the mud – followed by the elephant. Ford prevented anyone going to her assistance and ordered the camera operator to 'Keep 'em rolling'. I wondered if the final shots were worth risking millions of dollars of insurance on his leading lady.

One day, not being called for work myself, I was on the location watching a scene. The Continuity Girl suddenly remembered that immediately prior to this scene I should have emerged from a building in the background of the shot. This interruption irritated Ford: 'OK – OK! Donald, get back there and come out on Action.'

With considerable trepidation I said, 'The only trouble is that the clothes I am wearing are not those that I wore in the previous scene – they are all back at the camp.'

'If anyone notices, tell 'em to write to me and I'll give 'em their money back – get in there.'

He was quite right; of course no one would be looking at me in the distance when Ava and Clark were in the foreground.

In the course of the film we discover that a 'hostile tribe' (played in the film by the Samburu, a magnificent race of people, akin more to the Sudanese than the Kikuyu) will only allow the characters free passage if one of them will undergo a test. Gable, our hero, agrees to subject himself. He is to stand against a wall with arms and legs spread-eagled while the natives throw spears into the wall around his body: if he flinches, he is a coward and he has failed the test. The rest of us are fearful for his safety, but he tells us that he has done it several times before (and of course he is Clark Gable). He stands against the wooden wall and spreads his arms and legs: a spear hurtles through the air and sticks into the wall inches from Gable's leg; another just misses his waist; another misses his right arm; another his other leg; another his left hand; another lands three inches from his chest . . . As each lands he checks its point of impact. Suddenly one jabs into the wall not more than an inch from his eye! But Gable doesn't flinch, he merely glances at it. He has passed the test. We are all given safe conduct.

Not even a stunt man would stand there and have real spears thrown at him by – in this case – inexpert spearsmen. The technical trick of doing a scene like this is to attach fine piano wires to the wall at the spots where the spears are to land: these are drawn tight and fixed to a frame several yards away. Each spear has a little eyelet at each end of the shaft which runs along its individual wire. The actor stands in position with all the spears embedded in the wall. One by one they are pulled *out* by a fine thread in *reverse order*. After the film has been processed it is then printed backwards – a spear being pulled out appears to be thudding in. Very clever. But the problem is enormous for the actor: he has to react in reverse. He must start with his eyes on the final spear. As it is pulled out he must then look straight ahead. The 'concern' in his eyes must disappear, not grow. To do this with one spear would be bad enough, but Gable was required to do it with nine!

Clark and I arrived on the scene as they were setting it up. Ford came towards us and Clark nonchalantly asked, 'How are you doing this, Jack? – Reverse?'

'Yup – OK with you?'

'Yup.'

When they were ready Clark stood in position and merely asked in which order the spears were to be removed – eye; chest right; chest left; hand left; leg right . . . During his many years in films he had had to do many similar shots.

'Roll 'em, Action.'

I watched in abject admiration at his expertise while his eyes cracked back to centre as each spear was yanked out. Just one take was all Clark needed. 'Print it!' yelled Ford, and the unit gave Clark a round of applause.

Many years later, in a film called *The Siege of Sydney Street*, I was required to do a scene when my extended hand had to be pinned to a wall by a knife thrown at me. I immediately remembered Clark: 'How are you doing this?' I nonchalantly asked the director. 'Reverse?'

'Yes.'

I clenched my hand with the knife on its wire between my fingers.

'Turn over. Action.'

I stared at the knife and as it was pulled out I cracked my head back to centre. 'Print it!' yelled the director. 'Where did you learn to do that?'

But Clark had done it nine times.

The MGM unit now moved back to Nairobi for a short respite before setting off to the next location at Mount Kenya.

Our main camp had been on the Kagera river, in Uganda, at that time still a British colony under the Governorship of Sir Andrew Cohen. During our stay he had visited the camp: a special tent was erected in a central clearing, with two soldiers permanently on guard at the entrance. (Any marauder with a knife could have got in at the rear!) The Union Jack fluttered from a flagpole three yards in front of the tent. It was all wonderfully British. Sir Andrew stayed with us for several days and in return he now invited Ava, Grace, Clark, Frank, Ford and me to stay for a weekend in Government House, Entebbe, near the capital, Kampala. At the last moment Ford decided that he was too busy to join the rest of us in the Dakota which was to fly us there – he would travel by himself in the small Anson aircraft which, I have so far failed to mention, was also under exclusive contract to MGM. Actually Ford wasn't busy at all – he was merely practising his one-upmanship. A special car would now have to stand by at Entebbe airport for the unscheduled arrival of an Anson.

In the film Clark and I wore white dinner jackets and these we were allowed to borrow for the weekend; Frank had brought his, and both Ava and Grace had brought enough clothes for any contingency. We were greeted at the airport and whisked off to Government House, idyllically situated on a hill overlooking Lake Victoria, where Sir Andrew awaited us. We wandered around the grounds and were given tea on the verandah – the girls had changed into charming dresses. At five thirty Ford arrived, wearing crease-less baggy grey trousers, an ancient sports jacket, a washed-out blue shirt, a dark blue tie with a dripping egg-stain motif on it, plimsolls on his feet and a baseball cap on his head. (He must have borrowed the outfit – I never saw him wear any of the items again.) He had really put himself out for a visit to the Queen's representative. At about six o'clock the governor suggested that it was time to dress for dinner. 'Dress for dinner?' said Ford. 'This is all I've brought with me!' After the briefest hesitation Sir Andrew tactfully announced, 'Very well, we will not dress for dinner.' Ava and Grace were bitterly disappointed – they had been looking forward to wearing 'the lot', and bang went our white dinner jackets.

Drinks were served and shortly two members of the governor's staff turned up in full dinner jackets. They cast distressed glances at us and discreetly withdrew, only to appear fifteen minutes later in ordinary suits.

Towards the end of dinner I was intrigued to notice that the electric lights were dimmed as a result of an unseen signal, the governor rose and proposed the health of 'Her Majesty the Queen'. Lady Cohen took the ladies off and then Sir Andrew asked, 'Would anyone care to look at Africa by night?'

All the men dutifully trooped out on to the lawn which stretched away to a balustrade. The sight was magical: a full moon hovered over the great lake and was perfectly reflected in the glass-like water, lights twinkled from the town below us, cicadas creaked in the surrounding undergrowth and the scent from the flowers and shrubs was powerful on the hot air, the Union Jack hung limply from the flag post; the whole effect was dreamlike. I just stood there drinking it all in . . . Suddenly I was aware of a splashing sound. I looked round and there was the entire hierarchy of Government House peeing on the lawn!

'Would anyone care to look at Africa by night?' has since become a euphemism in the Sinden household.

The next day the Cohens took us over to a garden party given, in the grounds of his palace, by the Kabaka of Buganda – King Freddie as he was affectionately known. No one was to know that within a very short time he would be deposed and forced into exile in England, where I met him on many occasions before he died at a tragically early age.

Back to earth again, Frank returned to Hollywood and the rest of us set off for Mount Kenya where we were accommodated at the Mwingo Hotel. Originally a large private house, it had been transformed into a hotel by building several identical 'blocks' in the grounds joined to the house by a covered way. Each block contained six identical suites of rooms. Late on Saturday night, when we were not due to work the following day, Ava and I joined another couple for a little party in one of these suites after dinner. We all had rather a lot to drink and at about two a.m. Ava decided that she must go to bed but was a little apprehensive of the longish walk back to the main house where her rooms were: she asked me to accompany her. The other couple insisted that I should return afterwards to 'finish off the bottle'. We were all in a merry mood. Having deposited Ava, I began my return journey and, knowing the situation between the couple I was about to rejoin, I was sure that they would now be in bed together . . . In my inebriated state I thought what a lark it would be to surprise them by flinging open the door and saying, 'Put her down – you don't know where she's been!' Not very funny in the cold light of print, but at that moment I thought it hilarious and giggled to myself at the prospect. I tiptoed up the stairs and along the corridor. I could hardly stop myself from laughing aloud. What a jape! Silently I took hold of the door knob and slowly turned it . . . I took a deep breath and threw open the door. 'PUT HER DOWN – YOU DON'T KNOW WHERE SHE'S BEEN!' The room was in darkness, but a light was immediately turned on . . .

Disaster!

I had returned to the wrong block: sitting up in bed and staring at me with horror was Clark and beside him a girl – both of them starkers . . . Unfortunately I could not stop myself smiling as I said, 'Oh my God – I'm so sorry – I thought it was room 18.' My predicament was worsened because it *was* 18 and I wanted 24. I backed out of the room mumbling excuses.

The next day I had to try to make my peace with Clark who remained convinced that I had done it intentionally. 'Yeah – Yeah,' he said.

We now had to return to the MGM studios in London to shoot all the interior scenes. Someone must have pointed out to Ford that he had not been exactly charming to me and when I arrived for my first day's work I found that he had caused a large notice – BE KIND TO DONALD WEEK – to be painted at the entrance to the sound stage.

One scene concerned a dinner party with six of us around a table: having done the master shot we were then filmed in pairs. I was seated beside Ava who by this time in the scene was supposed to be quite tiddly and she delivered herself of a long speech attacking Gable, at the end of which she wheeled on me saying: '. . . What do you think?' to which I had to answer in a sober stuffy, English way, 'I entirely agree with you.' Apart from listening, this was my only contribution to the dialogue and it finished the scene.

After Take One Ford said, 'Cut. – No Ava. I want you to . . .' and he gave her several bits of advice. As I listened during Take Two I knew that she had not fully comprehended what he had said . . .

'. . . What do you think?'

'I entirely agree with you.'

'Cut. No, Ava . . .'

It is a strange thing that, more often than not, when a director gives notes everyone seems to understand what is wanted – except the person to whom he is talking. We embarked upon Take Three. Watching and listening to Ava I knew that she still wasn't giving him what he wanted . . .

'. . . What do you think?'

'I entirely agree with you.'

'Cut. No, Ava . . .'

On and on we went; Take Four; Five; Six . . . As we started on Take Eleven I just knew it was right – not only right but splendid; everything inside of me was willing Ava to keep it up! That's it! That's it! Jolly good, Ava! Don't drop it now! Hold on – hold on! She wheeled on me:

'. . . What do you think?'

And I dried stone dead. My jaw dropped – I could think of no answer . . . There was a terrible silence . . . No one said 'Cut'. Everyone on the set knew that it was a splendid take. The silence continued. An arc lamp hissed. Ford moved in my direction. Of course he is going to kill me. He came close to my other side, away from Ava, and glowered at me through the dark glasses. At long last he said very gently, 'Donald, I could kick your arse.'

Thank God Take Twelve went smoothly and was, if anything, even better.

One morning I awoke with a ghastly pain in my stomach (colitis it turned out to be) – it was agony, but I had been brought up in the tradition that the show must go on so I made for the studio and sat quietly on the set waiting for my call. Ford passed by and enquired if I was all right. I pulled myself together and said, 'Fine, thank you.' I didn't want any more trouble. In my first scene, a duologue with Clark, I thought that I managed to conceal my discomfort, but at the end of the rehearsal Ford again enquired if I was all right. I knew that I was capable of continuing and again assured him that I was. We completed that part of the scene, but when we finished a rehearsal of the next part Clark asked me quietly if there was something troubling me. Actor to actor I confided to him that indeed I did have a pain in my stomach.

'Then why the hell don't you admit it? We can all go home for the day.'

'I can't do that,' I remonstrated. 'I can keep going.'

'To hell with that — it all comes off the insurance,' replied Clark.

At the end of the next rehearsal Ford again asked if I was all right. 'Well as a matter of fact, I do have a slight pain . . .' I began but was interrupted by Ford springing into action.

'Bring him over here! Sit him down! Send for the nurse!' and then, inexplicably, he sent for the make-up man: 'Spray his forehead and neck with glycerine — put some bags under his eyes.' Shortly the nurse hurried on to the set. 'Just look at him,' Ford ordered. ' — He looks terrible — look how he's sweating — he should be sent home.' The nurse agreed. 'OK. It's a wrap for the day,' announced Ford.

Ford disliked any interference in the making of any of his films. He was despotic. It was then customary in Hollywood for all the footage of a film to be handed over at the end of shooting to the editor who could then impose his ideas on how it was cut together. Ford did everything he could to forestall any possible alternatives to what he wanted. I saw him many times actually walk in front of the camera at the precise moment that he intended that shot to finish.

During the time in the studio he never started work before nine a.m. and always finished at four thirty p.m. and still got about as much 'in the can' as other directors working from eight thirty a.m. to six p.m. He also disliked producers. At our very first meeting I had asked him who was the producer of *Mogambo*. 'The office boy back in the States,' he snapped. I was present one day when the producer came on to the set. Ford caught sight of him and ordered all work to cease immediately. He then advanced on poor Sam Zimbalist: 'Yes?'

'Don't let me interrupt,' said Sam.

'If I come into your office I expect you to stop work, so I stop for you. What do you want?'

Sam explained that he was a little worried that we were three days behind schedule . . . 'How many pages represent three days?' asked Ford (who knew perfectly well).

'Well, about three pages,' ventured Sam.

'Bring me my script,' roared Ford to a minion. When it arrived he opened it at random and tore out three pages. 'We're on schedule. Back to work.'

We never shot those three pages.

My character had to collapse and be put to bed in delirium. After diagnosing the fever Gable tells my distraught wife (Grace) what attention I am to be given and the two of them then go out on to the verandah to play a scene talking in whispers so as not to disturb the patient. We did the scene on the bed with me tossing and turning and sprayed with glycerine to simulate sweat. The camera and lights were then taken outside for the next part of the scene and the assistant director told me that as I looked so comfortable, I might just as well stay where I was. Grace and Clark then rehearsed the next part and then the stand-ins came in while their scene was lit, which took about an hour. Grace and Clark then returned for the take.

'OK. Quiet please. Roll 'em. Action.'

The scene started, but suddenly the sound-man broke in, 'Sorry. I can hear the camera humming.' The camera was checked. 'Quiet please. Roll 'em. Action' . . . Again the sound-man broke in: 'I think it could be a loose board on the verandah.' The verandah was checked and again, 'Quiet please. Roll 'em. Action,' but once more the sound-man complained, 'I think it must be a squeaking arc.' This meant checking four different arc lamps and changing the carbons. 'Quiet please. Roll 'em. Action.' Still the sound-man interrupted: 'I can't think what it can be. Come and listen through the earphones, Mr Ford.' At long last they discovered the source. Oh dear. Why did it have to be me? I had dozed off and was gently whistling in my sleep. This time Ford didn't say 'I could kick your arse.' He did. That's what woke me up.

One evening, as filming drew to a close, we were all invited, plus husbands and wives, to a party given by Anne Holland-Martin and her husband whom we had met in Entebbe. I asked Clark if he would be wearing a dinner jacket: 'A dinner jacket? Gee, no.' I turned up in a lounge suit only to find everyone else in dinner jackets and Clark laughing his head off: he had turned the tables on me because I had worn one in the African bush.

In the crowded room I was talking to Diana when over her shoulder I saw Clark coming towards us. I chose my moment. 'Diana, you haven't met Clark.' She turned and came face to face with her idolised Rhett Butler from *Gone With the Wind*.

Clark turned on the full charm, the jaw set and the mouth twisted into his famous smile, his eyes twinkled and the eyebrows quirked: 'Hi, Diana' . . . I have never before or since known Diana speechless. Her knees buckled and her mouth tried 'Hello', but no sound came out. She walked on air for days.

Poor Clark could go nowhere without being recognised and accosted. He was even asked for autographs in remote African grass-hutted villages. It was the first time I had encountered such fame and I asked if it worried him to be pestered for autographs: 'The time to worry is when it stops,' he said.

Meanwhile, as a new member of the Rank Organisation, I began to receive invitations to film premieres. Diana and I had been seeing a lot of Ava during the hours off from shooting and one day she asked what we were doing that evening and I told her that we were attending the premiere of the latest comedy from Ealing Studios, *The Titfield Thunderbolt*. 'I love those Ealing films – do you think I could come with you?' I telephoned the office and asked if I could have an extra ticket.

'Not a hope.'

'Not even one?'

'No. It is also the night of the British Film Academy Awards – the seats were allocated weeks ago.'

'Oh dear. Do you think there will be any returns?'

'I doubt it. Why do you want another one?'

'Ava Gardner wants to come.'

After a stunned silence – 'I'll call you back, Donald.'

A little later: 'You've got your extra ticket – we've moved J. Arthur' (Rank).

10

THE RANKERY

J. Arthur Rank once said, 'I know nothing about films but I can mix
a good bag of flour and I can buy the brains that do know about
films.'

As a devout Methodist who taught in Sunday School, he thought
that his efforts could be helped by showing religious films and being
a millionaire he therefore founded a studio to make them. Later, as
the studio was not fully occupied, he expanded into making secular
films. Finding that no one would distribute them, he bought a chain
of cinemas, which devoured more films than his studio could make,
which meant a bigger studio. The Rank empire just grew and grew.

J. Arthur was the chairman of the vast conglomerate and John
Davis the managing director. J.D., as everyone called him (some of
the braver ones even to his face), was a terrifying figure: a tycoon
who ruled his empire from an office in South Street, Mayfair. Heads
rolled – important heads – when he was displeased. Our only contact with him came at large functions when we shook his hand on
arrival. Otherwise we only glimpsed him sitting at the top table
surrounded by henchmen at film trade dinners. The main studios,
at Iver Heath in Buckinghamshire, were called Pinewood (which
we knew as Buchenwald, on the mistaken assumption that this was
the literal German translation). The head of production was an
American with a lined, florid face and silvery hair named Earl St
John (not 'Sinjon'). I was once seated opposite him at a film-world
luncheon. The talk was naturally of films. He suddenly addressed
me: 'What do you think is the most important ingredient in a film?'

Playing for time I said, 'Well, I must admit it helps to have a good
script . . .', but before I could add anything he jumped in and said,
You hear that everybody? The boy's got something – tell 'em
Donald!'

Below Earl St John came the individual producers and directors
who could hire the services of actors like me, who were under

contract to a company within the Rank group, for half their annual salary. Thus a contract artist needed to make only two films a year to be worth his contract: anything over two and he was making a theoretical profit. (He wasn't, but the company within the company was.) I managed to keep up an average 3.14 films per year over seven years.

The heads of the Contract Artists Department was a charming woman named Olive Dodds. Beside her worked – or, rather, overworked – Theo Cowan who was responsible for publicity and all the nefarious extra-mural activities, such as endless personal appearances which averaged two a week per head. Olive and Theo were the perfect people for their jobs – Olive always serene, kind and attentive, Theo always snowed under with paper, but able to smooth over any difficulty with a quip. He had been likened to Groucho Marx. His remarks always sprang so easily from the situation. When our second son Marc was born he sent Diana a beautiful bouquet. The next day I thanked him and he was rather abashed, 'Oh, no – it's the least I could do.'

'Ah, but it was sweet of you, Theo.'

'No – it *is* the least – I checked.'

On another occasion an actress was in his office having hysterics at the prospect of travelling in an aeroplane. Theo tried to pacify her and said, '. . . But there is nothing safer than flying – it's crashing that is dangerous.'

I really loved every minute of my time with the Rankery – for eight years Diana and I were cocooned. My biggest mistake was to believe that, because I was attached to that famous stable, someone somewhere was looking after me and moulding my career. When a new script arrived I automatically thought that it had been specially chosen as the perfect vehicle for me. Much, much later I discovered that·most of them had already been turned down by more senior contract artists. If I hadn't liked them I, too, should have turned them down, but it was a precarious path to tread – actors who turned down too many found that their contracts were not renewed at the end of the year.

Hot from *Mogambo* I was cast as the romantic lead opposite the French actress Odile Versois in *A Day to Remember*, produced by Betty Box and directed by Ralph Thomas. I was to work with Betty and Ralph many times over the years: Betty the most feminine of women in a tough man's world and Ralph the most cuddly of directors. Coming to him immediately after John Ford was quite a shock and it took some time to reassure me that all directors were not ogres.

What a delightful film this turned out to be (and I am still surprised that it is my only one never to have been shown on television). The plot concerned a darts club from a London pub going on a day's outing to Boulogne, where I was to meet a young French girl and fall for her head over heels. At the end of the day she comes to the quayside to bid farewell as the ferry leaves the harbour − will we ever see each other again?

Now it is rare for everything − camera, lights, background action, actors, and so on − to be perfect in one Take, and even if they are, another one for safety is always wise. The ferry we used was not, however, for our exclusive use, but plied in regular service between Boulogne and Dover. As the rules laid down that once this ship had left the quay it must continue its journey, the captain flatly refused to take it fifty yards out into the harbour and then return for a second Take. We had to do five, which meant that five times, with the camera mounted on the quay, Odile waving and me leaning over the side of the ship, the ferry slowly moved out of the harbour and chugged to Dover before returning to Boulogne to do it all over again. Five Takes took five days.

Betty Box had married Peter Rogers, a scriptwriter who was then starting a career as a producer and would in years to come achieve enormous success with the 'Carry On' series. I promise not to give the plot of every film I made, but Peter had secured the rights of *Sylvester*, a delightful satirical novel by Edward Hyams, about a young Naval officer who, at the end of a drunken evening, welds some old iron, including the frame of a pram and the balls from a pawnbroker's sign, to the mast of a warship. This is seen early next morning by the crew of a ship from 'a foreign power', who think it must be a new secret weapon. They make a report which ultimately reaches their President, who decrees that his country, too, must possess this 'secret weapon'. Soon spies of all nationalities are involved. Ours report this activity to the Prime Minister, who immediately questions the Admiralty, who of course know nothing about it, but dare not admit that they don't. They question their boffins who in turn dare not admit *their* own ignorance of the device. Questions are then asked of Sylvester, who tries to admit that it was all a joke − but too late − every ship in the Royal Navy is now being fitted with a similar 'weapon' and foreign countries are queueing up with orders. There is only one way to stop him from blowing the gaff: he must be silenced. But how? A *British* government could not possibly liquidate him; instead he is given a new name and passport and exiled after his apparent 'demise'. That was the novel. In the film I would like to have said that I played the title role, but *Sylvester* was retitled *You Know What Sailors Are* and the plot ceased to bear much relation to the original. Invited to a Middle East country, Sylvester becomes heavily involved in high jinks in the harem of the President, played by the Russian actor Akim Tamiroff. Tamiroff had emigrated to America in 1923 and since made scores of films in Hollywood. *You Know What Sailors Are* was my fourth.

My first scene with Akim was a 'tracking' shot: rails were laid across the set and as we walked beside them the camera was pulled along on a 'dolly' ahead of us. Akim and I had only just been introduced and at the first rehearsal he took me by the arm and we walked along together. This was quite in character – he was the 'President'. It was also friendly – apparently. At each rehearsal he repeated this gesture. We were then ready for the first Take. Akim now held my arm in a grip of iron (he was a very strong man, anyway). Too late I realised that he was holding me half a step ahead of him. While he was happily facing the camera I was forced to talk to him in profile!

Clever, I thought, but don't get caught again – but time and again I did.

We were seated side by side on a very low eastern couch and during our conversation he first offered me a glass of tea and then some Turkish delight, saying, 'Your drink? . . . Turkish delight?' The camera was on a level with our heads, but the director, Ken Annakin, was standing – his eyeline was therefore above the lens. We first did the 'two-shot' 'Your drink? . . . Turkish delight?' 'Print it.' Then we did Akim's close up: I watched as expertly he raised the glass and held it – closer to himself than before – so that it was perfectly framed in the shot, before passing it to me. (This is something the beginner has to be taught – and very unnatural it seems. If something is not *seen* to be passed it is quite possible that it is never seen at all by the audience who will be mystified.) He then raised the dish, again perfectly framed – 'Turkish delight?' There is nothing prettier to watch than expertise.

It was now my turn: again Akim's hand offered me the glass of tea but this time the rim was about half an inch above the bottom of my chin and closer to it than previously. The Turkish delight followed, again exactly half an inch above my chin and again closer than I expected. Akim had foreseen that from Ken Annakin's higher eyeline that half an inch would be undetected. Yet when the editor got to work later he found that at those two moments he could only use Akim's close-up or the two-shot – my close-up was unusable: not only was my face partly obscured, but I also had to look down my nose at what I was being offered. By his expertise Akim established that 'Your drink,' and 'Turkish delight?' were best seen in his own close-up.

Another trick of his was to rehearse a duologue with great intensity until a very positive sequence of timing was built up – a set rhythm. This timing took us through the 'two-shots' and through his own close-ups (which were always done first, because he was the elder), but when it came to mine – or any other unfortunate actor's – he would brilliantly vary the timing of his own lines, which he delivered standing behind the camera. Lines which earlier had been fast would become slow and vice versa (the difference was almost imperceptible, but enough). On reflex the other actor would unconsciously change his own timing so that once again the editor could not match that close-up to the rhythm of the scene – the only usable one was Akim's.

In spite of this, Akim and I became great friends: he was a superb technician and I learnt much from him. He explained that he had developed many of his upstaging tricks in Hollywood to counter the leading players who were always covered in close-up for every inch of the film: the character actor had to fight to get his face seen at all. He then proceeded to teach me the parries to all his tricks – on condition that I never passed on the secrets. Sorry! My lips must remain sealed.

In the course of the film a demonstration model of Sylvester's 'secret weapon' has been set up on the coast of England in a sand-bagged enclosure, surrounded by a group of interested RN personnel. Sylvester is trying to prove that it is nothing but a pile of scrap iron. At that moment an aeroplane flies overhead in which – unbeknown to us – a bomb has been planted. As it passes over the 'sights' of the 'weapon' it blows up. The RN personnel are now convinced the weapon is genuine. We were to film this scene at eight thirty a.m. on the coast near Weymouth, in the flight path of a plane in regular service between Blackbushe airport and the Chan-

nel Islands. Arrangements had been made that the pilot would fly
on out to sea and then circle back to give us a chance of a second Take
before continuing his journey. And the explosion and disintegra-
tion of the plane? That would all be done by an optical trick later.

We stayed the night in Dorchester where we were called at five
thirty in the morning; make-up at six fifteen a.m., a quick breakfast
and off to the coast to be in position by eight a.m. The prop
department had got up even earlier to erect the 'weapon' and the
wall of sand bags. More cars arrive bearing the producer, director,
art director, hair-dressers, make-up men, wardrobe men: the whole
vast unit slowly builds up. The actors are checked and double-
checked – we have only this chance to get the shot – the weather
does not really matter, but thank goodness it is a clear, bright, if
chilly morning. People begin to check their watches . . . Ssh!
Listen! Yes. We can hear the distant sound of the approaching plane.
Someone can actually see it, Tension. Here we go. 'Turn over . . .'
Unbelievable as it may seem, it is only now that we discover that we
have no camera. We watch the plane fly overhead, we see it turn and
circle back. There is no way we can tell the pilot that it has all been a
waste of his time. The camera and its crew were lost somewhere
between Weymouth and Dorchester.

When I first read the script I noticed a short stage direction that
slightly unnerved me: chased by the scantily dressed girls of the
harem, Sylvester swam to his escape across a pool. Ken Annakin
told me there was no alternative – I would have to learn to swim in
time to do the shot. So each evening after returning from Pinewood
I went off to the Chelsea public swimming baths. One evening – it
was in October – the water was ice cold as I dipped in my toe. I
know that under these circumstances one should dive in, but I went
down the steps at the shallow end and was standing, gibbering with
cold in three feet of water, waiting for the courage to duck under. A
nasty little boy at the deep end executed a beautiful dive and,
cleaving through the water, came to a skidding halt in front of me,
and with starry eyes asked, ' 'Ere, mister, wasn't you in *The Cruel
Sea*?'

My lips were numb but I managed to stammer, 'Nnno – nno –
nnot mme.'

After two months of intensive lessons all I could achieve was to
swim across the bath – underwater. But when we came to the scene
in the film, the pool was only two feet deep. I walked across!

★

The rights of a novel had been touted around the studios for some time, but no producer would make it. At last, for a pittance, it landed on Betty Box's desk. Being allowed only a very low budget, she used as many contract artists as possible and, with Ralph Thomas as director, shooting started on *Doctor in the House*. Apparently at that time films about doctors were thought to be death at the box office so none of the original publicity photographs showed us in white coats – we all had to wear sports jackets. They even thought of changing the title. Dirk Bogarde (the odds-on favourite in the Rank stable), Kenneth More (with *Genevieve* in the can, but not yet shown), Donald Houston and I were the four medical students with James Robertson Justice breathing fire down our necks as the eminent surgeon, Sir Lancelot Spratt.

With Betty and Ralph in charge, *Doctor in the House* was sheer *fun* to make – we were all young and exuberant. As Dirk, who was sporting his first status symbol, a Rolls-Royce, had discovered that the left side of his face was more attractive than his right, he always secured a position for himself on the right of the screen. Not for ten years, until he made *Victim*, was the public allowed to see his right profile – and then he was immediately hailed as an 'actor'. But Dirk is no fool – he knew that after fourteen years under contract one did not *suddenly* become a good actor. I soon discovered that I had the same problem – my left profile is better than my right – so sometimes there was a bit of a scramble for position. But Dirk had top billing.

We used University College, London, as our film hospital, 'St Swithin's'. For one scene I had to drive an ambulance, with Donald Houston beside me, down Gower Street at fifty miles per hour, with the traffic lights showing green. As we approached them they were to change red, but we were to continue against them. To do this we had the assistance of the police. The whole of Gower Street was closed to traffic, which was only allowed to cross it when their lights were at green. With the lights manually operated, the policeman changed ours from green to red while holding the crossing traffic on their red. (Are you with me?) Certain other cars belonging to the film company and driven by stunt men were to be narrowly avoided by the ambulance as they proceeded up and down Gower Street. All was ready. The red lights halted all crossing traffic and from the end of the street I saw the director's signal to go. I was doing fifty miles per hour as we approached the lights . . . but the policeman pressed the wrong button. Instead of our lights changing from green to red, the crossing lights changed from red to green. I was suddenly faced by a stream of traffic across my bows! I clamped on my brakes and by a miracle slithered and threaded my way through.

With no great optimism the Rank Organisation subjected the film to a sneak preview at a suburban cinema. A small group of us sat in the circle and *Doctor in the House* flashed on to the screen. It was soon being greeted with ecstatic laughter. When James Robertson Justice asked Dirk, as they examined a patient, 'What's the bleeding time?' to which Dirk answered, 'Half past two, sir' the laugh was so enormous that it drowned lines of the next scene. Two days later we were called back to the studio to film a short scene with no dialogue that was then inserted to cover the laugh. We were a success.

Doctor in the House created a record by being seen by more people in its first year on release than any previous film: 17,000,000 tickets were sold. Someone speculated that there were 34,000,000 people of cinema-going age in the country, so 'why didn't the other 17,000,000 go?'

Being under contract to the Rankery also meant that one had the backing of an enormous and extremely efficient publicity department and we were all expected to cooperate in their schemes. Numerous interviews were arranged: reporters and gossip columnists had apparently endless inches of column space and the Rankery was eager that these should be filled with news of their 'stars'. Any excuse for a photograph or a story was leaped on. It was not uncommon for the face of a beautiful budding actress to be blazoned across the pages of the national press long before she ever appeared in a film – if she ever did.

Almost every week a new film opened in the West End and was given the ballyhoo of a gala premiere. Each contract artist was allotted a chauffeur-driven Rolls-Royce. I would race home after filming all day at Pinewood to find the gleaming monster purring at my front door. A quick shower and dive into a dinner jacket. Diana would be putting the last touches to her make-up before donning a long evening gown. (The number of these she required nearly broke me.) Then into the Rolls trying to look as if we owned it. The journey to the West End was usually occupied in exchanging news of the day's happenings.

In Leicester Square the great cinemas were the scenes of gala premieres: the Empire, Odeon, Warner and Leicester Square Theatre, and in the Haymarket, the Carlton and the Gaumont. Psychologically there was a 'perfect' time to arrive, but as everyone knew it, invariably a queue of cars developed – it was essential to alight directly outside the main door, because only a narrow red carpeted corridor was kept clear by harassed commissionaires. Arc lamps flooded the area around the cinema, police, mounted and on foot, fought to keep the fans at bay. We were instructed to turn on the car's interior lights once we were in the vicinity of the cinema. At last the car pulled up at the required spot and the door was opened by a bemedalled commissionaire: I stepped out and assisted Diana, praying that neither of us would trip. Immediately, numberless cameras – professional and amateur – flashed. Quite blinded, we beamed toothy smiles in their direction. As each car arrived the crowd screamed. (The keen ones had been waiting there for hours to secure a front position.) From all around one heard 'Donald! Donald!' and one hoped that colleagues did not hear that occasional voice, seemingly louder than the others, which said, 'Who is it?' Autograph books were pushed forward, but we had been advised not to stop – bow ties and handkerchiefs were often 'acquired' by eager fans. Ahead of us more arc lamps positioned in the foyer glared at us through the glass doors and we aimed ourselves towards them in the fond hope that no steps lay before us. Inside newsreel cameras were whirring and from the blackness an apparently body-less hand greeted us. Sometimes the hand held a microphone which was clutched by mistake before a voice asked us to 'say a few words'. Out of the lights our eyes slowly adjusted to the comparatively dimly-lit foyer and we could see friends who had just witnessed our ordeal, grouped around the stairs. But first there was the official welcoming party – the cinema manager and his staff – and there was Theo and his team of mother hens ready to smooth down any ruffled feathers while trying to get the brood into their seats before the film began. More screams announced a new arrival and everyone turned to see who it was as more dinner-jacketed photographers tried to get us away from our wives to be photographed with beautiful, semi-dressed starlets.

These prints so often saw the light of day captioned, 'Mr Actor and Miss Actress attending last night's premiere' and caused many rumours.

More often than not, if the performance was not followed by a party or reception, pairs or individuals would team up and go off to a restaurant. In the early hours there was invariably an invitation:

'Everyone back to Anthony Steel's for coffee'. It was easy to forget that some of us were due on the set at eight thirty a.m. which meant a make-up call at seven forty-five a.m.

When one of our films was on release, we were expected to make personal appearances at cinemas where it was being shown. These were known as PAs and they became part of our lives.

The visit has been well publicised in advance, so crowds can be expected outside the cinema lit by flood lamps like a mini-premiere. Wearing a dinner jacket and accompanied by a Rank publicity man, I step out of a limousine (the door opened by a uniformed commissionaire) to more shouts of 'Donald! Donald!' to be greeted by the cinema's manager and taken to his office to be offered drinks from a bottle-laden table (to be cleared and locked away the moment we leave). A pimply, dinner-jacketed youth, invariably introduced as 'My assistant, David', enters breathlessly, announces, 'Nine minutes to go' and we make our way back stage along corridors, beaming at smiling usherettes, to stand at the side of the gigantic screen as the last few minutes of the trailers are shown: strange elongated figures, hideously foreshortened, dance about to the amplified sound on giant loudspeakers only a few feet away.

The stabbing lights from the projector fade, the house lights glow from crevices in the ornate plasterwork, and satin curtains are drawn in front of the screen. A microphone on a stand is carried on, or appears from the floor, and is encircled by a beam from a spotlight. A pause. The manager wipes his brow, clears his throat and marches on: 'Thank you . . . those of you who saw . . . will remember . . . and in . . . and later in . . . It gives me great pleasure to introduce . . . the ever-popular star of . . . Mr (a quick look at the paper in his hand) Donald Sinden.' (Without that 'paper in his hand' I was once introduced as 'Mr Donald Shiner' and even, once, as 'Mr Ronald Swindon'.)

I step forward to a storm of applause and shake the extended hand of the manager, who departs leaving me at the microphone. 'Thank you – thank you. Good evening, ladies and gentlemen . . .' followed by some well-rehearsed jokes pertinent to the film they are about to see, then an exit into the wings and back to the office to meet various friends of the local management. Photographs, which will later hang on the wall of the office, are autographed; more autographs on the way out, into the limousine with its interior lights on, and the twinkling 'star' shoots off.

If we were free from the studio we might be sent out of town for an intensive week or two visiting a different cinema each night, although this more often applied to the attractive young girls who were not otherwise finding themselves overworked. If busy at the studio we were still expected to do the London suburbs on one evening a week. It was quite possible to appear on stage in Greenford before the start of the film and then race off to appear at the end of the film in Ilford. On one occasion I did three in one evening (at the second the film was stopped halfway through). Place names became irrevocably connected with the local cinema: Regal/Barnet, Gaumont/Finchley, Commodore/Orpington, Odeon/Greenford, Gaumont-State/Kilburn, Carlton/Haymarket, Dominion/Tottenham Court Road.

One night at a party a South American Ambassador made a pass at Kay Kendall and tried to make an assignation for dinner one evening the following week. Kay was equally desperately trying to escape from his clutches and protested that next week every evening was booked for a series of PAs.

'PAs? What are they?'

'Personal appearances – in a different place each evening.'

'Perhaps I could accompany you?' He took out and consulted a diary. 'Would Wednesday be convenient?'

Cornered, Kay consulted her diary: 'Wednesday is the Commodore/Orpington.'

'Very well, Wednesday. I will call for you in my car. What do you have to wear?'

'Oh, I shall be wearing full evening dress.'

On Wednesday Kay opened the door of her flat to find the Ambassador in white tie and tails, a sash, a collar decoration and a row of miniature medals. After a drink they went down to his chauffeur-driven Cadillac and off they whooshed to Orpington where they drew up outside the flood-lit cinema. The Ambassador emerged from the car and gripped the hand of the uniformed and bemedalled commissionaire:

'Commodore Orpington, I am delighted to meet you!'

My worst experience was at the Gaumont-State in Kilburn, which was one of the largest in the country, holding 4,000 people. As we waited in the wings I noticed that the manager was very nervous and sweating profusely – his job called for him to appear on stage only twice a year at the most; we had to do it all the time and were hardened to it. For the fourth time he told me that he '. . . will go on first, make a short speech of introduction, and as I mention your name I will extend my left arm towards you. It's a very big auditorium, you know, but we've got two microphones . . .' With that the house lights came on, two microphones rose, like snakes charmed from the floor, and were immediately bathed in a pool of white spotlight.

I was rather shaken to find that, after the manager had made his way to the centre and begun his speech, I could not hear a word he was saying. Just how big was that auditorium? Did it eat up the sound? There was no possibility of hearing my name. So that was why he would 'extend his arm!' . . . And there it was . . . I strode on to a recorded fanfare and as I shook the extended arm he looked at me in apologetic desperation, hoarsely whispering 'The microphones aren't working!' and left me . . .

I gazed out at the great void and my mind raced: I had been a stage actor for eleven years and had never failed to make myself heard: having first checked that the microphones were indeed not working, I moved in front of them, filled my diaphragm, and asked if those sitting at the back could hear me: little elfin voices assured me that they could, and I embarked on my speech. I had only uttered two or three sentences when I heard 'Psst, Psst,' coming from the wings. I looked across and saw the manager pointing at the microphones and giving me a thumbs-up signal so I returned to my first position – but no; they were still out of order. Luckily the audience was amused by the whole business. I again started my speech from the front. But again I heard, 'Psst, Psst, Psst,' and saw the thumbs up . . . but yet again the microphones were defunct.

I remembered having seen Danny Kaye at the Palladium sit nonchalantly on the footlights, dangling his feet in the orchestra pit and taking the audience into his confidence: perhaps I could do the same . . . the audience loved it and I again started my speech when, to my horror, down the centre aisle came a girl carrying an illuminated tray and crying, 'Chocolates! Ices! Chocolates! Ices!'

I could not believe it. I called her to me and asked for a choc-ice, which she solemnly gave me in return for my sixpence and returned up the aisle as if nothing were untoward. The audience could see the joke and from that moment roared with laughter at anything I said. I stayed on for twenty minutes. I did not know that off stage all hell had broken out. Heads were rolling.

As the publicity man said: 'Suppose it had happened to one of our new starlets!'

★

Before moving on to my next film, let me add a postscript to *Mogambo*. The Rank Organisation had received what sounded like stupendous sums for sub-letting me to MGM and I looked forward eagerly to my half share of the profits. At the end of the year came the grand reckoning. All the omens were good – I had not had one week out of work in the previous year, nor had I had a holiday. The moment I finished one film I began discussions and costume fittings for the next. In twelve months I had spent twenty-six weeks on *Mogambo*, made *A Day to Remember*, *You Know What Sailors Are* and started *Doctor in the House*. I must be in for some lovely lolly . . . At last a cheque arrived – for £600. All right, I know that £600 is not to be sniffed at, but it was nothing to what I expected. My contract had said '. . . half the profits after deductions of expenses and idle weeks'. I complained bitterly and received a detailed statement from the accounts department.

First, the 'deal' had had to be negotiated between MGM and the Rank Organisation who, having no machinery for this, had appointed my own agent, Frederick Joachim, to do it in return for ten per cent of the total fee. I had spent twenty-six weeks on the film, during which the Rankery had paid my weekly salary, so that sum had then to be deducted. Next I was told that I had had six and a half 'idle weeks'. Not at all, I said. Oh yes, you have, they answered, and they pointed out in the small print of my contract that my involvement in a film began on my *first shooting day* and ended on my *last*: I had finished *Mogambo* on Tuesday and started shooting *A Day to Remember* seventeen days later . . . all these odd days added up to six and a half 'idle' weeks. Discussions, costume fittings, post-synching, stills sessions did not count. This resulted in X pounds 'profit' of which I was to get half. But first my agent took ten per cent of my share. He actually made more money out of *Mogambo* than I did.

Producer William MacQuitty decided that the time was ripe for a remake of Somerset Maugham's *Beachcomber* (originally made into a film under the title *The Vessel of Wrath*). Who better than Robert Newton for the part originally played by Charles Laughton and Glynis Johns to follow Elsa Lanchester. I was cast as the Resident of the island so I thought I should acquaint myself with the original novel: I got to the first entrance of my character – and was shaken to find that, to paraphrase Maugham, he was short, fat, with a freckled bald head . . . and there was I, thirty years old, with a full head of hair; so I settled for playing it as 'myself' – which was what was really required of me, anyway.

Robert Newton should have been perfect in the part – he was a born Beachcomber (the title of our film). It is no secret that he was a very heavy drinker and recently, but not for the first time, he had been warned by his doctors that if he did not stop he would more than likely pop off in the very near future. When we began *Beachcomber* he had been on the wagon for three months and a sorry sight he was: gone were the thrown-back head and the fiery eyes; the jerky gestures made by his arms were now limp and seemed to lack purpose. It was tragic to realise that he had now reached a stage when he relied so totally on alcohol to inject spirit into his perform-ance. He was listless and just moped around the studio, hardly talking to anyone. He knew he was not giving his best and this worried him. Every morning we greeted each other in the make-up room, where he stripped himself down to a pair of none too clean shorts-style baggy underpants, sat down, leaned back against the head-rest and stared with his large bloodshot eyes at the ceiling. Occasionally a low moan escaped his lips. He confided to me that he was not happy with certain elements connected with the film; things were not altogether successful in his private life; he was toying with an idea of doing Shakespeare's *Richard III* in Australia, but generally his career was not going as well as he could wish . . .

Early one morning I was seated silently in my make-up chair when suddenly the door crashed open – what the hell? – there stood Newton, absolutely plastered, his eyes blazing. He staggered across the room, thrust his face into mine and with slobbering lips and flashing eyes he embarked on the most thrilling rendering I have ever heard of 'Now is the winter of our discontent made glorious summer . . .' (What a Richard III he would have been!) From that moment he really took off in the film, but sadly there were only a few days to go – and sadder still, that last bout of drinking was followed shortly after by his death.

Once again Betty Box and Ralph Thomas came up with a script. Some years before, their film *Miranda* in which Glynis Johns played a mermaid had been an enormous success and the time was ripe for a sequel, *Mad About Men*. Betty and Ralph were noted for choosing the most delightful locations for making their films and this time we all set off for Polperro in Cornwall. I was to provide the romantic interest for Glynis, a fisherman who lived in a house on the edge of the quay where his boat was moored. Unfortunately the beautiful thatched house that the designer wanted was not to be found in Polperro, but in the village of Long Crendon, Oxfordshire. This was my first experience of the incongruities of film-making: heavily sun-tanned and wearing a seaman's sweater and trousers tucked into Wellington boots, I was seen in the film unloading a large basket of live lobsters on to a Cornish quay, carrying it across the road and entering a house – in Oxfordshire. The inhabitants of Long Crendon were vastly amused when we filmed their end of the sequence, and I was told that for a long time after the release of the film, visitors to Polperro asked the whereabouts of the thatched house.

I had adored Glynis from the first time I saw her in Esther McCracken's play, *Quiet Wedding*, at the Wyndhams Theatre. I loved her attractive, husky voice and round limpid eyes, and now I was playing opposite her. My colleagues had warned me that she was a superb technician and I would have my work cut out to look after my own interests.

Dirk Bogarde was not the only one beset with profile problems: Glynis preferred her right profile to be seen, which, luckily, matched my left side. In our first scene together we were seated on the beach leaning back against the side of a boat, my arm around her. At the first rehearsal I took notice that the camera was directly in front of us, favouring neither one nor the other. (All's fair in love and film making!) We then went away while the scene was lit using the stand-ins. When we again took our places I cast a beady eye at the camera: it hadn't been moved – neither had the boat – it was still fifty fifty. We then shot the scene. The following day we saw the 'rushes' of the previous day's work: there was Glynis in full face and me in profile! As we emerged from the viewing room I said to her, 'Congratulations. I don't mind you doing it – but how did you do it?'

'Experience,' she answered as her eyes twinkled. We developed a perfect working relationship, but it took me years to discover how much trickery was involved in filming.

Margaret Rutherford played the nurse appointed to look after the 'mermaid'. Late in life she had married a not exactly overworked actor by the name of Stringer Davis and now, both in their sixties, they were a devoted couple. Stringer, whose entry in the *Spotlight Casting Directory* was headed 'Have you thought of Stringer Davis?', dedicated his life to her well being. He came with her to the studio every day and never left her side. In one sequence Margaret had to wade fully dressed into the sea to catch the elusive 'mermaid'. The scenes where Glynis, wearing a long fish tail, was supposed to be immersed in the sea were done for safety reasons in a studio tank, the floor of which sloped from nothing to six feet. Everything was ready, Glynis was placed on a hidden support in the deep end, the lights were on, the camera turning. 'Action.' Margaret, her jowls trembling, waded in. Three times she had to do it, which involved changing into a new, dry costume each time. We had noticed Stringer standing close to the camera, wearing an overcoat which we thought a little excessive in the heat of the studio. Only when the scene was finally completed did we discover that beneath the overcoat he was wearing bathing trunks, ready for any life-saving emergency.

For some months the gaunt faces of producer Peter de Sarigny and director Brian Desmond Hurst, pictures of misery and dejection, had haunted the bar and restaurant at Pinewood. Possessing a splendid screenplay called *Simba*, concerning the Mau–Mau, they had taken advantage of the weather and a brief respite in the political situation and had gone off to Kenya with a camera crew and shot miles and miles of film using doubles for the main characters, intending to do all the dialogue and interior scenes involving the actors back at the studio. This is not an uncommon practice, but they had failed to cast the actors first and they were now faced with the sizeable problem of finding actors to match the doubles, instead of vice versa. Having hoped, indeed expected, to get Jack Hawkins to play the lead, they had used a double who looked like him, but was an inch or two taller. The second best part was a police inspector and while in Kenya they were given great assistance by a local police inspector, who was young, blond, athletic and a bit of a dare-devil – they decided to use him as the double of his counter-part in the film. Each day we saw Peter and Brian standing gloomily at the bar with thousands of pounds already involved in a film which possibly might never be made. Their problems seemed insuperable. First they found that Jack Hawkins was not available. Although Dirk Bogarde, as the next in line, was given the part, he was shorter than Jack, which would mean a noticeable discrepancy in height when the film cut from double to actor. But their other problem was far greater – where could they find a young blond actor to match the police inspector; the ranks of Equity appeared devoid of blond actors.

The weeks went by: Peter and Brian became the butt of our facetious remarks as each day we tried to cheer them up.

I was then about to start on *Mad About Men* and Betty Box suggested that as I was playing a fisherman leading an outdoor life I should have my hair streaked – 'sun kissed', as she put it. I spent the morning in the hair-dressing department and at lunch time, I went through the bar where as usual I found Peter and Brian slouched: 'Good morning.' 'Good morning.'

They looked up and Peter did a perfect double-take. He peered at my hair: 'Would you bleach it all over?'

'Of course I would.'

'You've got your next part!'

One weekend Diana and I went to stay near Chinnor with John Harrison who had married Daphne Slater a week after our own wedding. They were living in an enchanting thatched house, which had been two cottages; a second staircase led from our bedroom down to the kitchen. On Sunday morning we awoke to hear John and Daphne talking downstairs – we had better get up and join them, but Daphne's voice was insistent '. . . All right – all right. So what *is* the staple diet of the Russians?' Diana and I looked at each other. Neither of us felt capable of contributing so early in the morning. Nine months later Marc was born.

During the war the presence of one of Germany's largest battle-ships, *Tirpitz*, sheltering in Trondheim Fjord in Norway, was a great threat to Allied shipping as she could slip out at a moment's notice. Overhanging cliffs protected her from aerial attack, batter-ies of guns lining the fjord and anti-torpedo nets prevented assault from above or below water. As her destruction was imperative to the Allies the British decided to try launching an assault using midget submarines. Known as 'X Craft', they were powered by London bus diesel engines on the surface and by electric batteries below, but to conserve fuel each was towed across the North Sea at night by a 'mother' submarine. At a given point the passage crew was replaced by an operational crew of four men, who were to make their way up the fjord and attempt to dive under the netting. Once below the *Tirpitz*, they would unloose their side cargoes (bolted to the hull, each containing a ton of TNT) which would sink to the shallow bottom of the fjord. These were set to explode when the X Craft were safely on their way back to rendezvous with the mother sub. That was the plan and although in practice they did not succeed in totally destroying the *Tirpitz*, they did at least render her useless for the length of time required by the Allies to get vital food supplies through. Two of the commanders were awarded the VC for their bravery.

This remarkable exploit was turned into a best-selling book called *Above Us The Waves*. The film rights were snapped up by William MacQuitty and, using the same title, work began on the film with, once again, Ralph Thomas directing (four out of my nine films had now been with the same director). John Mills, John Gregson and I (the captains of the three X Craft), were to be seen going through the best part of a real submariner's training; thus the unit set off for Fort Blockhouse, the Naval Training Establishment at Gosport.

I had not known before that submariners are all Royal Navy volunteers. One of the first exercises is for the men to be dressed in frogmen's rubber suits, and from the deck of a small ship they are told to go 'over the side'. They can either jump or go down a ladder. One of the instructors told me that almost invariably those who choose to go down the ladder will ultimately fail in their training.

Why I ever agreed to do this film, I don't know. So many scenes involved my being in the water and still I could not swim. If I had thought the staff at the Training Establishment would be scathing I was wrong: they put me through some tests, one of which involved blowing into a mouthpiece connected to a sort of gas meter to measure my lung capacity. Apparently we all have air floating around our bodies but those with less than others are deemed to have 'negative buoyancy'. A normal person lying on his back totally relaxed in a swimming pool will have toes, tummy, chest, mouth and nose breaking the surface of the water. But when the negatively buoyant lie totally relaxed in the same pool they are three inches under the surface. At last I understood why I never had any difficulty swimming under water for as long as I could hold my breath, but when trying to swim normally at least half my energy was being used in keeping my nose clear of the water. Worse still, once in the water I could never stop swimming: as soon as I did, I sank below the surface, which was not altogether acceptable. But my negative buoyancy is hardly a rare complaint – one in twenty-five volunteers for the submarine service is unacceptable for the same reason.

To teach sailors to escape from a submerged submarine the Training Establishment uses a water-filled cylindrical tower, a hundred feet high and twelve feet in diameter, with a gallery round the top. It is possible to enter the water through hatches in the tower at depths of thirty, sixty or a hundred feet. You open a water-tight door into a small coffin-sized compartment, close the door securely behind you and open valves which allow water from the tank to enter the compartment at foot level. As the water reaches the level of your chin you take a deep breath and open a second door into the tank. You then find yourself thirty (or sixty or a hundred) feet below the surface. Quite illogically it is essential to breathe *out* as you make your way upwards because otherwise, owing to the pressure of the air you have gulped in, by the time you reach the surface your lungs would burst. The idea of actually breathing out is against all normal instincts, so an instructor swims down inside the tank and as you emerge from your doorway, if he does not see the tell-tale air bubbles coming from your lips or nose, he punches you in the stomach until they do!

Recruits usually spend a week entering the tank at thirty feet, another week at sixty and another at a hundred. As actors could not possibly spare all that time they immediately pushed us in at a hundred. The experience was quite unnerving, but at the same time rather exciting (especially if you can't swim). From a depth of a hundred feet you shoot up and come out at the top like a cork from a champagne bottle – you actually pop right out of the water before falling back in. When I did it, knowing my little problem, they had an instructor just out of camera range to support me as I flopped back.

We went into the English Channel to film the sequence when the operation crew takes over from the passage crew. The mother submarine has been towing the midget on a long length of steel cable; now an inflatable raft is launched from the mother (only a thin cord preventing it from floating away), the operational crew of four men get in, pull themselves along the cable to the midget and clamber out, the passage crew wish them luck, get into the raft, pull themselves back to the mother and climb on board. The Ops crew cast off the cable and go into action. When this exercise actually took place in wartime, it was done at night on a calm sea in the lee of the Norwegian coastal cliffs, but this was not exciting enough for the cinema. Instead of night we did it at dusk – so that we could be seen – on a fairly rough sea. It was easy enough to get out of the raft – you had something to hold on to – but getting in was hair-raising. As the belly of a submarine curves dramatically from the flat deck to the waterline and there are no footholds we had to jump – and jump diagonally – into the raft as it rose and fell and swirled around, below and away from us in the churning sea. It is the dubious privilege of the captain to be the last in and first out. Picture the scene. The raft is thrown in and immediately starts bobbing about. The first man has a four feet diameter target to aim at, the next man a little less, and the third less still and then the captain can only see a small patch, the size of his two feet to aim at. Not only that, but it is vital that you sit at exactly the same time as you land – otherwise the rubber raft acts as a trampoline and you take a somersaulting header straight over the other side. I don't mind admitting that I was very nervous. We used the same mother and the same midget to shoot the change-over of each of our three crews: John Mills and his crew in X1, John Gregson and his in X2, and me and mine in X3. I watched as John Mills performed his jump and the most amazing thing happened: as he landed with his two feet on target a sudden wave took the raft away; for a brief second he was suspended horizontally over the water; at the same moment he was bending his knees ready to sit; suddenly another wave took the raft back and he landed safely in position.

I enjoyed working with John enormously: he has developed a superb film technique over the years. I cannot resist mentioning here a little trick of his: whether he invented it or picked it up from another actor I do not know. By clenching his teeth he is able to tighten the tendons in the region of his temples. By doing this when he has three-quarters of his back to camera in an over-the-shoulder shot on another actor, the eye of the viewer is immediately arrested by the movement. I have always been fascinated by technique – some people will call it trickery – adapted to a particular medium. It is very important when the camera can pick out every wart and blemish on a face. I used to blink too much until a cameraman told me that the screen then used at the Odeon, Leicester Square, was forty feet wide and that when my face was seen in large close-up, each eye was ten feet long. Every blink would look like a garage door coming down.

For another sequence I had to re-enact a deed originally per-formed by Commander Donald Cameron: While his X Craft was being towed across the North Sea, the cable picked up a floating mine which then moved along the cable and made straight for his midget. Cameron rushed forward and, lowering himself over the prow of his craft, managed gingerly to push the mine clear with his feet. Donald was our adviser on the film and told me modestly, 'I couldn't think of anything else to do.' He was awarded the VC. I wasn't because we used a dummy. But Donald could swim.

For only the second time I was sub-let to another company, this time to the Boulting brothers (John the producer, Roy the director), for a film called *Josephine and Men*, with Glynis Johns as Josephine and Jack Buchanan, Peter Finch and I as the men in her life. I had known Finchy over the years, but we had never worked together. One evening I had gone into the Pinewood bar with him. 'All right, I'll get you a tomato juice,' he groaned. Leaning on the bar was the sad figure of the director Robert Hamer (*Kind Hearts and Coronets*) who had had a drink problem for years which was finally to kill him. He was now well away and his bloodshot eyes looked up as Finchy arrived.

'Good evening, Mr. Hamer. May I get you a drink?'

Hamer merely slid his glass across the counter and mumbled, 'Scotch.'

'Will you have a single or a double?'

Hamer wheeled on Finchy with his eyes blazing. 'You – Ignorant – Australian – Bastard! When I want a single I'll ask for one!'

In the film Glynis is expecting the arrival of someone she does not want to see. There is a knock at the door; she opens it and is confronted with – of all people – a vacuum-cleaner salesman, who injects himself into the room and immediately assembles and demonstrates his wares while talking non-stop. The actor cast for this part was very nervous: he had a lot of dialogue and he had to say it all very quickly. Everything was ready.

'Turn over. Action.'

Glynis opened the door and in he came but his nervousness made him stumble over his lines and the more nervous he became. After several Takes the poor fellow was getting worse, perspiration was dripping off him. Roy could see this and called a halt while the tension relaxed and everyone calmed down. He talked very quietly to the actor and eventually enquired if he was ready to go on. Quietly he told the crew to get ready and then addressed himself again to the actor who was positioned outside the door. 'There is nothing to worry about – take it gently – no rush – we can always do it again – relax – relax.' His voice got quieter and quieter. The actor visibly relaxed. 'All right then, shall we try it? – don't worry.' The door was closed. 'Turn over,' Roy whispered and then barked, '*Action!*' On the word every muscle of the actor tightened and sweat poured down his face.

Certain animals inspire love and affection – dogs and cats especially, horses, donkeys, goats, hamsters, even bears, but on the whole the public pulse is not quickened by reptiles. It was probably a mistake, therefore, to make a film in which the dumb heroine was *An Alligator Named Daisy*, even if surrounded by a cast that read like *Who's Who in the Theatre*.

Having accidentally shared a sleeping compartment on a train with an elderly gentleman (played by Wilfrid Lawson), my character finds that in the morning the old man has departed leaving behind a five-foot long alligator with a note asking me to look after it. From there the story and the problems proceed.

Cast for the part, still fondly thinking that 'someone up there' was looking after my best interests, I was called to Pinewood for a press photo call. Raymond Stross, the producer, and J. Lee Thompson, the director, met me on one of the stages.

'How are you with alligators?' Ray asked. 'Come over and meet Daisy.'

She was lying on a bed of straw in a metal tank surrounded by a group of photographers.

'Let's get a shot of you with Daisy.'

'What does she eat?'

'Fish. OK, feed her fish, Donald.'

Daisy's keeper handed me a fish about fifteen inches long which I held at the ready over the tank. Until this moment Daisy had been lying quite still and apparently lifeless, but slowly she opened her upper jaw and exposed rows of lethal looking teeth, her eyelids slid back and her beady eyes swivelled round to look at me. From the back of her throat came a sinister hissing sound.

'OK, Donald – drop the fish.'

I did and Daisy's jaws snapped closed with a crack over the middle of this substantial fish – the head and tail fell to the floor of the tank. And I was to work for the next three weeks in close proximity to Daisy!

The next day was devoted to getting to know Daisy and learning how she should be carried. Her keeper was a strange woman known as Koringa, famous at the time for her performances with alligators and snakes in a circus, who explained that the natural habitat for alligators is in or near water in a hot climate. If they are kept in the cold and away from water they become docile and lethargic and that in this condition they can only move forward very slowly. She also explained that they cannot lift their heads above the horizontal, but they have extremely rapid lateral movement. In front or above an alligator you are quite safe, but watch out from the side. She then showed me the technique of picking one up: you approach from the back so that it cannot see you, you grip the end of its tail in your right hand and pull it sharply back. This unnerves the alligator and, taking advantage of this, you place your left forearm under its body behind the front legs and hold it tight: quickly put your right arm over and round its tail just behind the back legs. The tail is immensely powerful, but will now be out of harm's way. Likewise its head can snap from side to side ineffectually. But don't let it tip on one side – it could bite your head off.

Nothing could scare me – I had worked with John Ford.

It was now my turn to try. What surprised me most was the actual touch – no different from touching an alligator handbag: cold and horny. After lifting her up and putting her down several times I fondly hoped that we had forged a bond, but I discovered later that that was quite out of the question – two months later she took Koringa by the arm and fractured it in seventeen places.

The only other actor in the film who had to carry Daisy was my old friend Harry Kendall, who was playing a valet in the large house where my character was staying. He had to discover Daisy in the bottom drawer of my wardrobe, pick her up and say, 'Oh, you sweet little thing – I'll take you out for a walk in the garden if you behave yourself.'

Harry was given exactly the same instructions as me, but when it came to the Take he picked her up and – turned her on her side! The camera was turning. In the middle of his line Daisy saw her chance, opened her jaws wide and snapped them, missing Harry's face by a hairsbreadth. Being the totally professional actor, Harry continued, so that the dialogue as seen in the film runs like this: 'Oh, you sweet little thing – I'll take you for a walk in the garden (a gnashing of fearsome teeth) – *if* you behave yourself!'

I really thought I was developing a relationship with Daisy. As each new actor arrived to take part and every time we had visitors to the set, I was asked to demonstrate my expertise in handling her. I could kneel on the floor with my nose two inches from Daisy's and I even thought I detected a gleam of affection in her eyes. I was amused that anyone meeting her for the first time kept a respectful distance. I learned that if I failed to keep a firm grip on her tail it would lash round and give me a resounding smack on my backside.

Once again the cast included the gloriously eccentric Margaret Rutherford, who this time appeared as a vet to whom I took Daisy. Apart from Harry Kendall and myself she was the only other person to touch her. I placed Daisy on the examining table and Margaret applied a stethoscope to her snout, looking thoughtfully upwards. (Very brave, I thought. I had never taken my eyes off Daisy.) Once again I noticed her husband Stringer standing beside the camera in his overcoat but this time he had one hand tucked inside. When the scene was completed he relaxed and we found that the hand was holding a large hammer – just in case.

Another sequence involved a ballroom scene in full swing – the ladies in long dresses and the men in dinner jackets. Suddenly the double doors opened and there was I carrying Daisy. The band stopped, the ladies screamed and everyone backed away. Everything was rehearsed and we were ready for the first Take.

'Turn over. Action.'

The door opened and I came through, but instead of screams I was greeted by howls of laughter which grew louder and louder. Someone shouted, 'Cut!' The director came up to me. 'What on earth is the matter?' I asked.

'Just take a look at Daisy!' he replied.

I looked down and saw that in the region of her belly a pair of 'bombdoors' had opened and from them was hanging a long wet thing like a banana, but pink. 'Daisy' was a boy! Nothing would make her/him retract it and we had a hundred and fifty 'extras' and all the principals hanging around waiting.

The director had a bright idea: 'Couldn't you put your hand over it?' I didn't altogether fancy that: Daisy could have taken it as a token of affection, but 'he' might have been outraged and turned nasty. We just had to wait.

As I suspected, audiences did not take Daisy to their hearts. Even more galling, everyone I knew who saw the film said, 'What a very good model you used – it looked almost like a real alligator.'

One evening Diana and I dined with our friends Bob and

Elizabeth Monkhouse. (Arriving at the restaurant, the commissionaire approached: 'Hello, Bob. Say something funny!' Bob said, 'Knickers', and the commissionaire went away chuckling uncontrollably and perfectly satisfied.) Bob mentioned that he had been sent the script of a play which he thought extremely funny, but, unfortunately, he had other commitments and could not do it. The next day my agent arranged an appointment with the impresario and shortly I found myself climbing the stairs to meet Henry Sherek.

A fresh chapter in my life was about to begin.

11
ANOTHER WONDERFUL DAY FOR HENRY SHEREK

Henry Sherek had begun his theatrical career booking artists in the 1920s when a live variety show was always a part of the bill at larger cinemas. Following a distinguished record in the Army during the Second World War, he returned to theatrical management and produced a string of successes, including *Edward My Son*, *The Caine Mutiny* and *Under Milk Wood* and plays by T. S. Eliot such as *The Cocktail Party* and *The Confidential Clerk*. He had married the elegant and Honourable Pamela Boscawen, and at this time they were living in an apartment in the palatial Arlington House in St James's above the Caprice, the fashionable theatrical restaurant started by Mario, former manager of the Ivy.

Although I had known Sherek's name for years I had never actually set eyes on him: Diana had worked seven years before in his ill-fated production of *The Philadelphia Story*, but I was quite unprepared for what met my eyes. Hunched behind a desk and puffing on a fat cigar was the largest man I had ever seen: as I entered he rose to a height of six feet three inches and side-stepped round the desk. The impression was astonishing. He was vast. He was enormous. He was gross. (More of his outsize anon.) But his personality was delightfully attractive; his eyes twinkled and his sensual mouth quirked beneath a bristling moustache. He was extrovertly ebullient and as I discovered later he was wonderful with children, having a great store of tricks to keep them amused. He spoke several languages fluently and wherever he found himself in the British Isles he adopted the appropriate regional accent. This sometimes made one cringe with embarrassment: in Edinburgh Derek Farr and I opted out of a group of Scotsmen dominated by Henry in a broad Robert Burns accent. Their laughter was interrupted by Henry saying, 'What's the matter, Donald – you used to laugh at my jokes before you signed your contract.' But there was no getting away from it – his heart was relatively as big as his frame. His smile could light up a room. He once told me that every morning of his life he looked into the bathroom mirror and said aloud, 'Today is going to be another wonderful day for Henry Sherek!' He and Pamela were to become two of our dearest and most loyal friends and to influence our thinking and living. We placed them in the position of surrogate parents and they took us under their protective wings.

Like Bob Monkhouse, I found the script hilarious. Translated by Robin Maugham from a French play by Claude Magnier called *Monsieur Mazure*, it lacked an English title until Henry's secretary suggested *Odd Man In*. There were only three characters, a husband and wife (to be played by Derek Farr and his own wife Muriel Pavlow) and an interloper, the odd man in – which Henry offered me. I accepted immediately. Rehearsals were not due to start for several weeks and I had to get permission from the Rankery. They agreed on the grounds that I would be free to film during the day once the play had opened in the West End: my contract was suspended for the length of time I was unavailable.

I had not bargained for Henry's villainous sense of humour. You could never be sure when he was joking: the moment you assumed that he was, you found that he wasn't and vice versa. I was to find that Henry never made one phone call when six would do. Sitting quietly at home I answered his call and without announcing himself he embarked, 'Bad news. Muriel can't do the play – she's tied up to do a film' and down went the phone . . . I was left gulping on the other end.

Ten minutes later the ring again: 'Have you given any thought as to who could play the part?' and he cut off . . .

Another ten minutes: 'Well? Any ideas?'

Just before he replaced the receiver I managed to blurt out, 'What about Barbara Murray?'

I wasn't sure if he had heard me, but some minutes later, ring-ring . . . 'Her agent says she is free.'

The moment I walked away from the phone it rang again, 'I'm sending the script round to her now.'

I could now imagine Barbara being subjected to the same calls because her reactions to the script were relayed to me act by act: 'She likes it.' 'She's finished it.' 'She wants to do it.'

And then silence for twenty-four hours until I raced in from the garden to be told, 'The panic is over! Muriel's film has been cancelled: I can't think why you don't like her.'

I had to call him back to ask, 'Who don't I like?'

'Muriel.'

'But I do like her!'

'No, you don't. You wanted Barbara Murray to play the part!' and I was cut off . . .

Our director was Harold French, by then a legend. As a young man he had been an actor and had starred in the original stage version of *The Blue Lagoon* before turning to musical comedies and then to directing – among many other plays – the original production of Rattigan's *French Without Tears*. He was a joyous man with whom to work and his gaiety was infectious. Some directors have the unfortunate ability to make actors feel inadequate, but not Harold: each day he encouraged us to invent more and more 'business' and character idiosyncracies at which he would chuckle outrageously and the more he chuckled the more we invented. It all seemed like a wonderful game – rehearsals were sheer fun and with Harold as our audience we felt we could climb the highest peaks of comic invention. Only in the final week of rehearsal did he apply his innate critical judgment: 'I think we can do without that,' 'and that', 'and that'. And we did not mind losing five per cent of what we had put in.

Every day the four of us lunched together and Harold would regale us with stories of the glamorous theatre he had known in the 1920s and 1930s. Occasionally he would go off into silent reveries as he remembered incidents and personalities. One day he sat smiling to himself ecstatically.

'What is it this time, Harold?'

'Oh, my darlings – can you imagine this play done by Kay Hammond, Rex Harrison and Roland Culver!'

We could and it didn't exactly cheer us up.

On several occasions rehearsals were attended by the play's adaptor Robin Maugham, but Harold soon had to discourage him from joining us for lunch when, for the third time, we found ourselves incapable of rehearsing during the afternoon without continual giggling, due to a too convivial two-hour lunch break, with Robin in full flight.

Robin and his sisters, the artist Honor (Earl) and Diana (Marr-Johnson), were the children of Viscount Maugham, the sometime Lord Chancellor. Their uncle was Willie Somerset Maugham.

Robin was outrageous: only a few weeks before he had been asked
to leave a country house, after his hostess, a horsy woman who
looked like a horse, asked him to pass the sugar. Robin put two
lumps on the palm of his hand and held it out to her! He adored his
uncle Willie, but disliked his severe father who in turn was not
exactly overfond of Robin, but once a month they tried to do their
duty by each other, the Viscount – quite old now – inviting his son
to lunch at his house in Cadogan Square. Invariably, it was a
miserable experience. Robin lived in Hove and late one night was at
a party, very much the worse for wear when at five o'clock in the
morning his friends remembered that *today* was the day for his
monthly paternal visit. Quantities of black coffee were poured
down him and, having done everything they could to sober him
up, not very successfully, they got him on to the London train.
An hour or so later, feeling and looking absolutely awful, his eyes
bleary and his face puckered, he arrived at his father's house. The
butler sucked his teeth and shook his head in saddened disbelief as he
let him in. Father and son ate lunch in complete silence, much to
Robin's relief as he felt incapable of contributing to any conversation. When the butler placed the port on the table he thankfully
accepted the first alcoholic drink he had been offered. Suddenly his
father spoke, 'What port would you say it was?'

'It's – it's your '28 isn't it?' (It always was.)

His father was delighted. 'It is – it is! – now tell me, who would
you say painted that picture?'

Robin could only just see it, but assumed that it was the same
which had hung there for decades. 'It's a Guardi, isn't it?'

Me, Derek Farr and Muriel Parlow.

'It is – it is! Oh this modern generation! – Do you think, Willie, my son Robin could have told me that?'

After a provincial tour *Odd Man In* opened at the St Martin's Theatre in July 1957 and ran for a respectable six months. It may give you some idea of Henry's size to know that one evening Derek and I saw a suit of his which had just been returned to the stage door from the theatrical cleaners. With inches to spare we both got into the trousers, Derek in one leg and I in the other, and then, managing to button the jacket around our combined shoulders we hopped up the stairs to present ourselves to Muriel.

We were a happy trio and, to celebrate our one hundredth performance, Henry took the *entire* cast – all three of us – to supper at the Ivy restaurant, and feeling in a festive mood I said, 'Oh Henry – there's caviare on the menu!'

Henry's smile collapsed. 'Yes. And there's a two weeks' notice clause in your contract!'

Was he joking? I thought it advisable to forget the caviare.

I did two more plays for Henry over the next two years but unfortunately neither ran. The first, *All in The Family*, lasted for only five weeks, but worse was to come. During my time in *The Heiress* I had appeared in a Sunday night performance of Dennis Cannan's first play *Max* and now he had written an excellent comedy called *Who's Your Father?* But the time was out of joint – following an ecstatic tour it closed at the Cambridge Theatre after only two and a half weeks.

Over this production I was once again subjected to Henry's telephone technique when he was trying to find a director for the play. I lifted the receiver and with no preamble Henry's voice said, 'What about X?' (mentioning the name of a well known actor).

'To play which part?' I asked.

'No. To direct,' and down went the phone. I was left pondering the question.

Ring-ring. 'Well?'

'Well . . .' I began.

'I see. You don't like the idea.' I just caught him before he cut off.

'No – it's just that I know him as a fine actor . . .'

'And you don't think he can direct?'

I tried to control the situation: 'I didn't know he was also a director.'

'You mean you wouldn't have confidence in him?'

'No – no – he's a good actor and I'm sure he's a good director . . .'

'So you wouldn't mind working with him?'

'Not at all.'

'I'm glad to hear that – he's sitting in front of me now.'

Some months later Henry asked me if I would care to go with
him to see the same play being done by the repertory company in
Worthing. I explained that Diana was tied up looking after Marc
who had measles but could I bring Jeremy (aged seven).

'Lovely. Yes, bring him,' cried Henry.

I need not have gone. Henry spent the whole journey entertaining Jeremy, chocolates and lemonade were laid on in the theatre and
at the end of the performance he was asked what he thought of the
production.

Ingenuously Jeremy said, 'I think it is much funnier than it was in
London!'

Henry never let me forget it and from then on always referred to
Jeremy as 'the boy who always tells the truth'.

After he retired from theatrical management Henry and Pamela
resided in Switzerland and travelled the world seeing their friends
and visiting the finest restaurants. Fittingly this great man died in
his beloved Venice.

Today, Pamela, more beautiful than ever, reigns alone in Geneva, still maintaining her high standards of elegance and sophistica-
tion; and every year making her regular visits to see her friends in
London, Paris, Venice, New York and Washington. As often as we
can, Diana and I visit her in Geneva from where she whisks us off
around Lac Leman and into France to restaurants – most of them
accompanied by myriad stars in *Michelin* – that she and Henry
discovered together and where the name Sherek still commands the
best tables and the finest service.

12

RANKERY TAKE TWO

Every Christmas the Rankery gave a sumptuous dinner at one or other of the large Mayfair hotels to which were invited all the producers, directors, contract artists and leading figures of the hierarchy, accompanied by their respective spouses. The festive season notwithstanding, these could be either exhilarating or frightening affairs. Long tables radiated from the epicentre where John Davis sat and one's place at the tables indicated one's position in the Rankery for the following year. If within touching distance of J.D., your star shone brightly in the firmament: if at the far end you were likely to be extinguished within the next twelve months. You checked on the seating plan with some trepidation. However as the person next to you was in the same position, the chat over the excellent food and drink was always optimistic and comradely . . . until the time came for speeches. The first was traditionally made by J.D.'s beautiful wife Dinah Sheridan and was always delightful: she spoke – always without notes – with a mixture of charm, sincerity and emotion and we responded with laughter and tears. J.D. would then rise and give a résumé of the year's achievements and then outline the plans for next year. One by one the names concerned would come like hammer blows: would one be mentioned? A colleague named for a plum part and suddenly, in the season of good will to all men, you feel like murder. For seven years Diana and I had almost the same seats, halfway down the table, and went home relieved that I was still a useful member of the stable.

The Rankery were remarkably generous with their dinners for film trade bodies such as the Cinema Managers' Association and the Cinema Exhibitors' Association, as well as for visiting foreign film delegations, and on each occasion contract artists and their wives/ husbands were invited. You needed a pretty good excuse to refuse. In evening dress Diana and I would arrive with the other guests at the Grosvenor House or the Dorchester, descend the great staircase to the ballroom, give our names to the toastmaster who roared them out to those already assembled, and pass along the receiving line to shake hands with J.D. and Dinah. This procedure was followed with almost monotonous frequency and one evening my sense of humour (if you can call it that) got the better of me. On fifty-six previous occasions I had behaved myself impeccably, but this time, as we paused before the toastmaster, I said, 'Mr and Mrs Anthony Steel.' The toastmaster faced the room and roared, 'Mister and Missus Antunny Still.' This got quite a good laugh from those who knew that we weren't, but on reaching J.D. I was greeted by tight lips and furious eyes. His hand yanked me past him.

The next morning I had a telephone call from Olive Dodds; her voice was serious: 'Donald, what happened last night?'

The rest of the previous evening had been so enjoyable that I could not immediately think what she meant.

'Nothing in particular,' I said.

'Well *something* happened – J.D. is furious.'

Then I remembered and recounted the incident.

'Oh, Donald, Donald, will you never learn? J.D. wants to see you in South Street (the head office) at ten thirty on Thursday morning.'

I put the phone down with trembling fingers. Oh God. The Chop. All the next day I fretted. Diana was no help – 'Well it *was* a silly thing to do.' On Thursday morning I arrived at South Street at ten fifteen and the door was opened by the commissionaire – normally a sunny face, but that morning even he was frosty. Over the telephone he announced, 'Mr Sinden to see Mr Davis' instead of the usual, 'Donald to see J.D.' I went up the stairs to the outer office where six typists sat at their machines. Normally it was chatter-chatter and cups of coffee, but now six compassionate faces looked up briefly with saddened eyes and returned to their tapping. Every-one seemed to know that I was to be carpeted. I sat down, despised and rejected, and tried to read a copy of *Kine Weekly*. Ten thirty came and went followed by ten thirty-five – ten forty – ten forty-five.

At ten fifty J.D.'s personal secretary came out and said, 'Mr Davis will see you now.' Henrietta saying farewell to Charles the First could not have been more mournful. She led the way into her inner office and sat at her desk. I braced myself and opened the door into J.D.'s room . . . He sat behind his desk engrossed in paper work.

'Close the door,' I was ordered. I did so and stood there. He continued to look at his papers. Minutes ticked by and still I stood, the blood pounding in my head. I began to shake – why couldn't he just say 'you're sacked' and let me go . . .

Slowly he stood up and glowered at me, slowly he extricated himself from the desk and slowly, slowly, moved towards me, his eyes never leaving mine. 'If he hits me,' I thought, 'do I hit him back?' He arrived inches in front of me and his jaw jutted into my face. For several seconds he just stood there. Suddenly the glower dissolved into a smile – a dangerous smile, but nevertheless a smile – and he spoke in a paternally severe voice, 'That was very funny, Donald – *but never do it again.*'

It was not the first, nor the last time that my sense of humour landed me in hot water. In this case I should have known that J.D. would not countenance anything that undermined the dignity of his beloved Rankery.

It was a small incestuous world in which I was working. William MacQuitty (*Above Us The Waves*) – this time in conjunction with Brian Desmond Hurst (*Simba*) as director – came up with a script called *The Black Tent*, written by Bryan Forbes (just beginning to make the transition from acting into writing) and Robin Maugham (*Odd Man In*).

At the end of the war a British officer (played by Anthony Steel), fails to return from North Africa and his brother (me) sets out from England in search of him and discovers that he joined a tribe of Bedouin Arabs and married the chief's daughter (played by a beautiful girl named Anna Maria Sandri, who, shortly after the film was made, married a millionaire and gave up being an actress). Almost the entire film was made on location in the Sahara desert in Libya. We were accommodated in Tripoli: Anna Maria, Tony Steel and I were at the Grand Hotel and the rest of the unit were at the Waddan Hotel. The heat was intense – in the desert it was 120 in the shade – so a continuous supply of drink was essential. Beer and soft drinks were at the expense of the production company, so when we foregathered at the Waddan we ordered what we wanted and chalked it up to 'Room 39', the unit office. We could not speak Arabic, but as Italian had become the Libyan's second language (thanks to Mussolini's occupation) we thought we could help the waiters by having the drinks put down to 'Camera trenta-nove'. After two weeks of the entire unit chalking up their drinks we discovered that the waiters had no idea that we were trying to speak Italian and thought we were saying 'twenty-nove' (29), the room of an American oil magnate who had left that morning, fortunately for us without querying his astronomic drinks bill!

It really was an exotic location in which to be paid to work. Diana came out to join us and together we visited the glorious Roman cities of Leptis Magna and Sabratha and were able to walk about the extensive ruins with not another tourist in sight. We were neither of us particularly enamoured of the desert – it never seemed to be the romantic Garden of Allah we had expected. Meal times were the worst: no sooner was a plate placed on the table than five thousand flies came out of a clear sky and settled on it. We found that the only answer was to keep one's knife permanently waving over the plate while stabbing at the food with a fork and hoping to get it into one's mouth before the flies saw it.

Filming one day, miles out into the desert, we were in the middle of a scene when someone detected a little cloud of dust on the horizon moving rapidly towards us. As it approached we perceived a magnificent Arab sheik, his white robes streaming behind him, mounted on the most beautiful white stallion with silver-studded bridle and saddle. Reining in the horse, he demanded to know what we were doing, as this was his territory. He received his answer through our interpreter. Meanwhile Brian Desmond Hurst was thrilling to the dramatic possibilities of using the galloping horse-man in his film and, through the interpreter, asked if the sheik would, on 'Action', ride like the wind from A. to B. The sheik looked slowly round at our motley crew and after a moment's hesitation agreed. It was like a group of schoolboys asking Don Bradman to demonstrate a hook or a cut. The sheik rode into the mid-distance amid his own cloud of exalted dust.

'Action.'

It was a sight I shall never forget. Previously we had only seen him approaching head on, but now we saw him in profile, the sharply outlined heads of horse and rider dissolved into billowing robes and streaking tail, racing across the sands with a spume of dust following from the animal's hooves . . .

But all was not well with the camera and the operator asked if it could be done again. The director asked the interpreter who asked the sheik who had now rejoined us with a round of applause from the unit. No, he could not spend more time with us as he had to return. Brian was distraught and pleaded. The interpreter had already had problems dealing with hundreds of 'extras', and now made a hideous social gaffe: he offered the sheik 'twice the fee' . . . Up till then no mention had been made of any payment: the sheik had been asked to do something, he had graciously agreed, but now there was an insulting suggestion that he was being *paid*. He drew himself up in his saddle, his eyes pierced the interpreter and then travelled from one to the other of the unit as if to say, 'You come to my country and behave like this . . . to me . . .' He spat on the ground, reared up his steed and, without a word, was gone.

Magnificent.

During the making of *Beachcomber* I had indulged in a touch of nepotism and asked if a part could be found for my old friend from the Bristol Old Vic, Donald Pleasence. The only one they could think of was that of an Indian servant – but Donald had light blue eyes. Conscientious actor that he is, Donald had himself fitted with dark brown contact lenses and he got the part. We hoped that his film career might blossom, but no: although busy in the theatre, nobody wanted him in films until *The Black Tent*, in which there was a good part of an Arab servant: 'Who has dark brown eyes? Ah yes – Donald Pleasence,' so once again he and I worked together.

Near the location was a colony of Troglodytes and we were privileged to be invited into their dwellings. Before seeing them I must admit that I was rather shocked by the idea of people living in holes in the ground. I certainly never expected to find only comparatively wealthy families, because it costs time and money to dig holes of that size – thirty feet deep and thirty feet square. This formed a sort of courtyard: the entrance was a sloping tunnel which started some distance away. Radiating from this courtyard, rooms of considerable size had been hewn out of the sandstone, with beautiful carpets on the floors and areas curtained off with rich hangings. Once down there you were immediately aware of the attraction of living like that – it was so wonderfully cool. Compared with the surface temperature, it was almost an icebox. The inhabitants were charming and gave us tea as we sat around on cushions.

In the city of Tripoli we encountered a most bizarre problem. At that time the population was divided into almost equal sections of Moslems, Jews and Roman Catholics. Sunday being the holy day for the Roman Catholics, Saturday for the Jews and Friday for the Moslems meant that for three days a week *everything* closed, which left a four-day working week. The unit manager was considerably relieved when we finally left that romantic location and returned to the norm of Pinewood.

I saw something more of the Mediterranean at this time, but not in front of the cameras.

In the mid-Fifties the Rankery decided to strike out and conquer new frontiers by a show of strength at the Venice Film Festival. A gleaming Viscount airliner, chartered from BEA and specially polished, was boarded at London's Heathrow Airport by John Davis and his team of Ranklets: Jack Hawkins, Belinda Lee, John Gregson, Diana Dors, James Robertson Justice, Eunice Gavson and their respective spouses. With us came a posse of publicity men under the redoubtable Theo Cowan, a gaggle of gossip columnists and a frame of photographers headed by the best taker of female portraits in the business, Cornel Lucas, who was also married to Belinda Lee.

From Treviso Airport a fleet of limousines took us to the water's edge where we transferred to motor boats: down the Grand Canal, across the Lagoon to the long narrow island of the Lido, and right to the door of the plush Excelsior Hotel, the focal point of the Festival. That year the British dominated the festivities: the Union Jack fluttered from countless flagpoles on the island while on the Lagoon the white ensign was proudly hoisted on the flagship of the Royal Navy's Mediterranean Fleet, the cruiser HMS *Sheffield*, which was anchored within a cable's length of the Doge's Palace, and escorted by the yacht of the Commander-in-chief, Sir Guy Grantham. (To call it a yacht is rather belittling – it was actually a modified frigate.) By night both ships were outlined by strings of lights. One evening the British film contingent were floated across the placid waters to the yacht, piped aboard, greeted by our host and his flag officer, Captain Jephthah West, weighed down by a Fort Knox of gold braid, and entertained by Sir Guy at a marvellous party under a dreamy star-lit sky.

Every other evening, watched by crowds, we attended film shows with parties and receptions before and after, and every day we had 'official sightseeing'. All the time we were haunted by hoards of Leicable, but predatory photographers whose negatives were rushed back to England for apparently copy-hungry newspapers. Diana Dors stole a march on the other girls by appearing in a mink bikini. We knew nothing about it; the scoop was effected at seven o'clock in the morning to avoid the crowds.

Diana – my Diana – and I had never been to Venice before. We were delighted on our one free day to get a phone call – even if it was far too early in the morning – from John Davis and his wife Dinah, asking if we would join them in a private tour of several of the churches and art galleries. That tour so whetted our cultural appetites that we have since returned to Venice many times.

Fortunately the Festival coincided with the annual regatta on the Grand Canal, which our small group of Ranklets was privileged to watch from the balcony of the British Consulate, overlooking the canal beside the Accademia Bridge. Surely this regatta must be one of the most colourful sights in the world? Every gondola in the city, beautifully decorated and rowed by flat-hatted gondoliers in their Sunday best, escorts magnificent gilded barges trailing long lengths of crimson material in the water as they glide along the canal powered by countless colourfully costumed oarsmen.

Every balcony, loggia and window along the route is crammed with spectators. The procession is followed by gondola races, when the crowds become dangerously partisan.

Towards the end of the week each nation gave a party for all the other nations attending the Festival and these were strikingly representative of each nation's character.

The French took over the Doge's Palace: candles flickered on every sill as on a warm evening we mounted the stairs while fountains gently plopped in the courtyards and a string orchestra on the balcony played Saint-Saëns. Champagne popped and fizzed and pink cloths covered the tables in the magnificent rooms of the Palace where we sat for salmon and asparagus by the light of silver candelabra.

The Americans chose the Casino for their shindig for which the invitations requested that 'Western' costumes be worn. Hamburgers and fried chicken were served by 'cowboys' at tables covered by checked gingham cloths, dampened to prevent them blowing about. A hill-billy group played guitars, accordions, fiddles, and mouth-organs for barn-dancing. But the slatted chairs had all been freshly painted, with disastrous results: everyone went home with green-striped bottoms.

The British invitations insisted on black ties for a formal dinner at the Excelsior Hotel. Sedate ballroom dancing followed, to the band of the Royal Marines from HMS *Sheffield* 'by kind permission of the Commander-in-Chief', who brought along his officers resplendent in their snow white uniforms, gold braid and medals.

The following year J.D. decreed that we should attend the Cannes Film Festival, but this time wives and husbands would not be allowed because the publicity department had discovered that our other halves were – let's face it – an encumbrance when they were trying to set up situations for photographs geared for publicity. Instead, contract artists were to escort each other to film shows and on 'official sightseeing'.

Although not exactly overjoyed by this decision, Diana and I decided to take advantage of my presence on the Riviera for a holiday on Cap Ferrat immediately after the Festival. The Rankery even agreed that we could drive down and stay the night at the magnificent Negresco Hotel in Nice (at their expense!), so that the following day I would be on the spot to join my colleagues on their arrival at Nice airport and participate in the Rankery's triumphal entry into Cannes. Diana would take the car on to Cap Ferrat and await my arrival. Our room at the Negresco was reserved by telephone from the Rank Paris office and when we registered we found that Peter Finch – at that time a contract artist – had also been booked in. After dinner we all repaired to his room (779) and ordered alternate rounds of drinks on our two room numbers. I have never been very good at heart-to-heart, in depth, soul searching, self-analysing, *mea culpa* confessionalising, but Diana loves it and she and Peter settled down to a classic seven-hour marathon. I tried to take an intelligent interest, but eventually fell asleep. Long before all was revealed in the Sunday papers, Finchy bared his soul to Diana who was so intrigued and flattered by the enormity of his disclosure that she never breathed a word to anyone (except to me).

The following morning we checked out of our rooms, but were stopped at the reception desk by an intransigent clerk who insisted that we should pay our bills. We explained that they were to be settled by the Rank Organisation. They agreed that indeed the rooms had been reserved as a result of a telephone call from someone purporting to be from the Rank Organisation but they had nothing in writing. We announced our names rather loudly, but to our horror – and chagrin – Peter and I were told that no one on the desk had ever heard of us. We would not be allowed to leave until the account was paid. Between the three of us we did not have enough money. What could we do? Peter and I would miss our appointment with the Rankery at the airport. J.D. would be furious. Heads might roll . . . At that moment a small group arrived and one of them asked for the room reserved in the name of

Butlin . . . Butlin? We looked around and sure enough there was our old friend Billy Butlin, surrounded by his entourage.

'Billy!'

'Peter! Donald!'

We explained our situation and Billy assured a genuflecting manager that all was well – he would personally guarantee our accounts.

This time the Ranklets were installed at one of the world's great hotels, the grandiose Carlton, and once again it was the round of film shows and 'official sightseeing' accompanied by the statutory hordes of press photographers. But this time there was no British Navy to back us up; in lieu of the admiral's yacht, our contingent was invited to a party at the glamorous Villa Yakimoor, the home of the old Aga Khan. Reputed to be one of the wealthiest men in the world – if not *the* wealthiest – he seemed to have been around all my life; as a boy I had seen pictures of him leading in a Derby winner and read accounts of him being weighed on his birthday against diamonds presented by his followers. Now there he sat, well advanced in years, in a deck chair on a verandah, his head shaded by a soft white hat and peering through thick, tinted spectacles. We stood in a receiving line to be presented and I found myself immediately behind J.D. – God to some, and also the managing director of the vast Rank empire which owned film studios, chains of cinemas, countless subsidiary companies, and us; but now he was presented quite simply as 'Mr John Davis, Managing Director of the Rank Organisation.'

The Aga Khan countered with a showstopper: 'What's your capital investment?'

Taken aback but determined not to show it, J.D. answered proudly, 'Sixty million pounds.'

And then came the Aga Khan's trump card.

'Oh, is that all?' (He must have learned it from John Ford.)

He was much kinder to me and I responded by waxing poetical about his villa, positioned perfectly a third of the way up a mountain, with Cannes at his feet and nothing but the top two-thirds of the rugged terrain sloping away behind him. 'The only drawback would be if someone built a house up there,' I said.

'They can't – I own it!'

Later I talked to his wife, the beautiful Begum – next to the Duchess of Windsor probably the most celebrated wife in the world – who, on learning that I was married, asked why my wife was not there. I explained the situation and said that she awaited me at Cap Ferrat. 'But you must bring her over and use our swimming pool.' Needless to say I did, and we spent many hours splashing around in a vast pool that could be divided by great glass doors making half of it an indoor pool, and having tea from the thinnest of porcelain, brought to the poolside by a maid straight out of a Feydeau farce: dressed in a short frilly black dress, with a whiter than white cap and apron of ordandie. The Villa Yakimoor apart, our *pension* at Cap Ferrat was a welcome relief from the unreal celluloid existence of Cannes.

The Rankery certainly made a lasting impression on both Venice and Cannes but the experiment was never repeated.

Meanwhile, back at Pinewood . . .

Sydney Box, who had administered the famous Gainsborough Studios in Shepherds Bush, was not only the elder brother of Betty Box, but, like his sister, an independent producer working under the Rank umbrella. His wife Muriel had already directed me in *Beachcomber*. Noël Coward had earlier called them 'the Brontes of Shepherds Bush'. Now the husband and wife partnership offered me a thriller to be called *Eyewitness*.

I had never played a villain before and my casting in this film caused some speculation. Donald Zec, the film gossip columnist of the *Daily Mirror*, took me down to a series of pubs in the East End of London with the object of picking up some local colour and perhaps finding a prototype on which I could base my characterisation. Oscar Wilde says somewhere that nature imitates art and we were disappointed not to find one original 'character'. In our travels we saw several Jack Palances, Robert Mitchums, Tony Curtises, Alan Ladds, but no originals. The regulars of those pubs had all emulated their screen heroes. The tour was of no use to me, but it provided Donald Zec with a good twist to his article.

My partner in crime was Nigel Stock and the object of our villainous attention was the delightful Muriel Pavlow. I first saw Muriel posing as the Blue Boy in a play called *The Gainsborough Girls* and now I was to have the pleasure of working with her in my next three films.

Eyewitness is now shown on television more frequently than any of my other films, but ironically when it first opened, to rather bad press reviews, commercial television was in its infancy and had yet to make the impact that was to change the lives of everyone in the country, not least those in the Rankery.

Within days of finishing *Eyewitness* we began shooting on *Tiger in the Smoke* in Brittany with Roy Baker directing. The location was miles from the normal tourist run, while the one and only hotel in the small village in which we were housed could only be described as primitive, and judging by the food one would never have known we were in France. One morning Roy told us that when scouting around looking for the location he had been taken to a fantastic restaurant near St Brieuc – he had now discovered precisely where it was and he would take us to dinner there next Thursday. We could hardly wait – our rooms were damp and cheerless, the sun for sorrow would not show his head and we were feeling dejected. Thursday came. We raced from work, changed our clothes, and Muriel, Roy, Geoff Unsworth the cameraman, and I set out, crammed into St Efflam's ancient and only taxi, to travel the seventy kilometres to the restaurant. We bumped along the uneven roads with the springs failing to take the shock – whoever sat in the middle at the back felt as if they were sitting directly on the differential, so we continually changed places. The engine clattered along and sent black smoke out of the exhaust, some of it finding its way into the car. Every so often we hit a rut, our heads would be thrown against the roof, our spines jarred as we landed on the cushionless seats.

All the way Roy gave us a eulogistic account of the goodies in store for us: a restaurateur from Paris had bought a disused mill which straddled the main street in a small village – some of the buildings, now housing the bar, were on one side of the road while the restaurant was on the other. It was furnished throughout with antiques. Old lace cloths covered the genuine old tables. The cutlery was of silver, every plate and every glass a collector's item. There was no menu. The patron himself chose the dishes for the day and he also chose the perfect wine for each course. Every client would get the same meal. Gourmets from as far afield as Paris made the pilgrimage to his establishment, secure in the knowledge that each dish would be perfection, and would be followed by another dish of greater perfection, washed down with wines of equal wonder.

Slowly we approached our destination and pulled up outside. Roy was beside himself with excitement as we entered the bar and was determined that we should savour every moment. 'Just look at that . . . and at that . . . and what about that . . .?' And we were determined not to let him down, 'Ooh' . . . 'Ohh' . . . 'Ahh!' Drinks were ordered and Roy went off to find le patron. Muriel, Geoff and I satiated our senses and recharged our Oohs, Ohhs and Ahhs. A few minutes later Roy returned, tears welling in his round eyes. 'The chef is ill and there is no food! Le patron tells me that he will not serve anything in his restaurant that is not of superlative quality, his whole reputation is at stake, so we cannot even have a boiled egg . . .'

We were permitted to see the inside of the deserted restaurant, but our Oohs, Ohhs and Ahhs were muted: we then began the seventy-kilometre return journey with Roy slumped in silent gloom astride the differential. Nothing that we said could rouse him.

The exterior shots completed, we returned to Pinewood for the interiors. My character is abducted by a group of street musicians led by Bernard Miles, who, having bound and gagged me, cram me into a pram and wheel me along the kerbside while playing their instruments – a most bizarre and sinister scene. They eventually reach their hide-out in the basement of a derelict building and, amid roars of laughter, send me and the pram hurtling down a flight of concrete steps.

'You won't have to worry about that,' said Roy. 'That will be done by the double.'

Once again Frankie Howerd of *Cruel Sea* fame was called in and I watched the preparations for the shot. Guide rails were fixed to keep the pram on its correct path before plunging down the stairs. At the bottom piles of empty cardboard boxes were covered by an old mattress. These would absorb the shock as the pram appeared to hit the opposite wall. Several times the pram was sent down empty so that the camera operator and others could calculate the speed. The first-aid department was brought in and red crosses clustered ominously in the gloom behind the camera. The possibility of a nasty accident is always a magnet and many more people than were actually needed hovered ghoulishly around the set. With no rails or banisters on the concrete steps, perhaps the pram plus Frankie would plunge over the side . . .

Everything was checked and double-checked.

Members of the prop department would send the pram on its course – apparently actors could not be relied upon. Frankie don-

ned my costume and his mouth was gagged like mine – all was
ready.

'Turn over. Action.'

Along the top and down the stairs shot the pram and ended up
embedded in the cardboard boxes. Roy dashed forward. 'Are you
all right, Frankie?'

'Yes, fine.'

The disappointed crowd melted away and the red crosses were
sent back to their humdrum job of pulling out splinters. Roy came
over to me. 'Now, Donald – I'm going to need close-ups on this.
Get your costume from Frankie.' It was not easy to get a bouncing
head travelling at speed down a concrete staircase, so I had to do
Frankie's journey four times before they were satisfied and the only
audience I had was the minimum crew!

I hardly had a moment to breathe before Betty Box and Ralph
Thomas whisked me off to Knokke-le-Zoute in Belgium to begin
shooting *Doctor at Large*, the sequel to *Doctor in the House* – the same
team, but this time without Kenny More and Donald Houston.
Also appearing in the film was Athene Seyler. I had known her for
some years while she and her husband were living opposite us in
Chelsea, but this was the first time we had worked together. She
was no longer young and I took it upon myself to look after her.
One day she called me over to where she was sitting.

'Donald, dear, I don't want you to panic but I feel you should call
a doctor. I think I have had a stroke. I was perfectly all right a few
minutes ago but now I can't move my neck . . .'

Before going in search of help I thought I should make her
comfortable by putting a cushion behind her head and in doing so I
discovered that she had caught her hairnet in the clasp of her
necklace. I released it.

'Oh Donald – how did you do that? I'm well again!' she cried.

My character of Benskin was now fully established. He was an
outrageous womaniser chasing anything in a skirt. I grew a moustache in emulation of Guy Middleton, who had played a similar
character in the original *French Without Tears*.

I decided that Benskin was a beer drinker and I fully developed
the wolf 'growl' that I had first used in *Two Dozen Red Roses* at the
'Q' Theatre in 1950. It was with this character more than any other
that I became identified with the cinema-going public. Three weeks
after returning from Belgium a full-page photograph appeared on

the front page of a Sunday tabloid showing me in a swimming costume lying on the sand with my head in the lap of a very attractive girl in a bikini and my arms around two similarly unclad beauties. The caption merely stated, 'Donald Sinden on holiday in Belgium'. The photograph had been specially staged by the publicity man, but there was no mention of the film in the caption. Diana was inundated with 'Oh, you poor thing' telephone calls from friends, but filmgoers demanded more of the character. However, before I could satisfy them, I was committed to doing another and rather different comedy, *Rockets Galore*.

The producer-director team of Basil Dearden and Michael Relph had decided to make *Rockets Galore* as a sequel to the successful Ealing comedy *Whisky Galore*, which had been based on Compton Mackenzie's novel, so we all set off for the island of Barra, the westernmost island of the Outer Hebrides, where the stories were set. Our little plane from Glasgow was to land on the sands which served as an airstrip. The plane was due to make a stop at Tiree but an ominous message came over the loudspeakers that we would not be landing there, 'because the tide was in'. We circled above Barra and were given the opportunity of sizing up the place where we were to be working for the next six weeks. Only eight miles long and four wide, at its southern end is a large bay with a castle built on a small island in the middle. Here also is the main centre of habitation named, quite logically, Castlebay. Rising behind it is 'the mountain' 1,260 feet high. At the northern extremity is the Cockle Strand, on which we landed just in time: while our bags were being unloaded the sea began to cover the strand. The small hotel in Castlebay could not possibly house all our unit so most people were accommodated in private houses. Once shooting had finished for the day there was practically nothing to do but sit around talking or playing cards or darts. One evening I decided to go for a solitary walk before dinner and I aimed at the top of the 'mountain' which has gently sloping sides, mainly grass covered – it was not exactly a challenge for a mountaineer. When I returned in time for dinner someone asked where I had been.

'To the top of the mountain.'

'Right to the top?'

'Yes.'

'But you couldn't have – you only left here at six fifteen.'

Nobody would believe me so the next day I was challenged to

take a stone with my initials on it and leave it on the ordnance survey pyramid which I said was at the top. The stone would be retrieved by the next person to go up, who would then leave his own stone. The race was on: each evening a contender would be timed from the moment he left the front door of the hotel to the moment he fell on the floor (as they invariably did) of the lounge where the rest of the unit were gathered. Boredom was our main enemy. Not only was there a lack of entertainment – television had yet to reach the Hebrides – but we had discovered a terrible monotony in our diet. Sheep were the only animals roaming the hills and all the lambs were immediately exported to the mainland, so the only meat obtainable on the island was ancient mutton from sheep that had outlived their usefulness. The caterers attached to the unit did their best to make it palatable, but we had nothing but mutton: roast mutton, boiled mutton, curried mutton, stewed mutton, grilled mutton, for every meal for a month until the unit showed signs of rebellion. Meals were prepared in a mobile kitchen which rendezvous-ed with us wherever we happened to be working on the island. We heard that the caterers had taken pity on us and imported a consignment of pork chops. When we broke for lunch on this particular day I happened to be first in the queue at the kitchen and a large tray of sizzling pork chops was placed on the counter. I find it difficult to describe the effect of a pork chop after four weeks of mutton. I cast a beady eye over the trayful and chose a magnificent specimen quite six inches in diameter and an inch thick, all lean with the smallest rim of crisp fat round the edge. Scrumptious. I added some mashed potato, a great knob of butter and, hugging my tray, I made for one of the caravans at our disposal. Already seated there was Jean Cadell, a highly prized character actress, a member of the cast and mother of my agent-to-be. As I entered carrying the tray I was drooling. Jean, who was then aged seventy-two, looked up and said, 'Oh Donald, how *sweet* of you!'

Was I a gentleman or not? Biting back my tears I handed over the tray and, before returning to the kitchen, I paused long enough to watch her knife glide through the tender meat . . . Sad to relate, when I got back all the chops had gone and they were busy heating up some mutton for the latecomers.

The islanders took us to their hearts and invited us to delightful ceilidhs at which they would sing traditional Hebridean songs to the drone of the bagpipes. Most of them were Roman Catholics in the charge of Father John MacCormick who had been born on the island, gone to Oxford University, had taken holy orders and returned to his homeland. Every Sunday, rain or shine, he took his little boat over to the neighbouring minute island of Vatersay to say Mass for the few remaining inhabitants. He told me of one old maiden lady there who when asked why she had not married replied, 'Pedestrians didn't interest me and equestrians never came my way.'

Around the coast of Barra lobsters bred in their thousands. French fishing boats made the long journey to very profitable advantage but the local fishermen seemed uninterested. I enquired of one the reason for this and he answered philosophically, 'If I catch a lobster, I can sell it and buy a sack of potatoes – I don't want two sacks of potatoes, so why catch another lobster?'

One of the locals carved delightful animals out of driftwood: 'I find a piece of wood on the beach and I just look at it: after looking at it for a long time I begin to see a rabbit or a squirrel or a dog and then with my knife I just cut the rest away.'

Did Michelangelo work like that?

While we were there one of the French fishing boats broke a propeller and was hauled up on the beach to effect the repairs. I joined a group of local fishermen who were leaning over the quay wall observing the Frenchmen with undisguised contempt, while making no effort at all to offer assistance. One of them muttered something to me out of the corner of his mouth. He had a thick Scottish accent and I had to apologise for failing to understand him. His second attempt was scarcely more intelligible than his first but I thought I detected the word liquor. 'Liquor?' I asked. He then realised that he was talking to a dim-witted Sassenach and spoke fractionally slower but still out of the side of his mouth. (I hadn't noticed that the other side was clamped around a pipe.)

'They've got liquor on that boat.' (He sucked through his teeth.) 'Wines – all kinds of wines' (more sucking). 'Cognac – Deutsch Cognac' (even more sucking).

'Deutsch?'

'Deutsch.'

I pondered this for a moment before asking, 'Do you prefer Deutsch Cognac?'

With no pause at all, as if continuing a sentence, he went on, flatly, 'I was walking along a road. I saw a man kissing a pig. I said why are you kissing a pig? He said tastes differ.'

In spite of the mutton we were all sorry when we had to leave

Barra to return to Pinewood to shoot the interiors. In my mind's
eye it represents the nearest I shall come to Shangri-la. As we left,
wild irises came out and covered the island in a yellow carpet and a
weather-beaten islander observed, 'Now isn't God the clever boy!'

Every so often the relative tranquillity of work at Pinewood was
disrupted by some visiting luminary from Hollywood who always
gave the impression that he was 'slumming'.

A cavalcade of limousines would drive through the studio gates
and continue right up to the dressing room block; black-felt hatted
men leaped out and opened doors and from the largest car stepped a
muffled figure wearing dark sun-glasses who was then hurried
furtively through. A hypochondriac passing through a leper colony
could not be better immunised. The 'star', hedged about by retainers – agents, managers, secretaries, personal hair-dresser,
make-up man, photographer, publicity man, sometimes even
bodyguards, had lost touch with gravity. Were they afraid of
catching acting? Why were they disguised? Who were they hiding
from? If they had walked, all alone, the twenty miles from their
West End hotel to the studio, they would not have been accosted.

As a breed their IQ level was pretty low: their rise to fame had
depended almost entirely on mammoth publicity campaigns
mounted by the studios to which they were under contract. Very
few had ever appeared in the theatre and so had no grounding in
their craft. Male or female, they had been selected for their bodies
and installed in the solar system. They were paid astronomic
salaries for being photogenic; salaries which they didn't know how
to spend. Most of them were neurotics.

For the first two or three weeks they always kept themselves very
much to themselves: the entourage accompanied them to and from
the set, their meals were taken to their dressing rooms. We 'residents' were all vastly amused by this and merely waited for them to
emerge from their cocoons. Sometimes it was worth the wait.

As a contract artist it cost a producer no more to call me to the
studio every day to be available at any time, so that economic use
could be made of the other actors who were paid what amounted
to a daily rate: this meant that I had a lot of free time just hanging
around the studio – time that I sometimes utilised by visiting the
stages where other films were being made (access was always easy
as I knew most of the people involved), and thus I was able to watch
some of these Hollywood 'stars' at work. I must be careful not to

give the impression that they were *all* morons. Most certainly not. Katharine Hepburn, for instance, was delightful and most professional; but what was deemed by some to be 'professional' can also be called 'temperamental' by others. I happened to be on the set of *The Iron Petticoat* while Miss Hepburn was blowing off steam about something in a professional/temperamental manner. Bob Hope – her leading man – came to the rescue with his superb sense of humour and said to her, 'If you don't behave yourself, I'll tell everyone that you are Audrey Hepburn's father!'

One star arrived to play the lead in an action-packed drama and brought in his entourage a 'double'-cum-stunt man who bore an uncanny resemblance to him. The double did all the long shots, most of the medium shots and even appeared in two-shots when the hero had his back to the camera. The star only did eleven days' work in the entire film.

Another star was extremely short in stature and, unless he was alone, the camera could never show his feet, because if he was stationary he was standing on a box; if walking, the other actors were in specially dug troughs or ditches; and for anything between, all other actors were required to stand with their legs apart and their knees bent.

A month before Marilyn Monroe arrived to start work on *The Sleeping Prince*, Pinewood's number-one dressing room was gutted and completely re-decorated in blue. A new carpet, curtains, couch, armchairs, dressing table were installed – all in blue. Then two weeks before she appeared a man arrived from Hollywood to vet the joint and ensure that everything would be to her satisfaction. He pronounced 'Miss Monroe doesn't like blue'. Back came the painters, upholsterers and carpet fitters and in six days everything was made white. On the seventh day they rested. My dressing room (which I had for eight years) was in the same block, four doors from hers, so I saw the comings and goings of the entourage. She was still suffering from the effects of The Method and one day I made up a notice which I fixed to my door saying:

Registered office of the   Prof. Donald Sinden
NAZAK ACADEMY
'You too can be inaudible'
Particularisation:
NEW EGOS SUPERIMPOSED

MOTIVATIONS IMMOBILISED
IMAGINARY STONE KICKING ERADICATED
UMS & ERS RENDERED OBSOLETE
FEES: Exorbitant but we can work on your minimum
Extra pockets provided by the school tailor
MOTTO. 'THOUGH TIS METHOD YET THERE'S
MADNESS IN IT'   (Bacon)

I waited inside and presently heard the footsteps of the entourage. They paused outside my door and from the entire group I only heard one laugh – immediately recognisable as Monroe's. The door burst open and in she came, slamming the door in the faces of her retainers. We introduced ourselves and from that moment whenever the poor girl could not face the problems of her hybrid existence – which was frequently – she popped in for a natter and a giggle.

Of course as a sex symbol she was stunning, but, sadly, she must be one of the silliest women I have ever met.

'How would you like three months cruising round the Greek Islands?' asked producer Jo Janni. 'I'm making a film of Richard Gordon's book *The Captain's Table*. Jack Lee is directing and all the action takes place during a cruise to Australia – so why not base ourselves in the Mediterranean?' I was asked this before I started on *Rockets Galore*; the schedule fitted in exactly so of course I accepted with alacrity: three months around the Greek Islands – whoopee. I was to play the First Officer to John Gregson's Ship's Captain, with Peggy Cummins, Nadia Gray and a bevy of beauties.

While on Barra I received a letter from Jo – his budget would not after all run to the Mediterranean – it was now to be around the Channel Islands. Not quite the same thing, but after all it was the middle of summer – a three months' working cruise was not to be sniffed at – and anyway I was committed. When I had completed *Rockets* I was immediately involved in costume fittings and discussions with Jack Lee about the script. My fans who wanted more of Benskin were to get what they wanted (but without the moustache – we were only allowed a full set). I had, however, noticed that one important scene featured a bathing beauty contest, and I was not involved, which seemed a pity as I was sure that my character would have been in the thick of such an event. Jack said that it was too late to do much re-writing of the script, but if I could think of something he would go along with me. I suggested that I could be a sort of Master of Ceremonies – I could check on the girls' vital statistics with a tape-measure – my mind was already running on the eminent possibilities of using a retractable steel tape-measure . . .

'Oh, by the way, when do we embark for the Channel Islands?'

'Hasn't anyone told you? That idea fell through.'

'So where are we doing the film?'

'Tilbury Docks.'

So for three months we stayed in Southend and commuted to the Docks where myriad arc lamps simulated the Mediterranean sun while the girls tried to hide their goose pimples.

John Gregson had gone under contract shortly before me and along with Terence Morgan we formed a triumvirate and our wives became friends. All actors remember the stories against themselves and John used to tell one concerning one of his most successful films, *Genevieve*. John lived in Shepperton and one evening was standing quietly alone at the bar of his local when over his shoulder a beery voice said, 'Old cars. London to Brighton. Need I say more?'

Actors become inured to such opening gambits and John rather wearily said, 'Yes. You're quite right.' Whereupon the man behind the voice turned back to some companions seated at the end of the room, made a thumbs-up signal and mouthed, 'Yes it is!' Then, turning back, said, 'What do you say your name is?' Not feeling inclined to shout, John whispered, 'John Gregson.'

'I'm sorry, I'm a bit hard of hearing. What did you say?'

John placed his lips nearer to the man's ear and articulated, 'John Gregson.'

The man's face fell and he again turned to his friends, mouthing, 'No – it's not him' and turning back to John asked, ' 'Ere – what was the name of the *funny* one in that film?' Rather exasperated John replied, 'Do you mean Kenneth More?'

The man fell about laughing. 'Yeah, yeah – Kenneth More – cor *he* was *funny*!' and he rejoined his friends repeating, 'Kenneth More. Yeah. Kenneth More.'

One evening John, his wife Thea, Diana and I were in a restaurant when a man approached me saying, 'You're Terence Morgan aren't you.' John butted in: 'No he's not – but you're very lucky tonight because neither am I.' The man was delighted and went away muttering, 'Thank you – thank you.'

John hated flying and avoided any possibility of doing so, but shortly after taking his family abroad – by car – for a holiday he received a telegram telling him that he must return immediately to do some retakes on his last film. There was no alternative – he would have to fly. His friends decided that the only way to get him on the plane was to get him drunk. Tight as a tick, he was driven to the airport and they poured him into the aircraft which duly took off. Once in the air the steward came round taking orders for drinks. John was now in an expansive mood: 'A large scotch! Beautiful day for flying!'

'Do you fly a lot?' enquired the steward.

'Yes – Yes! Do it all the time!'

'And doesn't it worry you, sir?'

'Worry me?! Not a bit – not a bit! Love it!'

'Oh, you don't know how lucky you are, sir – I'm giving it up – can't stand it any more. If you knew the thin thread by which your life is hanging . . .'

It now dawned upon me that 'somebody up there' was no longer looking after me. A rather good comedy script on the subject of the ATS, with the ambiguous title of *Girls in Arms*, was my next assignment. Many of my scenes were with my batman and I was not overjoyed when they told me that the part was to be played by Ronald Shiner: a nice enough chap but his comedy playing was of the broadest: there would be no chance of anything subtle. My heart sank even further when the title was changed to *Operation Bullshine*. Apart from working with some splendid actors such as Barbara Murray and Naunton Wayne it was a fairly joyless experience.

I then found myself cast in the film version of a stage play now to be called *Your Money or Your Wife*. Oh dear. Unfortunately it was made on the cheap and little care had been taken turning a script, intended to be played in one permanent setting, into a film. It was merely chopped into sections: one to be played in the living room, another in the bedroom, the next in the garage, the next in the kitchen. This left endless shots of actors walking in silence from one place to another before continuing the dialogue. As someone wisely pointed out, a movie means that the *action* should move – not the *camera*.

★

It does seem strange that until Monty Berman and Robert Baker, no one had made a film of *The Siege of Sydney Street*, particularly as we will never know the true identity of 'Peter the Painter' and his nefarious colleagues, which leaves plenty of scope for invention. For the film we were faced with several problems: not only had many of the original locations in London's East End ceased to exist, but in streets similar enough to be used, every other house sported a TV aerial, hardly appropriate for a film set in 1911. Hence the decision to make the film in Ireland where few Dublin houses yet had television sets.

According to our version of the story, the revolutionaries, finding the house in Sydney Street surrounded by police as well as troops called in by the Home Secretary, Winston Churchill, effected their escape over the rooftops, leaving one of their number to create a diversion by firing a revolver from the windows of the house which was now on fire. The scene in the blazing room we filmed in the studio and I was vastly intrigued to watch the way the special effects department created the illusion. They began by making everything – the floors, walls, doors, windows, furniture, curtains – completely fireproof. They then spread an inflammable jelly over the sections that were to be seen burning and just before 'Action' it was set alight. Tables and chairs blazed away and at the end of the scene the flames were extinguished ready for the next Take. It was remarkable. Nothing was damaged.

Leonard Sachs was the actor left in the room with the revolver; his clothes had also been fireproofed and in the long-shot flames licked from the jelly which had been put on his back as blazing joists crashed down from the ceiling. For the next shot, his close-up, he was having the jelly placed strategically on his shoulders and arms. I was talking to someone in the background when one of the crew approached and whispered to his colleague, 'Have they fire proofed his hair?'

'No, I don't think they have.'

'But don't you think they should?'

'No – no – it would take twenty minutes.'

I was informed later that the explanation of this was that, had Leonard suffered any damage, the insurance company would have paid up, but twenty minutes of the crew's time on an hourly rate merely to fireproof an actor's hair would have had to have been paid for by the film company. Thankfully Leonard only suffered a slight singeing of his hair.

Not one of my last three films had been made by the Rank Organisation or at Pinewood Studios. It was clear that all was not well in the Rankery.

EPILOGUE

In 1960 my agent Freddie Joachim took Diana and me to lunch at a smart restaurant and at a chosen moment said, 'Well this is it. I have been informed that your contract will not be renewed at the end of the year.'

The blow was not totally unexpected as several of my colleagues had already suffered the same fate. Film attendances had been plunging since the advent of commercial television in 1956, and cinemas all over the country were closing. Where the Rank Organisation once had had fifty actors under contract, now there were less than ten. At one time the Rankery made sixteen films a year at Pinewood – now there were to be only three or four, with gala premieres no longer statutory. I had known that the films I had made in the past two years were not exactly of the calibre of *The Cruel Sea* and *Doctor in the House*, but however expected, the end of my contract came as a shock; for an actor to be paid fifty-two weeks of the year is rare enough, but Diana and I had led a cushioned existence for eight years. For the one and only period in my professional life I had been given security. Indeed I had begun to think I was there for life. I was and remain, most grateful to the Rank Organisation.

My assets were not inconsiderable. I was now a 'name', my face was known to millions of cinemagoers and, quite apart from making films, I had learnt to cope with events as varied as tours round hospitals and biscuit factories to Royal gala occasions. Head waiters and hall porters no longer terrorised me. I had made many friends (some of whose children are the same age as mine, and have remained their friends). But I also had responsibilities: a wife, two children, a house in London, a cottage in the country, a car and school fees and a standard of living to which we had become accustomed – and now I was out of work.

What was I to do? The theatre I had left in 1952 was now a very different animal. A play called *Look Back in Anger*, written by John Osborne, had been produced at the Royal Court Theatre in 1956 and completely revolutionised the theatre; it brought in its wake new critics who were telling their readers not to waste their time on 'drawing-room comedies' and 'well-made plays'; they must march forward with the New Drama of the Kitchen Sink (as the style became known). The story was told of a new play sent to George Devine at the Royal Court. The plot concerned a young man who in the first act had an affair with his sister, in the second act an affair with his mother and in the third act an affair with his father. At the end of the play he shot himself – he had found out he was adopted.

Coward and Rattigan were out; Osborne and Pinter were in. The new drama called for new actors. Anyone over twenty-five seemed too old. I was thirty-seven and, theatrically, labelled as a 'light comedian'.

In the classic theatre I had missed my opportunity. During my time in the Rankery, Richard Burton and John Neville were leading the company at the Old Vic. Three times Glen Byam Shaw had asked me to return to Stratford-upon-Avon: first in 1952 to play Orlando and Malcolm, again in 1957 to play Orlando and Mark Antony, and in 1960 to play Petruchio. But the Rankery said that if I went it would mean the end of my contract – a whole year away from the cinema would be detrimental to my film career. I chose to remain with the stable and in retrospect I still think I made the right decision, even though the vacancies at Stratford were filled the first year by Laurence Harvey, the second by Richard Johnson and the third by Peter O'Toole, all relatively unknown at the time.

I had not wedged my foot in the door of television. No one wanted me in any of the media. I was out: my world had collapsed. Walter Hudd had once said that a career in the theatre was a series of brick walls: you manage to surmount them one by one but always facing you is another. The wall that now faced me seemed insurmountable. I could not find the reserves to climb it.

I went down to our cottage in Kent and began to dig the garden. I dug and dug and as I dug I resolved to turn my back on acting. I speculated on what other jobs I could do: I was thirty-seven, not too late to change careers, but whatever happened I was no longer an actor. I dug my anger and frustration into the ground. I thought nobody knew where I was but suddenly a telephone call came from my friend John Cadell saying that he was going to Birmingham with his wife to see a new play called *Guilty Party* – would Diana and I care to go with them, just for the trip? I protested that I never wanted to set foot in a theatre again, even as a member of the audience but Diana argued that it might be fun to be with our friends. Reluctantly I agreed. But by the time we left London in the car I was in a bad temper and slouched silently in the back seat. We drew up outside Birmingham's Alexandra Theatre and made our way into the foyer. A tall, dark-haired, ebullient stranger bounded over to us: 'Donald – my name is Peter Bridge and I am presenting this play in London. You are going to play the lead.'

It is not outside the realms of possibility that but for that meeting I would still be digging up Kent. Instead of which I was still less than halfway through what has been up till now a not exactly uneventful career.

> There is a divinity that shapes our ends,
> rough-hew them how we will.

Perhaps I shall record another touch of my memoirs in the future?

INDEX

INDEX

255